Power in Pictures

Power in Pictures

Using Picturebooks to Energize Secondary ELA Instruction

Deborah Dean
Brigham Young University

National Council of Teachers of English
340 N. Neil St., Suite #104, Champaign, Illinois 61820
www.ncte.org

Staff Editor: Cynthia Gomez
Manuscript Editor: Bonny Graham
Interior Design: Jenny Jensen Greenleaf
Cover Design: Adrian Morgan
Cover Image: Nataliia Kozynska | Dreamstime.com

ISBN 978-0-8141-0218-3; EPUB eISBN 978-0-8141-0219-0; PDF eISBN: 978-0-8141-0220-6

It is the policy of NCTE in its journals and other publications to provide a forum for the open discussion of ideas concerning the content and the teaching of English and the language arts. Publicity accorded to any particular point of view does not imply endorsement by the Executive Committee, the Board of Directors, or the membership at large, except in announcements of policy, where such endorsement is clearly specified.

NCTE provides equal employment opportunity to all staff members and applicants for employment without regard to race, color, religion, sex, national origin, age, physical, mental or perceived handicap/disability, sexual orientation including gender identity or expression, ancestry, genetic information, marital status, military status, unfavorable discharge from military service, pregnancy, citizenship status, personal appearance, matriculation or political affiliation, or any other protected status under applicable federal, state, and local laws.

Every effort has been made to provide current URLs and email addresses, but, because of the rapidly changing nature of the web, some sites and addresses may no longer be accessible.

Library of Congress Control Number: 2024943854

Acknowledgments

To my students through the years who have responded in ways that encouraged me to keep using picturebooks and to seek better ways to teach picturebooks because of their responses when I tried new ideas.

To all the colleagues who have supported me in this journey and read drafts and given such good feedback.

To NCTE for letting me write the book I have wanted to write my whole career—and for helping it become a better book with your help.

To David for support and encouragement and foot rubs when I felt at the end of my rope. It's you. For now and always.

Thank you, all.

Contents

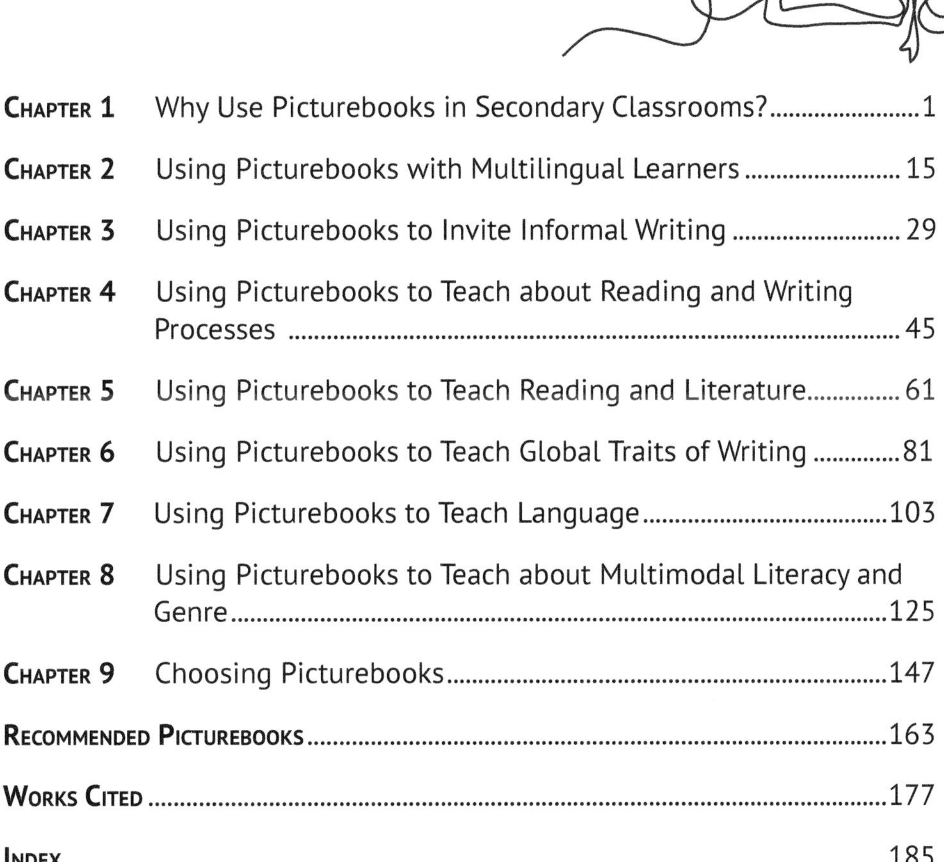

1

Why Use Picturebooks in Secondary Classrooms?

I began my teaching career in the middle of the school year, after my classes of seventh and eighth graders had had a series of substitute teachers from September through January. It was a rough start. Eventually I came to love teaching, but at first I wondered whether I would. I was scraping by each day, staying up late writing lesson plans, trying to find a way—any way—to interest these students who must have felt abandoned by a system that was supposed to teach them. I quickly found that I could engage them with a story. And if it had pictures as well, even better. I didn't have many picturebooks on my shelves at that time, but if I could use one for a lesson, I did. I began to feel success in my teaching, but I didn't think beyond the immediate effect: picturebooks interested my students in ways that helped engage them in learning.

When fall came around, with the first classes that would be mine from the start of the school year, I had some ideas about using picturebooks from that first half-year to help me begin. On the first day that year and for several years to follow, I started my classes with *The Teacher from the Black Lagoon* by Mike Thaler. The story is told from the perspective of a student who, like most students on the first day of school, is wondering about his new teacher, Mrs. Green. But instead of "Green," I would say "Dean" every time the story says her name. Mrs. Green/Dean looks and acts like a horror, eating students whole (or, to teach fractions, in half), burning them up, turning them into frogs, or shrinking their heads. When I got to the part of the book where Mrs. Green tells students to put their heads (if they still have them) on their desks, I closed the book and said, "I bet you are wondering about your English teacher this year."

That was their introduction to me and to the course—because picturebooks were going to be a part of it in one way or another. I could tell that a few students (especially later when I taught high school) wondered about my use of a picturebook. I can still see them sliding their eyes sideways to look around at each other, checking to see if it was okay to be engaged by a teacher reading a picturebook to them in high school. Usually they couldn't resist the lure—it is just too different from what they expect on the first day of classes. Besides that, there is something kind of comforting about being read to and having the book be one that reminds them, whether they think of it consciously or not, of being read to as a child, almost always by someone they know cared about them. And it felt fun.

When I tell people what I'm working on right now—a book about using picturebooks to teach secondary English language arts classes—I get mixed responses, mostly surprise. For most people, that surprise might come because we have been conditioned to think of picturebooks as books for young children. Books with pictures, I was told as a child, were meant for beginning readers or babies. "Growing up" as a reader meant reading chapter books—more words, no pictures. This is a "common misconception," according to Nikolajeva, among people who see picturebooks as merely books with few words and decorative pictures (110). But in the past few decades, we can find shifts in that thinking: from scholars who have presented research about the value of using picturebooks with older students and from teachers who have, as I did, tried using them in classrooms for a variety of purposes and found them to be effective.

Susan Hall's books from the 1990s were influential in my early thinking about effective use of picturebooks, both for her rationale for using the books with older students and her suggestions for specific books. *Using Picture Storybooks to Teach Literary Devices* was the first I read that talked about picturebooks that weren't meant—at least solely—for children; she called them "picturebooks for all ages." The names we have seen for the types of picturebooks that are useful in secondary classes have varied over time and across different writers, from *picturebooks for all ages*, to *postmodern picturebooks* (Anstey), to *challenging picturebooks* (Evans), to *crossover picturebooks* (Beckett), even to *picturebooks written and marketed only for adults*, some perhaps not appropriate even for secondary students in school (Ommundson). Clearly, the shift shows a growing acceptance of picturebooks for all readers. Indeed, Beckett finds in her research that "[m]ore than any other literary genre, picturebooks can genuinely be books for all ages" (209). Whatever the term, research from across the world supports using picturebooks with older students for a variety of instructional purposes.

One of the clearest of those instructional purposes is to develop students as readers. Ommundsen's work shows that "as all students can read visual texts, read-alouds of carefully selected picturebooks may increase both the students' reading motivation and self-efficacy" (102). Tiedt explains that reading picturebooks may actually benefit reading development more than other texts because they have a lyrical quality that makes reading them aloud very pleasant. She notes that teachers, reading picturebooks, can model intonation and the pleasure of reading (6), two important aspects of helping students develop as lifelong readers. Massey agrees, explaining that "using picturebooks can motivate reluctant readers to read and find reading enjoyable" (45).

Additionally, because of the multimodal nature of picturebooks, students are using multiple sign systems to create meaning, gaining important skills in the way they read in the world outside of school—moving back and forth between words and images and actively constructing meaning from both. Ommundsen and colleagues make this important point: that modern picturebooks, with their options for different ways of reading, "invite the reader to think, explore and interpret the word-image interplay" (8), all activities we hope for from maturing readers both in and outside of school.

Students generally show interest in lessons that involve picturebooks, largely because of the visual element. Their exposure to online texts that mix words and images means students today are more inclined to pay attention to picturebooks (Vercelletto). The use of picturebooks thus helps span the gap between traditional school texts and digital texts. Farrer and colleagues go further, calling picturebooks "training fields for multiliteracies" (43). Schools in Finland are starting to implement picturebooks from kindergarten through university for this very reason—to help students develop visual and aesthetic literacy skills (Österlund).

Reading picturebooks engages students' emotions. "Pictures are an immediate conduit to emotional connection" (Vercelletto). Nikolajeva sees picturebooks as an "efficient implement" to increase students' emotional intelligence (114), partly because "unlike novels, picturebooks evoke emotional engagement through images as well as words, through amplification of words by images, and through ambiguity created in the interaction between media" (114). Massey also sees the emotional value of picturebooks because they "stimulate the imagination and serve as a receptacle for coping with psychosocial issues" (45). I too have seen this aspect in my use of picturebooks, as students often get emotional or open to discussion of important ideas because of picturebooks. Something about looking at the images as I read to them creates this emotionally safe and creative space.

Reading picturebooks together in secondary classes contributes to building a classroom community. There is something about being read to, especially the kinds of stories we can find in picturebooks, that brings us together in a shared experience. When we read the books, we show the pictures. The pattern creates a reassuring rhythm to our reading—words, pause to look at pictures, words, and so on—that calms classes and provides a space to come together and just "be." When some teachers commented that graphic novels also combine images and words, Lukehart noted that despite the similarities, "picturebooks are uniquely designed to be a shared experience" (qtd. in Vercelletto). Certainly, teachers who have shared picturebooks in a secondary classroom can note this same effect: reading picturebooks as a whole group can bring a class together in emotional ways and build community.

Moving beyond aesthetic pleasures in reading, which picturebooks definitely provide, Massey explains how picturebooks also present content and perspectives that often are not found in textbooks (45), allowing teachers to engage students more deeply in classroom content and help them see multiple perspectives that textbooks might limit. When reading novels set in historical eras, for example, also reading multiple picturebooks about the time period can give students access to multiple points of view and to content outside of the textbooks or novels we are reading together. Picturebooks allow us to see the world and people's experiences in it from a variety of lenses, something that prompts a more accepting attitude.

Picturebooks can do even more in our classrooms. They can stimulate creativity (Sundmark and Jers), motivate reading and writing (Mueller), encourage critical thinking (Beckett), and "help students develop as readers, writers, and imaginative thinkers" (Ommundsen 116, citing Pantaleo studies from 2012). In her graduate thesis, Foster presents a lengthy list of educational benefits from reading picturebooks aloud that she compiled from researchers and teachers. Many of these meet ELA pedagogical needs: building vocabulary; teaching grammar and style; exposing students to ideas, places, concepts, and genres that might be unfamiliar; and broadening their understanding of the world, among many others (14–16). Without including the long list here, I am convinced that teachers can, with confidence, use picturebooks to address almost any learning objective they have for their older students. It's just a matter of finding the right book for each purpose. Additionally, we know that students enjoy picturebooks, so their interest can work to enhance their learning in any of these areas.

As teachers, we have many options for texts to use in our classrooms—novels we love and short stories we savor, plays we live for and poetry that feeds our soul. With so many options, what makes picturebooks a choice we should not only consider but prioritize? They have three qualities that set them apart:

- ✓ They are **efficient**. Because most picturebooks are short, they allow teachers to use complete texts for instruction. When we read novels, we can certainly use passages from the books as mentors for writing or language lessons. And we should. But sometimes a wider context is important, such as for a lesson on sentence fluency or tone, something that requires contextual knowledge. In these cases, using a passage from a novel can be more time-consuming in establishing context. When using a picturebook to engage students in a topic or concept to help them enter a longer novel for class reading, the length of the picturebook allows for reading and discussion in less than a class period, reducing teachers' constant tension with "having enough time." Some picturebooks are longer, of course, but in general the length is one advantage of using picturebooks in secondary classrooms as they can be efficient tools for concept and language lessons.

- ✓ They **engage** students. Because picturebooks are not the texts students are used to seeing in their secondary classrooms, students respond with high interest. The novelty and the connection to the memories students have of being read to have an immediate positive effect, and—pictures! Vercelletto notes the appeal of images for students, and Lukeheart agrees: "If you want people to really engage with a topic, . . . show a picture" (qtd. in Vercelletto). Ommundsen says it straight out; picturebooks in the classroom "lend fun to learning and teaching" (118). Reiker's observations for her thesis on the use of picturebooks in secondary classrooms include that students respond audibly and physically when a teacher shares a picturebook. And once students understand the clear purposes of the books in their classrooms, repeated uses of picturebooks seems to encourage even more positive physical reactions, something she attributes to both positive past experiences and novelty in a secondary classroom context. Picturebooks are something different—and novelty usually means fun.
- ✓ Students find picturebooks **accessible**. Perhaps partly because they incorporate images, picturebooks may seem easier in some ways, maybe because they remind students of their childhood. Studies show that multilingual students also find picturebooks accessible because the images help them understand the words they might not otherwise comprehend (Hadaway and Young). As mentioned earlier, the best books use images to add meaning to the words, so even reluctant readers can begin to see levels of meaning beyond the words they can understand. Despite students often thinking picturebooks are simple and easy, they are not. Students have asked me if they could write picturebooks—and we have tried it. When they try and realize that it's harder than they thought, we really see how accessible these picturebooks are; they just seem easy when in truth they are complex.

If picturebooks can do so much for our students and our instruction, we should consider what we mean by picturebooks, especially the ones we want to use in secondary classes. As I mentioned earlier, a common view is that picturebooks are simplistic, for children, without much substance. That view might represent some examples, but it certainly isn't representative of currently available picturebooks or the ones we want to use in our secondary classrooms. Indeed, even the different ways to spell the term (*picture books or picturebooks*) is evidence of the shifting types of books available now. These are books with pictures, yes, but it is the nature of those pictures that is essential to today's understanding of the genre. Goldstone explains that picturebooks are not categorized by content (simple or only story based) but by "interdependence of the illustration and the text" (362); in fact, Sipe identifies interdependence as "the essence of the picturebook"

("How" 97). That interdependence leads scholars in this field to use the combined form of the word—*picturebook* as opposed to *picture book*, even when spell-check keeps wanting me to spell it differently—as a way to represent the integral and essential interactions of two modes in the current version of the genre (Kümmerling-Meibauer 6).

This interaction of image and word in current picturebooks is a big reason why today's picturebooks are even more appropriate for older students and mature readers. Historically, we have assumed that the images are merely illustrations of the words, but today's picturebooks make more thoughtful and complex use of the image–text relationship. Ommundson et al. assert, "[T]he multimodal character of picturebooks is of fundamental importance" (3) and summarize the range of interactions theorists have considered between the modes. At one end of this range, as expected, pictures can represent the words, but today's picturebooks can also use images to complete the words, filling in gaps left by the words (for instance, *Where the Wild Things Are* by Maurice Sendak). It's also possible that images can present a view or narrative different from the one the words portray, telling a different story altogether (for example, *Come Away from the Water, Shirley* by John Burningham). Some picturebooks might even use a variety of these interactions in the same text, leaving considerable interpretation to the reader, producing a sophisticated reading experience (such as *Wolves* by Emily Gravett). Sipe calls the reader's interaction with images and textual elements a kind of "oscillation," noting that the "possibilities of meaning in the word-picture relationship are inexhaustible" ("How" 103). Reading today's picturebooks is not always the straightforward endeavor it might have been in the past.

Several elements beyond the relationship of images and words can also contribute to a picturebook's sophistication. In her explanation of what constitutes a challenging picturebook, Kümmerling-Meibauer notes that elements of (1) content, (2) structure, and (3) design might all play a role. Picturebooks with content that challenges readers' thinking can be more appropriate for older students, such as ideas of what it means to be an immigrant (e.g., *Wishes* by Múón Thi Văn) or what really happened in history (e.g., *The Mary Celeste* by Jane Yolen and Heidi Yolen Stemple). *Michael Rosen's Sad Book* (Rosen) is one that I would not recommend for younger students and caution even for older students as it deals with the death of Rosen's son and the grief he feels. Despite the value I see in using this book—helping students deal with loss as well as academic objectives—I think some of the content might be triggering, so I would suggest teachers use it with care. It is a picturebook—but on its back cover we can see the identifying label: All ages. More sophisticated than we might anticipate.

Structurally challenging picturebooks might require readers to interact with two or more types of content (narrative and informational, for example) simultaneously. At the same time, as in Nicola Davies's *Ice Bear*, picturebooks may use a variety of font types and multiple types of font design (straight and wavy, for example) that require sophisticated reading skills. More and more, we find picturebooks that also use font size and type, as well as their placement and direction, as a kind of visual element to contribute to meaning, in addition to the kinds of images and other visual elements we expect to see in a picturebook (see, for example, *Wolf Won't Bite!* by Emily Gravett). And if we also consider picturebooks that depend on an understanding of what colors symbolize (e.g., *Chester* by Mélanie Watt) or how image placement affects interpretation (e.g., *The Three Pigs* by David Wiesner and *Zoom* by Istvan Banyai), we can see that today's picturebooks might push the boundaries of what we mean by "reading"—and also prepare students to be more effective readers of the world outside of traditional print texts.

Other characteristics of postmodern and crossover picturebooks make them useful for secondary classrooms. The nature of their construction creates multiple ways to "read" them, or, as Sipe explains, these picturebooks allow readers "to have multiple experiences as they engage in creating new meanings and constructing new worlds" ("How" 107). Postmodern picturebooks are characterized by uncertainty and playfulness, blurred boundaries and deviations from expected forms and patterns. Crossover picturebooks are those written intentionally for dual readers—adults and children—and may also reflect intertextuality (references to other texts or world events), parody, or irony. Beyond challenging structure, content, and design, picturebooks for secondary students might also have the following elements that make them more appropriate for older readers:

- ✓ More complex or nuanced illustrations
- ✓ More text on a page
- ✓ Layers of meaning, sometimes in words, sometimes in images, and often in the interactions between the two
- ✓ Mature themes or storylines
- ✓ Complex peritextual features

One of the ways that we can help students see the complexities of current picturebooks is to ask them to do a genre study. For this assignment, I depend on students' prior knowledge of and experience with picturebooks. I give student groups about ten pages of blank paper stapled together and access to black-and-white images, glue, markers, etc., with the directions that they are to write the worst picturebook they can imagine. The discussion is lively and the classroom is full of laughter. The hardest thing for me is figuring out how much time to give them—they could take days! They love being directed to write the worst something—they are used to having to try for the opposite. And a picturebook? How fun is that?

It's possible that, in today's world, some students might have been exposed to *The Book with No Pictures* by B. J. Novak and know that one option is to make a picturebook without pictures, completing their task by defying what they see as essential (it *is* in the name of the genre, after all). But even students who have not seen the book occasionally try that. Additionally, they write what they consider stories inappropriate for children: scary ones or ones with "bad words kids shouldn't read or hear" (although we *** them for appropriateness). Illustrations show dragons smoking ("kids shouldn't see stuff like

The Book With No Pictures

B.J. Novak

that in books—smoking is bad for them") and images that don't have anything to do with the words on the page ("this would be confusing to a kid"). Sometimes they use what they consider bad grammar or just write stories that make no sense, both of which they identify as things you never find in picturebooks. It's always interesting to see what students come up with.

When they are done, we mainly discuss their choices. Why did they choose to do what they did to create the worst picturebook? As they give their responses, I ask them how they knew that their choices would make it the worst. They generally acknowledge that their exposure to picturebooks as children helped them work against the genre's expectations. Although this is a good lesson to start them thinking about writing other, less familiar genres and how exposure matters, it also establishes the value I see in picturebooks and students' exposure to them.

When we have established what they already know, I like to give students some postmodern picturebooks that might do some of the things they said picturebooks would not do, characteristics that might identify them as "bad" picturebooks. In groups, they can examine their books to determine whether these really are bad. Most of the time, students decide the books are good, so we can begin a discussion of why picturebooks that "break the rules" of the picturebooks they knew as children might be good—and useful for secondary classrooms. It is a good way to get them to think about picturebooks from a more current viewpoint.

I encourage using picturebooks in the preservice courses I teach, and then, when I observe my students as student teachers, I watch them pull a stool to the front of the room and invite high school students to "come to the front and find a seat" so they can read a picturebook. Students sit cross-legged on the floor, attention rapt for once on a book and not a phone or a screen. Reiker noted in her observations of secondary classrooms using picturebooks that there was a visceral response when teachers pulled out picturebooks. I have observed the same thing many times in my own teaching in classes of all ages—adults and teens—and in classes that I have observed. Picturebooks make magic.

Principles

- ✓ Pragmatics
- ✓ Reading aloud
- ✓ Teaching approaches

Pragmatics

Teachers often ask me about the physical act of using picturebooks in the classroom—and it can be challenging. As Massey notes, "[I]t is imperative that students have access to both the text and illustrations to render picturebooks beneficial to the learning process" (46). I agree. Figuring out how to do that varies depending on the class size, for one thing, and how each class manages movement. But it also depends in part on the purpose of using the book.

When I read a book to prompt informal writing, for instance, or to introduce a concept, I read the book aloud at the front of the class. Students can come to the front and sit on the floor (if the class can manage that) or stay at their desks. I try to make sure that everyone gets to see the images, so the pacing is often slower as I read a spread and then make sure everyone gets to see the image for that spread. Once I had a sophomore honors class that had such difficulty with managing personal space that they could not get out of their seats to sit on the floor for a reading. I walked around the room while I read the book, showing them pages as I moved around the room and read. It wasn't ideal, but it was the best option for that situation.

If I have access to a document camera, I love using that. Students are better able to see the images, and, because the image–text relationship is so essential to many picturebooks, it is important for students to see the images. Sometimes I will note that a specific image is significant for some interpretation of the book, so I take a longer pause on that spread to make sure everyone can see the images. According to fair use, it is appropriate, if necessary, to scan one image of the book to put on a screen for deeper discussion as long as the document the image is screened into isn't distributed or shared in any way.

A surprising number of picturebooks are available online, either as PDFs or with someone reading them and showing the pages, so that teachers can share those versions on a screen. I am not always able to find every picturebook I want, but it's surprising how many are online, even newer books. I preview them, though, as some of the reading is more fluid than with other versions, and some of the filming of the pages is better too. I do sometimes request specific books from my school librarian—she has a budget that allows her to get some books for me each year—and that is another way to build a collection.

Sometimes, for other purposes, I have purchased several copies of a title (usually from used book sites) so that students could look at the book in groups (*Battle Bunny* by

Jon Scieszka and Mac Barnett, for example). In some cases, I took the books apart so that I could laminate pages and students could look at parts of the book in small groups and then trade the parts with other groups (e.g., *The Secret Knowledge of Grown-Ups* by David Wisniewski; *My House Has Stars* by Megan McDonald; *The Stinky Cheese Man* and *Squids Will Be Squids* by Jon Scieszka). In these cases, I usually needed only two or three copies.

And for other purposes, I collect sets of different books from the local library on a topic or by an author to use in groups and have students share their findings with the class: fractured fairy tales, for example, to develop revision concepts or several picturebooks about a historical period as context for reading a class novel. In these cases, students in small groups read different books and then share what they learned or trade books so that everyone gets to read a variety of picturebooks to achieve the objective of the lesson.

Ideally, we could have a book for each student to follow along in—or even one for every two or three students—but that just isn't realistic, either for cost or for storage. But considering the purpose of each book's use can help us choose the best option for the way to present the book to the class.

Reading Aloud

Lots of people think of reading aloud as something we do only with young children in elementary classes. However, Ommundsen reports on multiple studies to show the power of reading aloud to help motivate readers, including research that shows the power of students participating in experiences that held their attention and had an affective element to them—exactly what happens when students are read to (101). Merga reports her own and others' research supporting the same finding, noting particularly that "continuance of the practice encouraged [students] to read with greater frequency" (15). Gold and Gibson explain that "reading aloud is the foundation for literacy development." In fact, research shows that it can be the "single-most important activity for reading success" and can develop listeners' interest in language and help readers who are still building reading skills see the reading process in action (Gold and Gibson). Scoggin and Schneewind also note that teachers can use reading aloud from a wide variety of texts to validate all readers in the classroom, so reading picturebooks aloud can send the message that we value more than the novels we assign or read together in secondary school. Reading aloud is a good choice that teachers can make to improve students' reading, language, and writing skills.

Beyond the reading benefits, we gain other benefits from reading picturebooks aloud. An important one is that it makes those of us who are listening part of a community (Scoggin and Schneewind). This conclusion from research speaks to this point: "A child may enjoy being read to, for reasons beyond literacy, including closeness with a person or the shared experience with classmates" (McTigue et al. 130). When we are read to, we share an experience—both the cognitive and the emotional experience of reading together. That can have powerful effects in a classroom that I have seen happen many times.

Other benefits of reading aloud to children of all grade levels include the following: syntactic development, vocabulary acquisition, and comprehension (Layne 8–9). Reading aloud can improve students' writing, engagement, and attitude along with their understanding of new genres (9). The incredible body of research supporting teachers reading aloud to students is too much to ignore. We need to help secondary students develop in these important ways—and that means reading aloud to them.

Picturebooks, used for a variety of purposes in the secondary classroom but read aloud to students, can help us achieve these outcomes. We use picturebooks with intentionality—to meet learning objectives—but when we read them aloud in service of these other goals, we create layers of benefits to students, helping them read better independently, come to enjoy the language of books and the ideas they help us engage with, and build emotional connections with others. Yes, we can read class novels aloud to students. I have done that many times and even have passages memorized from reading some books aloud so many times a day over several years (think *An American Childhood* by Annie Dillard or *To Kill a Mockingbird* by Harper Lee). I have even read longer novels aloud to my secondary school classes, such as *The Right Stuff* by Tom Wolfe. Although some students didn't want to listen at first and accepted my invitation to read independently in the hallway, thinking they were beyond being read to, all of them eventually stayed in class when I read aloud because they found they understood more when they were read to than when they read silently. And they found that they enjoyed the shared experience. But reading novels takes time. And strong vocal chords. I think those read-alouds have benefits too. But they tend to happen less frequently. We can read a picturebook aloud for different purposes much more regularly in our classes, maybe even every day. Think of all the benefits we can accrue.

One thing we want to be sure about is that the picturebooks we choose are easy to read aloud, smooth and even. I particularly love books by Cynthia Rylant and Patricia MacLachlan, as they are so lovely to read aloud. A favorite is MacLachlan's *All the Places to Love*. As we visit the places around the farm—the mountain top, the river, the barn—we feel the peace and love in the place and totally understand why Eli wants his sister to love those places too. Sometimes this book brings me to tears as I read it aloud—I've had to have a student finish the reading a time or two. My students write after we read this book, and the experience always reminds me of the power of reading aloud when my students share their own deeply thoughtful pieces about places they love.

But we also need to practice our reading of the books so that we can read them smoothly. Sadly, more than once I have started reading a book aloud for an informal writing invitation and realized that my reading is bumpy—I can't see the page clearly and miss a line, the pages stick together and I have to put the book down to separate them, or it's been too long since I've read the book and I just can't catch the rhythm. At these times, I notice that my reading doesn't have quite the same effect on students, and I wonder if I miss some of the benefits possible from reading aloud as a result. We want our reading aloud, when it offers so many benefits to students, to be as effectively performed as possible.

Teaching Approaches

Most of the time, I read picturebooks aloud to students. That is partly because there is a limited number of books, but it's also partly the nature of picturebook interactions. They are meant to be read aloud. But as Foster notes, "[T]he way teachers read aloud to students is just as important as selecting quality books to read aloud. Reading aloud is more than simply standing in front of a group of students and reading the words on the pages" (28). So, although I spend a lot of time in this book discussing the selection of picturebooks, I will also spend some time discussing the presentation of those books.

Sipe presents five "conceptual categories" (Storytime 200–202) or roles for the ways that teachers interact with students when they are working with picturebooks. The first is as a reader, including reading the title and other peritext when it is useful and pointing to elements of note in the book. Sipe's research says this role constitutes about a quarter of the teacher's contribution to the class conversation. The second role is what he calls manager or encourager; in this role, the teacher poses questions and directs attention, either to something in the text or to a student's comment in discussion. The third role is that of clarifier or prober, where the teacher makes connections between student comments or poses questions to direct students' attention to an element of the picturebook that warrants special consideration. The fourth category he labels "fellow wonderer or speculator." In this case, teachers position themselves in the same role as students, questioning and speculating about what a text or image might mean. In Sipe's research, this role was the smallest, only 3 percent, and often identified by the teachers' silence, but it seems important because it can model for students how teachers can extend thinking, be creative or use their imaginations to make connections or predictions. The last role is as "extenders or refiners," where teachers expand on a student's insight or take advantage of a comment to introduce an important concept. This, according to Sipe's observation, is also a small category, only 5 percent of teachers talk.

I mention these roles as options for the many ways teachers can interact with students and picturebooks. Certainly, as a beginning point, we need to be able to read picturebooks well, with expression and good pacing, but when we are using picturebooks for instructional purposes, we can also consider other roles we might play to enhance student learning. I have had moments when a student's insight has surprised me, has been one I had never considered, and it encouraged me to take on the role of wonderer as it created a special moment in class. I have more often planned my comments ahead as an extender or prober as part of my lesson plan when I had a specific point for using the picturebook in a lesson. I hope that identifying these roles can encourage us to consider all the possibilities for using picturebooks in our classes and show us all the possible paths we can take as we do so.

The rest of this book builds on the strengths of picturebooks and students' affinity for them. I provide suggestions for picturebooks to use in the secondary classroom, for a variety of purposes that enhance reading and writing instruction. But I also give suggestions for other aspects of our instruction: working with multilingual learners, building community, and developing identities as readers and writers. I think the suggestions, focused as they are on a specific book and tasks, can be useful. But, since I don't know the books of the future—or even all the picturebooks teachers might have access to now—I know my suggestions are limited and might become dated.

To avoid that as much as possible, in each chapter I also provide **principles** to help teachers choose other books to help them in teaching similar lessons or for similar purposes. I hope these principles will guide us all to make effective future choices that fit our students' needs and the purposes of our classes. And with all the new picturebooks that will be published in the coming years, we will have some ideas for thinking about how to use them to help us do the important work in our classrooms. We just have to keep watch for the amazing books still to come. And how much fun is it to browse picturebooks?! Let's get going!

2

Using Picturebooks with Multilingual Learners

Learning a new language is hard work. I know. I've been trying for more than a year to learn Spanish, and if someone asks me how to say something or if I hear someone near me at the grocery store speaking Spanish and I try to listen—I am blank. It's awful. I want to learn. My friends from Bolivia encourage me and tell me to watch Spanish TV shows. I know I should, but watching Spanish shows is hard, even with the subtitles. At the end of the day, when I have time to watch something, my brain just wants to rest. I learned French when I was younger. I lived in France and went to school there. I can watch French shows, and a lot of the language comes back to me. But sometimes, when I want to do a Spanish lesson, the words of the two languages get mixed up in my head and I just can't remember what word I want. I want to mix the two. Or just use English. I don't have to think so hard when I do that.

I don't know how students in the United States with a home language other than English do it. When I was in school in France, I learned language more quickly than I am learning Spanish now, but there were so many other things that made the experience a challenge: different foods and different ways of doing everyday things like navigating subways and shopping. All the differences add to the complexity of learning the language. I don't know exactly how my multilingual learner (MLL) students might feel, but I know enough to try to find ways to make learning in my class just slightly easier, if I can.

I can try to remember my own experiences and consider what makes my class a challenging place to learn and use English. I can remember that the ELA classroom can be fast paced. As a teacher, I move quickly partly out of necessity (a lot to cover) and partly out of choice (too much free time and some students find "other" ways to entertain themselves). That pace could, in itself, be a challenge to my MLL students. I can also remember that the kinds of language we use in class may not be like the English my students encounter in social settings. Academic English can be a challenge; even for native English speakers, this might be an issue. I can also remember that classrooms are often conducted in a "recitation" style (Newkirk, *Literacy's Democratic Roots* 87), where the teacher poses a question and students answer and the process repeats. It's fast, and the pressure to find the right word in that moment is high. Picturebooks, chosen well, are a perfect antidote to these challenges, allowing for a shift in pace while still addressing the objectives of the lesson. When they are selected with care and thought for the MLL students in our classrooms, these books can also provide some relief from the intensity of English-only academic talk.

Lado asserts that picturebooks can motivate MLL students and improve learning, two important issues, and Roser et al. note that, whatever their levels of English, multilingual students are more engaged with picturebooks for a variety of tasks. Students learning English "can deeply process the limited text, because it is accompanied by visual and other scaffolds in a supportive social context" (Lado 30). In fact, Arizpe and Styles, looking at other research, conclude that our MLL students bring "a greater wealth of metacognitive and metalinguistic strategies" to their interpretation of picturebooks (219).

The challenge for teachers with multilingual learners in their regular classes is to select books that would be most helpful to our students with varying degrees of English knowledge. For example, a study reported in Hadaway and Young shows that multilingual students might have more difficulty with postmodern picturebooks, where the images tell a different story from the words. In the study they report, students learning English were able to participate in the discussion following a picturebook reading where the images and text complemented each other but were challenged when the images did not support the text (261). However, other researchers found that although the MLL students might have been challenged, as they discussed the unusual features of a postmodern picturebook they were able to "increase their enjoyment of the very features that had puzzled them" (Arizpe and Styles 219). Choosing books with care matters, but it might also be possible to scaffold our discussions of the books we choose with consideration of all the interpretive skills our MLL students bring with them.

Translanguaging

Translanguaging is a way to begin to approach the needs of MLL students in our classrooms and to think about selecting picturebooks to accomplish our desired instructional goals. At its heart, translanguaging values all the languages our students bring into our classrooms. In doing so, it challenges the idea of languages as "bounded" (Newkirk, *Literacy's Democratic Roots* 83). I first heard the term *Englishes* years ago, addressing the different ways English is used around the world and in different situations. Now, learning Spanish, I understand that there are "Spanishes": friends from Bolivia speak a Spanish different from that of friends from Ecuador or Peru. And, when we think about it, each one of us speaks different ways in different settings, sometimes blending our friend-slang with more business language at work. We do it for effect and because it makes better sense sometimes. It fits the need of the moment. Our multilingual students do the same thing, often shifting "in midsentence from one language to another, 'simultaneously using linguistic tools, knowledge, and features from all their languages,' adjusting them for the purpose and audience" (Newkirk, *Literacy's* 85, citing Fu et al. 6). In real life, language is fluid, without clear boundaries. It is even more true when speakers know multiple languages, and it's useful for teachers to be aware of this fluidity.

Allowing or even encouraging the fluidity of languages in our classroom begins with us and the artifacts we use that may, without even realizing it, suggest something about our language attitudes. Beyond simply the texts we choose—and the picturebooks we might include among those to accomplish multiple purposes—Herrera and España suggest reviewing the documents in our classroom that might suggest less flexibility toward language. One of their ideas is to look at rubrics that identify slang or informal language as something that will result in reduced scores. I have students who were told they could not use contractions in any school writing. We can imagine that these linguistic restrictions might send a message about not only who gets to speak in academics but also that the other ways we speak might not be accepted in this space. Considering genre is one way to think about language use: Do the genres we are writing really not have contractions? Slang? If so, instead of restricting language to "formal" only, we can design rubrics that ask student writers to use language in ways similar to that found in the genre we are writing. If they want to look for examples in the mentor texts we study of the kind of language they want to use, all the better. And our attitude becomes one of openness rather than restriction.

Newkirk (*Literacy's*) suggests some strategies for incorporating translanguaging into our classrooms: substitution, translation, transmediation, and strategic mixing—and picturebooks can help us implement these. Beyond the importance of helping multilingual learners in our classrooms feel seen and able to contribute, using picturebooks that exhibit these translanguaging characteristics can spark an interest in languages, potentially encouraging students to consider learning other languages. Substitution is writing in the first language instead of the new language. Transmediation—combining words with images to use readers' understanding of the pictures to improve understanding or communication—is the essence of picturebooks. Our use of these two options in our classes shows translanguaging explicitly.

Another strategy, translation, is writing in one language and then translating it into another. *Marisol McDonald Doesn't Match/Marisol McDonald No Combina* by Monica Brown is a lively picturebook about a girl who is full of life and loves all the contradictory aspects of it simultaneously. The story is about accepting yourself, so the

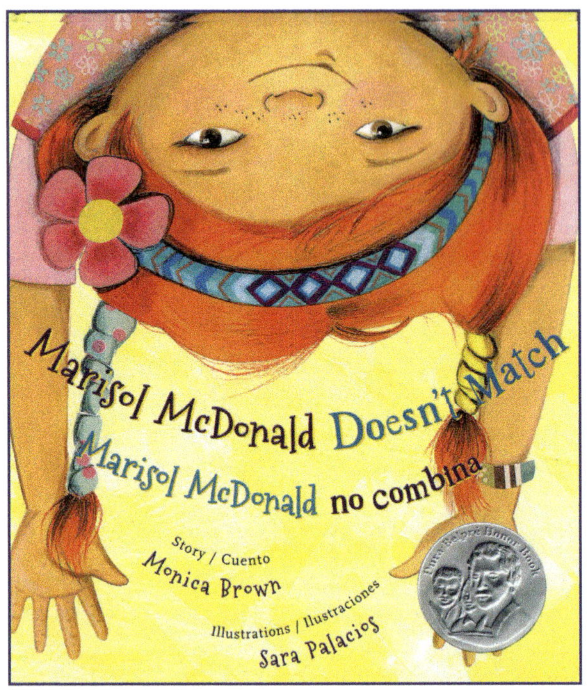

theme of the book can apply to a number of other texts we study and with any age, although the characters in this book are young. The book has English text on one page and Spanish on the facing page, so it is a good example of translation. I especially appreciate the example on one page where the family conversation is sprinkled with Spanish words on the English page and with English words on the Spanish page—also an excellent example of translanguaging, moving fluidly between the two languages and showing the full range of language. I like to use this book as an invitation for informal writing, with a Spanish-speaking student reading with me.

For a poetry unit, *Tierra, Tierrita/Earth, Little Earth* by Jorge Tetl Argueta is a great picturebook to share that also implements translation because it shows the poem in both Spanish and English on the pages and then in Nahuat, the author's first language, in the back. The poem can help teach literary devices as it provides MLL students access to the idea of texts written in one language and then translated into another, a process they might want to implement in their own writing processes.

I regularly taught Sandra Cisneros's *The House on Mango Street*, asking students to consider the book as a mentor text. In my tenth-grade classes, students would respond to some of the vignettes by writing similarly about their own lives. After we had read the entire book and written a number of vignettes, they selected five of their own to revise and link together for a memoir in Cisneros's style. Even when we didn't read the entire text, I used excerpts. One of the passages I often used to prompt writer's notebook entries was

"Hairs." I have found a picturebook of just this piece, told in both Spanish and English: *Hairs/Pelitos* (Cisneros). Illustrated, it is short enough to allow for both languages to be read aloud to prompt writing, engaging students who speak multiple languages and serving as a good example of translating.

Substitution could involve writing in students' first language (L1) and using English words where possible or writing in English and using L1 when necessary. Strategic mixing is the next step of substitution: knowing when to combine languages for the greatest effect, not solely out of necessity. Sometimes our students need to use substitution in their language development, but we can also encourage strategic mixing by including texts in our classes that show how to blend languages; we might see even stronger writing from the combination.

A book that I love for strategic mixing is also one that is useful with a reading fluency activity: asking students to practice reading picturebooks and then recording their reading for a class website so that classmates can hear a lot of different stories. *Digging for Words: José Alberto Gutiérrez and the Library He Built* by Angela Burke Kunkel tells the story of two Josés, an older one and a younger one. The older one collects garbage at night and finds books that he saves and shares with children (including the younger José) on Saturdays. I love this book as a shared reading for two students. For one thing, it is based on a true story, which I appreciate for the authenticity, but it also emphasizes the value of reading—another important aspect of the book that is emphasized by the repeated readings required to

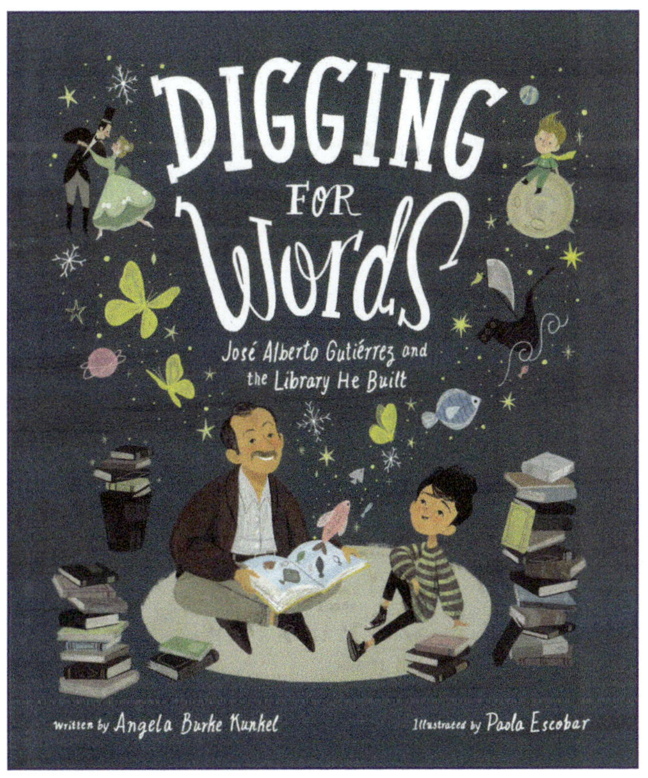

prepare for the recording. Spanish words are embedded throughout the text, so I think it helps Spanish speakers feel they are contributing to the recording in meaningful ways, teaching the Spanish to their partners (which is what happened with me).

Areli Is a Dreamer by Areli Morales is another example of strategic mixing in a text that recounts an immigrant experience directly; Morales is a DACA recipient who tells the story of her life in Mexico and her family's journey to being together in New York. In the early part of the book, Spanish words are used strategically—and even more so when she first arrives in New York and goes to school with little knowledge of English. By the end of the book, few words are in Spanish as she has developed her English fluency. The book would be a good starter for students to consider their own life journeys—from other places or from other stages—as they write their own stories, something that honors each person's life experiences just as this book honors the language each student brings to our classrooms.

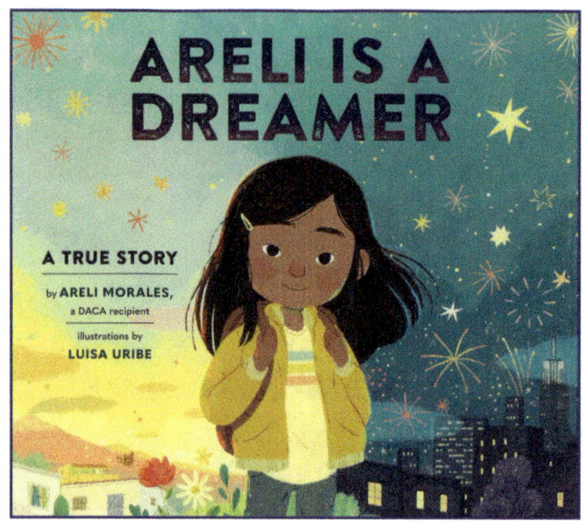

Another book that employs strategic mixing, *The Lotus Seed* by Sherry Garland, is useful for teaching either the element of symbolism or the skill of inference, both important lessons we often teach in secondary English classes. With Vietnamese words and place names woven throughout, the spare text includes images that support the words, meeting characteristics of picturebooks effective for MLL students. Narrated by a granddaughter, the story follows a young woman who saw Vietnam move from being governed by an emperor to a place of war, who lost her husband and moved to another country to raise her family. Through it all, the grandmother saved one special thing—a lotus seed. At one point in the story, the grandmother reveals what the seed symbolizes, but it is useful to have students stop before that to consider what they might see as the symbolism of the seed. At several points in the story there are also good places to have students practice inference; for example, we can consider what inferences readers

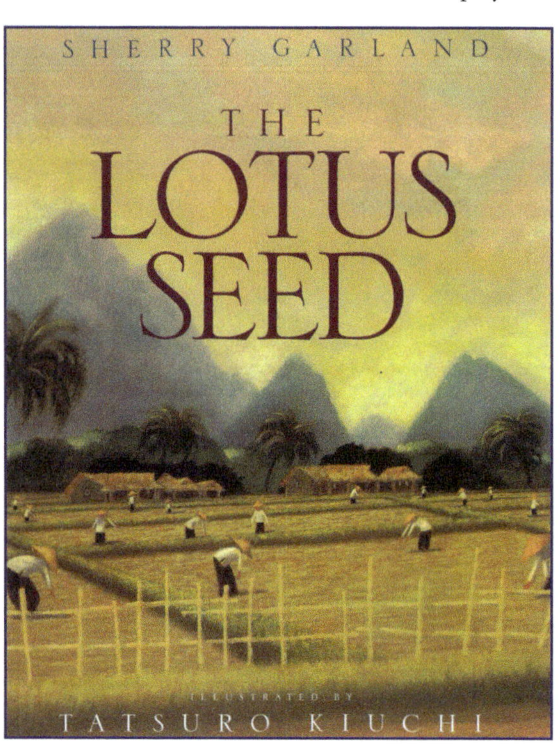

could draw from these sentences: "When her husband marched off to war, she raised her children alone" (10) or, on the next page, "when the bombs came and, in her hurry, she took her seed but not her mother-of-pearl hair combs" (11).

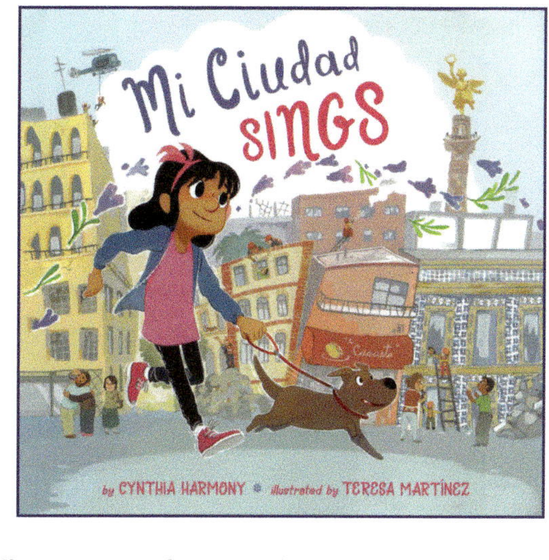

Mi Ciudad Sings by Cynthia Harmony is another example of strategic blending. It's a book that teachers might want to use to teach theme or for a lesson on active verbs in narrative writing. It blends Spanish words throughout (even in the title) and is a good example of how the blending can work smoothly to effectively communicate the ideas of the book.

A final example of strategic blending, *Nacho and Lolita* by Pam Muñoz Ryan can be a good book to use for a lesson on finding theme in literature—and differentiating it from moral or main point. It tells a Mexican folktale—and Ryan has an interesting story about her research for the book, finding out what kind of bird the tale is about since it's not a word she knew. It would also be useful to pair this text with books or units about overcoming differences and getting to know and like people who are not like us. I would suggest pairing it with James Hurst's "The Scarlet Ibis," a short story I taught with high school students because it raises the question of how the outcome of the story might have changed if Doodle's differences had been accepted by his brother and about what his brother would have needed to give up to accept Doodle. Paired with other picturebooks or other pieces of literature that have the same focus, this book could extend the idea of seeing beyond surface differences at the same time that it shows how we can use the full range of our linguistic resources in our classes.

Honoring Identity

Beyond language development, picturebooks and our classroom activities can help MLL students see our classrooms as places that value them as individuals. Goldy Muhammad explains that MLL students "are seeking to find curriculum and instructional practices that honor the multiple aspects of who they are" (69). Muhammad recommends classroom activities that help students consider their histories, their names, their cultures. Many

picturebooks provide either mentor texts for such writing or springboards for longer texts or writing activities to accomplish that goal.

I use Fran Nuño's *The Map of Good Memories* to invite informal writing, especially as we are preparing to write personal narratives, a genre that can accomplish Muhammad's goal of honoring who our MLL students are. The book tells the story of a girl who must leave her country because of war. Before she leaves, she takes out a map of her city and marks the places where she has been happiest in her life. She walks us through the places with a short memory attached to each: the library, the park, the movie theater. When she finishes marking the map, she realizes that she has written her name and that she will take these good memories with her all her life. I read the book to students, and they write whatever they want, but they usually write memories of important places in their lives. This works for multilingual students because the images help to clarify the story, and many of these students have places they miss. It works, too, for native speakers who also have places important to them.

While we use picturebooks for authentic purposes in our instruction, we can also show students we honor who they are by choosing from among the many options available books that show students who look like the learners in our classroom. Misty Copeland, author of *Firebird*, tells of feeling lost and alone. When she opened books about ballet, she didn't see herself in them. Now, in her book, she shares how others might find their dreams even in books that don't show people like them. *Firebird* is an example of this application of picturebooks: if we want to teach a concept (say, a theme about perseverance), we can use a large number of picturebooks, but to consider the MLL students in our classrooms, we

can look for picturebooks that also help those students see themselves in the stories, find their place in the classroom.

Joon was a student from Korea assigned to a class of eighth graders I was teaching, a class the district labeled "basic," for students who were more than two years below reading level. Because he spoke little English—and our district at that time had a very limited program to help English language learners—Joon was placed in this English class. At first he was mostly just angry. I could tell he was bright, but I needed to figure out a way to help him move beyond his anger. Because picturebooks were already included in the texts I used in all my classes, I continued to use them with Joon's class too. What I learned was that I could be more intentional about the picturebooks I chose for my classes to help my MLL students even more. Eventually, because of an assignment based on a picturebook at the end of ninth grade, when Joon was in my "regular" class, he and I both saw the flowering of his abilities and his confidence in himself as a learner.

Principles

- ✓ Have a clear, authentic (academic) purpose.
- ✓ Make sure the books are representative of the English levels and interests of students.
- ✓ Choose books that are sensitive to cultural issues.

Have a Clear, Authentic (Academic) Purpose

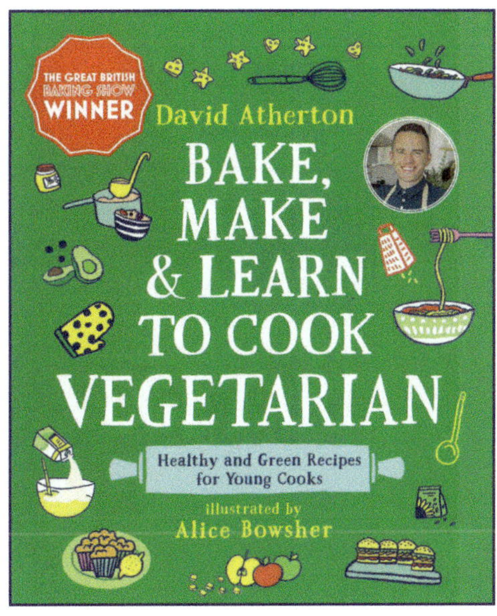

Secondary students, as mentioned in Chapter 1, can be very open to the use of picturebooks in the classroom, but they are also sensitive if in any way the books are meant to suggest that the students are not capable of higher-level reading or work. Having a clear academic purpose will shape the way teachers present and use picturebooks—and will mean that they can quickly address any questions about why they are using picturebooks. Knowing that I am using a picturebook to teach background knowledge for a novel or to develop students' understanding of theme means that I feel confident in my use of them.

Introducing *Bake, Make, and Learn to Cook Vegetarian* by David Atherton might seem like I am teaching students how to cook or encouraging vegetarianism. However, I know that I have several other objectives in mind: This book uses images with the written directions (transmediation) so that all students, not just multilingual students, can understand the ingredients and cooking tools being described (developing vocabulary). The foods included in the book are from a variety of countries across the globe, not just the ones that might be most familiar to many of our students (culturally affirming). And the text is a great mentor text for process writing (writing in a genre). So, despite first impressions, I have a solid rationale based on multiple academic objectives for using the book in my classroom.

O'Loughlin recommends using picturebooks to help multilingual learners understand difficult abstract principles since the images can help clarify abstractions. I have had my students write "Where I'm From" poems (http://www.georgeellalyon.com/where.html) at all grade levels. I find that some of their best writing comes from this prompt, and we get to know one another when we share our responses. But the poem is not literally about where a person is from; it's about the experiences, people, food, and talk of the people who make us who we are. Some of my multilingual students (and some of my younger students generally) don't seem to understand the abstraction of this task; they want to write "I'm from Alaska" and be done. Reading the picturebook, *Momma, Where Are You From?* by Marie Bradby is a perfect way to bridge students' understanding from literal to abstract. The book is set in the past—"I'm from Monday mornings, washing loads of clothes in the wringer washer"—but the images help clarify unfamiliar vocabulary. Repeated "I'm from" sentences with experiences instead of places makes clear the abstraction being developed in the writing so that students can begin to collect the experiences, people, and memories that make them who they are. This is a great way to build understanding of abstraction with the scaffolding of a picturebook.

Researchers (Mourão) and teachers (Gonzales) working with multilingual students recommend wordless picturebooks as a way to help students develop vocabulary and fluency through talking and activating creativity. However, Mourão specifically cautions that wordless picturebooks can be exhausting for some students without adequate language experience and should be accompanied by teacher scaffolding. When used effectively, wordless picturebooks can encourage listening, speaking, and writing. Choosing books with intriguing storylines is important as students can develop inferring skills.

Generally, the procedure I use is to allow students in partnerships to "read" the story to each other. This is especially useful if multilingual students feel comfortable pairing up with native speakers. If they don't, they might use partners who speak the same language to interpret the images. Partners don't have to tell the same story but can build off from what the other partner notices (or doesn't notice). Some books even allow for multiple storylines. When I taught junior high, I loved using *The Snowman* by Raymond Briggs, *Clown* by Quentin Blake, and *You Can't Take a Balloon into the Metropolitan Museum* by Jacqueline Preiss Weitzman. I usually had students "read" the book to each other, practicing inference and speaking and listening skills.

After they had practiced interpreting and sharing the stories orally, I liked to ask students to write the stories too, as the speaking before writing seemed a supportive practice. But I noticed that writing a whole story was sometimes challenging for students who were still learning English vocabulary, even after they had spoken the story or at least shared parts of it. I understand that challenge more now from trying to learn another language myself. I can read and even say some things, but writing is a different game. One way I address this issue is to give students a panel or two from one of the stories and ask them to write just that part of the story, limiting the amount of text they need to generate. Also, I encourage them to use strategic mixing in their writing, or even translation. They are already employing transmediation by putting words to the images. By writing for only a few pages or panels, students need to make sense of the page, but they can write significantly less. Some teachers have students write captions for different panels or pages, another way to lower the load of writing extended pieces. The back cover of *Clown* contains four illustrations and accompanying captions that summarize the complete story. These can serve as an example of summarizing, but I also liked to show the back cover and ask students to write a sentence of detail between each main idea, writing three to four sentences instead of the whole story.

Another option I sometimes used, especially with *You Can't Take a Balloon into the Metropolitan Museu*m, was to ask students to write extensions, such as what might be the next adventure the balloon has, to practice new skills (like dialogue) by writing two characters speaking directly to each other, or to have some of the characters write journal entries, telling the story from their individual perspectives. All of these options allow students to use their understanding to create meaning and to use language options (translating, substituting, or mixing) as needed.

Make Sure the Books Are Representative of the English Levels and Interests of Students

There are a lot of picturebooks that might be useful to teach something about reading and writing, even vocabulary. But if secondary students feel that the book is too juvenile, especially if they are still learning English, they could refuse to use the opportunity to learn. As it is, choosing picturebooks for secondary students must always be thoughtful of age appropriateness, but this is even more important for multilingual students. For example, numerous ABC books can help to build vocabulary. But the books we might give to a small child, with text such as "A is for apple," for example, might be best left on the shelf, allowing those students who need that level to choose those for themselves. Instead, *The Skull Alphabet* Book by Jerry Pallotta or *P Is for Pterodactyl* by Raj Haldar and Chris Carpenter are more age appropriate. The skull book doesn't tell the name of the animal but gives clues (answers are in the back). Multilingual students can learn a lot of vocabulary from this book, but it doesn't feel juvenile in any way. The pterodactyl book contains words that have silent first letters, so it turns the idea of an ABC book on its head: *G* is for gnat and *K* is for knight. Even though traditionally we consider ABC books to be for children, these books are examples of the types that are not meant for young children—and they can teach vocabulary to multilingual students (besides being of interest to many secondary students).

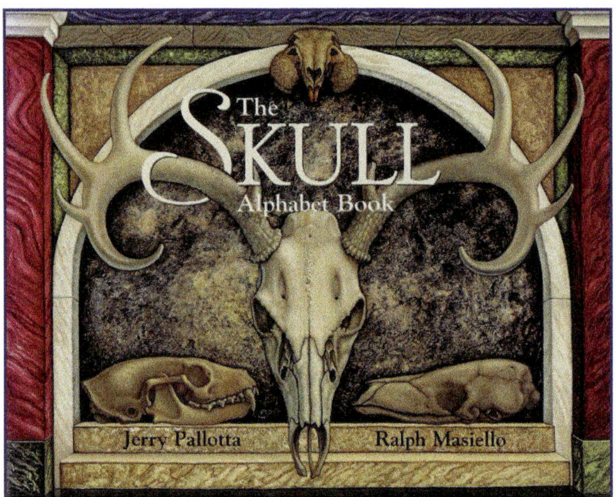

Depending somewhat on the students' proficiency with language, wordless picturebooks should be considered if they are for more mature students. As mentioned earlier, Mourão notes that interpreting wordless picturebooks can be "extremely demanding" for students with "low language proficiency" (60). Nevertheless, some classics, like *Good Dog, Carl* by Alexandra Day, might be useful for younger learners with less English since the concepts are fairly straightforward. Finding wordless picturebooks with layers of meaning may be more appropriate for older students. They are beneficial to all learners but don't feel as though they are suggesting that lack of English language means less ability to understand abstract concepts and ideas. *Rainstorm* by Barbara Lehman, for example, seems direct, with images that are easy to follow, but the storyline is more complex, appropriate for middle schoolers or above rather than younger children. About a boy, alone on a rainy day, who finds a key that opens a chest that takes him to another world of adventure and friends, it is reminiscent of C. S. Lewis's Narnia stories. The book can generate a lot of discussions about imagination, loneliness, and what matters in life for older students who can all "read" the book, no matter their level of English language development.

Choose Books That Are Sensitive to Cultural Issues

We want to make sure that the books we choose to represent other cultures accurately portray those cultures. For example, when speaking of books that represent Indigenous peoples, Reese recommends that teachers "choose books that are tribally specific (that name a specific tribal nation and accurately present that nation), written by Native writers, set in the present day, and relevant all year round, keeping Native peoples visible throughout the school year" (391). She recommends *Jingle Dancer* by Cynthia Leitich Smith as a good example for cultural understanding, but the principles she names might be good ones to consider for other cultures too.

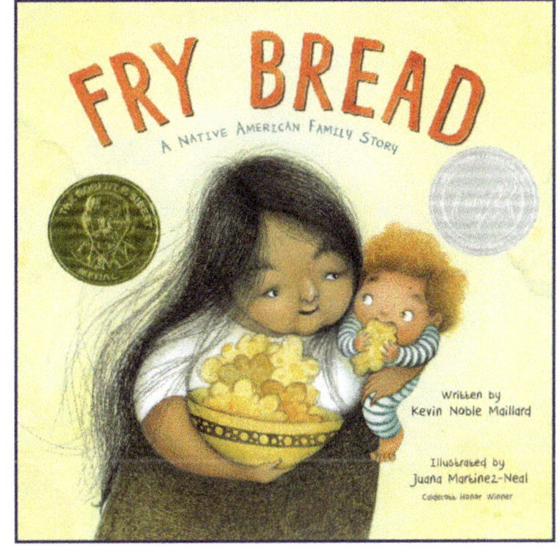

A popular picturebook right now is Kevin Noble Maillard's *Fry Bread*, which tells the story of a food and how it represents the culture and heritage of a broad group of peoples. The endpapers, with their names of villages and tribal names, are impressive in and of themselves, but in this spare book, they also help readers see the way food is both a reflection of culture and a connection between cultures. Although the text is spare, the ideas underlying the content in the endpapers that connect to the writer and illustrator and their traditions with fry bread are nuanced and complex enough (originally a food developed out of oppression) to create a strong foundation for a high school class unit on food narratives.

My favorite book for trying to help all students feel comfortable in my class no matter who they are is Shaun Tan's *The Arrival*. This wordless picturebook is the story of a man traveling to a new country, learning how to make his way through all the newness, and eventually having his family join him. Because it is illustrated in a way that doesn't align with any country on our planet, the story carries no stereotypes. Whenever I have used this book (or part of it, since it's quite long), everyone understands what it means to be new in some way. We all identify with adjustments we make to move from one place to another. Friends who have been teaching immigrant students in recent years find the book essential when language is limited; students totally understand the story of going to a new place, the unfamiliarity of what we see and hear, the confusion and initial feeling of being lost. Many of their students want to write their own stories after "reading" *The Arrival*; *Marianthe's Story* by Aliki is a good book to pair with *The Arrival*, possibly even as a way to help students who are gaining English language facility find alternate ways to communicate until they have the language they need.

3

Using Picturebooks to Invite Informal Writing

My students enter class and settle their bags next to their desks. Among the "getting ready for class" routines, they retrieve their writer's notebooks because they know they will be using them. The chatter is what I expect—greetings and laughter and commentary—that diminishes only slightly when the bell rings. But when I stand in front of the class and welcome them with a picturebook in my hands, the class settles and quiets. It's almost like a sigh.

I read the title of the picturebook and show the cover; then I open the book and start reading, pausing to turn and share the pages with the students. I walk in close and move around the room so that everyone can see what is happening on the pages, not just hear the words. There's a kind of rhythm to this oral reading, a little like mindful breathing, as we settle into the story the book unfolds for us. When I finish, I close the picturebook and say, "Let's write." And that is what we do. I might have them write for only a few minutes in some classes (if I have students who need more monitoring), but they know that I want to write, so they generally give me a little time to do so. When most of them have written what they have to say today, I ask the ones still writing to "find a good place to pause, write a note to yourself about where you were thinking of going next" and give them half a minute to do so. Then I ask, "Who is willing to share with us today?" and wait for hands to go up.

After students share, we clap. We have established that the applause is acknowledgment of willingness to share, not an evaluation of the writing, since we all just wrote spontaneously. Sometimes the sharing is more enthusiastic than at other times—and I have strategies for managing the slower days—but we always have sharing of some kind. Then I thank students for writing, and we move into the lesson for the day. This informal writing is an island in our day, a sanctuary away from whatever else we do. And that aspect of this writing is essential.

I start whatever class I am teaching, from junior high through high school and college, with informal writing in our writer's notebooks. My students depend on it. In fact, with rare exception—shortened class periods for assemblies or testing days—when time doesn't allow for the ritual, my students complain. They like writing informally. They like sharing. They like the freedom and creativity of the practice. They like the time in school that doesn't feel like school. Here, in their own words, are some of the reasons they appreciate regular, informal writing time:

- ✓ Reminded me that writing can be fun
- ✓ Helped me avoid the fear or pressure I feel to create a perfect piece of writing
- ✓ Revived my love for writing
- ✓ Gave a place in class to simply be yourself
- ✓ Appreciated the freedom and flexibility
- ✓ Made a time where I could unwind
- ✓ Created more unity in our class because of our shared entries
- ✓ Helped me improve my writing skills

My commitment to daily informal writing is strong. Now. That wasn't always the case, though.

Before I used writer's notebooks and committed to the regular and frequent practice of informal writing, I used either journals or class notebooks. The challenge with journals was that students associated it with very personal writing, a purpose at odds with school. I wondered at the time about the fit: Do we always want to share our journal entries? And how do I grade journals? What do they contribute to learning? The class notebooks were a combination of class notes, sentence play, and informal writing that I adapted from Ianacone and that kind of made the writing seem like class notes. With both these methods, journals and notebooks, we would write informally maybe two or three times a week. Maybe. If I had time for it. But I had a hard time making the time. I think I wasn't seeing results or connections, so it was easy to push these formats and practices aside. When we do it right, regular informal writing takes time. Committing to daily informal writing took risk on my part—I had to give it a chance, give up the time and the other content I wouldn't get to, before I could see the value. When I did, I learned that what we gained as writers and as a community was much more valuable than what we gave up.

I don't know why it took me so long to dedicate time to writer's notebooks. Lots of influential teachers I admire have written about using writer's notebooks and about the necessity of regular, informal writing: Donald Graves, Donald Murray, Nancie Atwell, Katie Wood Ray, Stacey Shibbutz, among others. Published writers often advise us to write regularly and informally: "It's important to pay attention to your ideas and write them down. If you do, you'll start having more and more of them. It's almost as if your imagination suddenly realizes it's being taken seriously," says Elise Broach, author of, among other books, *Masterpiece*, *Desert Crossing*, and *Shakespeare's Secret*. I should have believed.

Researchers (Graham; Smith) and teachers across the country (Gehr; Hubbard) also endorse regular informal writing, suggesting that it encourages the following traits we want writers to develop: risk-taking, awareness, ability to make connections, improved ease and perseverance with writing, and confidence, among others. These important attributes are ones that I can't really teach in a mini-lesson, and I began to notice those traits in my students too. That's what I learned from incorporating regular informal writing (writer's notebooks) in my classes. That's why it's important to make room for informal writing as a regular practice.

So, now that I am committed to regular informal writing in my classroom, how do I make it work? I'll admit that I've tried everything out there: Prompt? No prompt? Specific time? Open-ended with regard to time? Scored? Not scored? Sharing in small groups? Sharing with the whole class? This isn't the place to discuss all of that except to say I believe each teacher makes these decisions for their own class and their own students—which might mean changing things up with some classes.

For the purposes of this book, I address using prompts, but I prefer to call them "invitations to write." Someone recently asked me about this: Does it matter what we call whatever we do to invite writing? Prompt or invitation? It might for students; if we call our writing "journals," they usually think it's only about their personal lives—and some want to participate while others don't. What we call the invitations to write as teachers matters too. A prompt, to us, might mean something like "write about your most embarrassing moment." I've done that. Sometimes students respond, "I've never had one!" or "I can't write about *that*!" And I know how that feels—most of my embarrassing moments are not ones I want to relive. And I am not always sure that I want to ask students to share what they've written, but if they do . . . TMI.

I also advocate using the term *invitations* more than *prompts* because students usually need something to get them writing. I have found that students often don't know what to write about if they have total freedom. "Write about anything you want" can be as paralyzing as a too-specific topic I know nothing about. I have tried Atwell's writing territories, Heard's heart maps, and Anderson's "writer's eye" (35–37), and all have their value. What I finally ended up with, though, is a combination. I begin with picturebooks as invitations to write and then, early on, have students fill a page with possible writing ideas (through any of the methods just mentioned) so that when they don't feel inspired by the invitation I provide, they can go to that list and find something to write about. So, mostly, I invite writing through a picturebook.

As I experimented with different kinds of invitations, I found that when I used picturebooks, the time we spent together with the book provided us with a shared experience, one that opened possibilities for writing and that didn't feel like "school writing." I sometimes use short videos or poems as invitations to write, and there are benefits to those too. But there is something unique to using picturebooks for these invitations; there is a community in the shared experience of reading from the same book together. And that makes a lot of difference.

Let me illustrate a difference between a prompt and an invitation. Sometimes teachers ask students to write about their fears. That is the prompt. Some students will write, but it can be hard for others to respond to that request. Some might not like the risk it takes to share fears in a classroom setting, and with the prompt, there is nothing else to choose from. Instead, I can bring in a book that might get at the same topic, if that is the goal, but in a way that encourages lots of ways to respond: *Little Mouse's Big Book of Fears* by Emily Gravett. After we read it, some students write about the things they fear, and the tone of the book encourages them to write about even the fears we wouldn't normally think about. Students might also tell a story of a time as a child when they were afraid of a dog or of turtles (as one of my students did—who knew?). If they want, they can even write about the nursery rhyme alluded to in the book. There are lots of possibilities, and those possibilities invite more students to write.

The advantages of using picturebooks as writing invitations also include the time the book allows for writers to relax and get into the idea or concept. While we read the book together, students begin to absorb the concept. Being read to is relaxing, and I think that adds to the writing experience. We begin with a few minutes of relaxing enjoyment before we write. Additionally, well-written books provide multiple ways of seeing the concept, thus opening possibilities beyond the simple invitation to "write about a time that something didn't turn out as you planned." As writers listen to the book, they each experience it

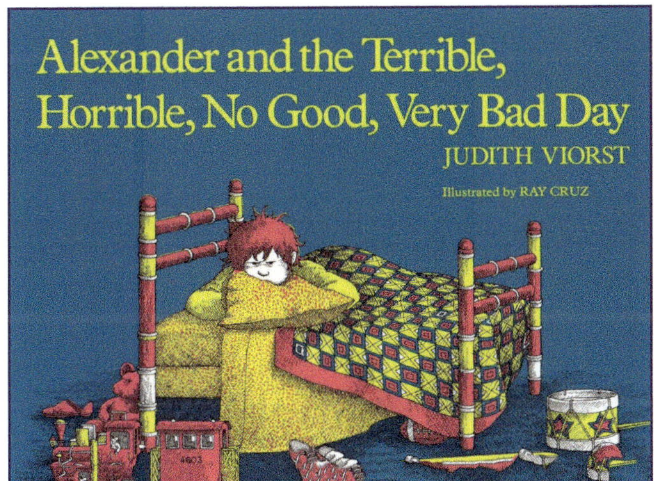

individually, allowing them to find a way into the concept that works for them and their lives.

When I look for books to use to invite informal writing, I try to imagine all the possibilities that the books might offer for writing. *The Most Magnificent Thing* by Ashley Spires is a good book for eliciting responses about a time when something didn't turn out the way we expected. Books of lists that have universal appeal are also provocative: Jenny Offill's *17 Things I'm Not Allowed to Do Anymore*, *One of Those Days* by Amy Krouse Rosenthal, and *Alexander and the Terrible, Horrible, No Good, Very Bad Day* by Judith Viorst each sets up the possibility for venting about common experiences of having a bad day or doing something that seemed like a good idea but didn't turn out as planned.

I would caution that the tone of the picturebook also matters for the response. Heavy books tend to elicit heavier responses than light-hearted treatments of topics do. Sometimes students respond to elements of the books in ways we should try to anticipate. At the beginning of the school year, one of the earliest invitations I give has to do with our names and how we feel about them. I have found that the book I use as an invitation has an effect on the tone of the writing students do.

So, for instance, *Chrysanthemum* by Kevin Henkes is about a little mouse who LOVES her name until she goes to school and others make fun of it. Although she eventually comes to appreciate its difference, the book acknowledges how others might respond to names. In Annika Dunklee's *My Name Is Elizabeth!*, the protagonist proceeds through her day with each person calling her by different nicknames. Tired of it, she corrects each person, repeatedly asserting that her name is Elizabeth. I have noticed that the different books tend to elicit different tones and responses in the informal writing that students share. The character Elizabeth is feisty; Chrysanthemum is more thoughtful. Students' responses tend to reflect those tones as well. I have wondered about using other books about names—*The Name Jar* by Yangsook Choi and *The Change Your Name Store* by Leanne Shirtliffe—and how they might alter the students' initial experiences and, thus, how and what they write informally. The key is to ensure that the books open up possibilities for writing instead of shutting them down.

Opening up possibilities is another benefit of using picturebooks for invitations to informal writing. They help students feel like writers. School writing tends to have specific topics and specific intended outcomes. Students feel like writers when they have room to make choices—and one major desired outcome of writing informally is to help writers feel like writers.

Sometimes teachers ask me how to get students to see all the possibilities for writing in the invitation. I usually start with a short mini-lesson in which I read a picturebook and then ask students to brainstorm all the things we could write about from that book. So, if we read Dave Eggers's *Tomorrow Most Likely*, we would list things like the following: what tomorrow will be, hopes and dreams, squirrels, bugs, breakfast, cities, clouds, ice cream, cousins, sticky stuff (gum on the ground), and more. I want students to see that anything from the book has potential for writing. We can talk about writing stories or memories or poems or whatever for any of the topics. It's up to each writer. That is what I hope the mini-lesson shows them.

I could use excerpts from literature or poems, and I have from time to time. But I find that the addition of a visual element encourages more ideas in my students, partly because of their innate interest in the visual elements but also because many choose to write about something that comes from the images in the book rather than the words. The pictures provide even more options for writers. In addition, today's picturebooks contain so many options of genres and topics, and they are accessible to all learners, including multilingual learners. Most important, to me, is that picturebooks are inherently about possibility—and that is the true value of using picturebooks as informal writing invitations.

Sharing our writing is an important community builder in our classroom. As students see how other students respond to the invitation, see how others use humor or reflection in meaningful ways, we come to know one another in ways that we can't in the usual activities of an English class. We don't expect the writing we do in ten minutes to be polished or perfect; we just expect that it exists. And we all clap or snap to show appreciation for the sharing—not for the quality of the writing. But we learn about each other, —and that is important.

✦✦✦

Principles

- ✓ Provide possibility for multiple and individual responses.
- ✓ Consider length.
- ✓ Consider content.

Provide Room for Multiple and Individual Responses

This seems fairly obvious, especially since I discussed the idea earlier, but it's important to consider in more depth. To encourage writing, the books we choose as invitations need to open up possibilities for writing, not close them down. A book that is about a topic too new or unfamiliar to writers usually doesn't open up possibilities. So, as good a book as Nicola Davies's *Surprising Sharks* is (and I use it as an example in another chapter), it doesn't create possibilities for informal writing. I imagine myself as a student after the teacher reads the book and invites me to write. These are some of my thoughts: What do I know about sharks? Just what the teacher read to me. So what do I write? I'm afraid of sharks. I heard a story about sharks once (and watched *Jaws*). . . . Now what?

Books about concepts or universal ideas are excellent for invitations. For example, *Night of the Veggie Monster* by George McClements always gets a good response because, after all, who doesn't have something to say about food—especially negative reactions to food? And all of us have foods we love or hate or love to hate, foods that make us cheer or foods that make us want to vomit. Everyone has something to say about food. Picturebooks about food usually offer lots of good possibilities and are accessible to the majority of our students.

The Loud Book and its partner, *The Quiet Book*, both by Deborah Underwood, are books I really like to use for inviting informal writing. I have used them with great results at all age levels. *The Loud Book* lists different kinds of "loud": last slurp loud and going-to-school song loud. The sounds seem to progress through a day, or at least come in an order of morning to evening, but the structure is not strained. The images are essential to a full understanding of the louds, so I suggest showing them on a screen, if possible, but be sure to show the images because they prompt ideas for writing too. Both books are short so there is time to spend on sharing the images, even if we have to walk the book around the room. Students always seem to enjoy these picturebooks and have lots to write about sounds in their lives. This invitation is one that appeals to all students. The responses can be embarrassing or funny, common or unique, but everyone has something they can relate to with this invitation.

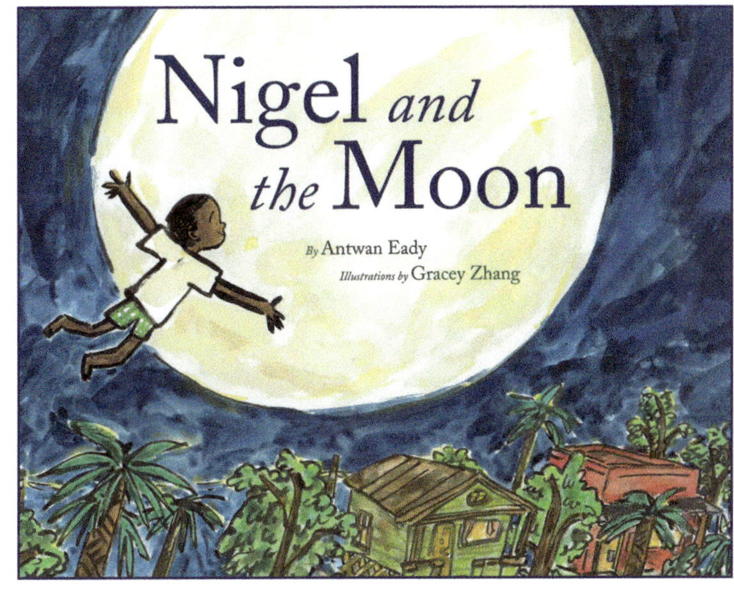

Nigel and the Moon by Antwan Eady is another book that opens up so many possibilities for students. It talks about dreams, about fitting in, about school and embarrassment, and about acceptance and growing confidence as it tells the story of a young boy who has dreams for his future that he is afraid to share. He is a little embarrassed by his parents coming to school to tell about their jobs, viewing them as perhaps less interesting than the other parents' jobs. Nigel's dreams may not be the same as those of other students (becoming an astronaut, a dancer, a superhero), but he feels his dreams deeply. The language of the book is as bright as Nigel's dreams, so this book inspires lots of responses.

Consider Length

Another principle when teachers use picturebooks as invitations for informal writing is to consider the length. Since most picturebooks are thirty-two pages long, what I really mean by length is not the number of pages but the time it takes to read a book aloud. Some picturebooks have more writing on each page; others let the images do more of the meaning-making work. Some books have more fluid text, making them easier to read aloud, while others take longer to read simply because the words aren't as easy to read. The time it takes to read a book doesn't mean the book isn't a good one; many picturebooks I use for other purposes are not as useful as writing invitations. But when we are taking class time for informal writing, we need to be careful about how much time simply reading the book takes. We want to leave time for writing and time for sharing. If reading the book takes too long, those other activities are often cut short, or we end up taking so much class time that even more content is cut, and that can sometimes be a problem too.

What this consideration means is that teachers should practice reading a book aloud before they use it as a writing invitation. Ryan T. Higgins's *Mother ~~Goose~~ Bruce* (a book I recommend later for teaching character in literature) is a funny book that takes longer to read aloud than it would appear. Part of that has to do with the way the illustrations are needed for the full meaning of the text—you simply must stop to show the pictures! Additionally, the book is about a grumpy bear, so many of the sentences reflect that: they are abrupt and choppy, just like the bear. As a result, they don't flow the way other books might.

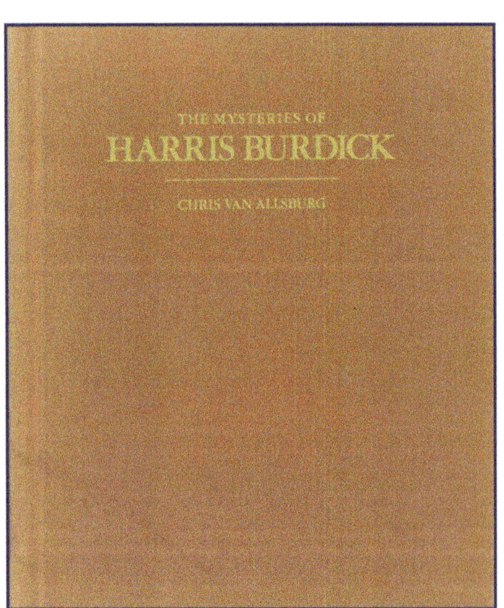

An option for using longer books might be to provide the overall frame and then read only a portion to students. This works well for some books such as Pamela Zagarenski's *The Whisper*, where it's possible to set up the storyline and then read one of the pages as an invitation for informal writing. For this book, I read the first six pages, which have a lot of words, and then choose one of the double-frame pages with the start of a story and use that as the entire invitation. It takes a little more time to set it up the first time I use the book, but I can return to other parts from the book as invitations later without having to read the beginning again, saving time at those points.

With another longer book that's great for inviting informal writing, *The Mysteries of Harris Burdick* by Chris Van Allsburg, I read the introduction, which is about an author who dropped off the illustrations, titles, and first lines of several stories to an editor, who wanted the author to return with the rest of the stories. The author never did, so the editor published only what he had: illustrations, titles, and first lines. Then I pick one or two of the images with their first lines to inspire informal writing. As with *The Whisper*, we can return to future images and opening lines on other days if students wish to do so—and on those days, giving the invitation is shorter because students already have the initial frame of the book. And I will say that this book is a favorite with my students of all ages.

Some books, however, as effective as they may be for other purposes, are too long for inviting informal writing and just can't be used in this way. For example, although Megan McDonald's *My House Has Stars* works well for teaching about genre and structure (and is used in another chapter), it doesn't work well as an invitation for informal writing. Reading the entire book just takes too much time. And, although the frame could be read separately, the individual pages are fairly long, so they don't work effectively as independent invitations. I love *My House Has Stars*; it is a mentor text for writing a longer piece that elicits the best response of any piece of writing I have ever asked students to write. My reference to it here is meant to highlight the importance of considering length as part of purpose. Just because a picturebook is too long for the purpose of inspiring informal writing doesn't mean the book might not be very useful for other purposes.

Consider Content and Genre

While we want to choose books that open up possibilities for informal writing, we also want to consider the ways a picturebook might influence student writing, especially if it contains complicated content and structure. For example, I was a little surprised the first time I used *A Pig Parade Is a Terrible Idea* by Michael Ian Black as an informal writing invitation. It's a funny book, and I thought students would like the imaginative stretch it takes to consider what kinds of parades might be good or bad ideas. Students did have a lot of fun with the creativity of the invitation, but I noticed that their writing mirrored the structure of the picturebook, which is somewhat like a five-paragraph essay. Not all students followed that structure—in fact, one student wrote her ideas in the shape of a poem!—but most of the responses followed a thesis, reason, explanation, reason, explanation, etc. format that sounded remarkably alike as students read them, much more alike than I usually see with informal writing responses. Although I was aware of the structure of the picturebook, it didn't occur to me that it would have this kind of influence on students. I have since moved the title to our genre study of standardized tests because it provides a good introduction for students' natural inclination to use the structures valued in writing tests. And I hope that says something important about the use of picturebooks: even if a book is a good one, it might not be good for all purposes. Choosing it to meet our specific goals is essential.

So, if a book is written in rhyme, will writers feel inspired or compelled to also write in rhyme? And do we want that? I'm not saying teachers should avoid books with particular structures; I just think we need to consider the influence of the picturebook on student writing.

Sometimes we might want students to explore sensitive topics or social issues in their informal writing—and I don't think that's a bad idea. I would give a few cautions here. First, if our choices for specific topics for informal writing become too tied to the topic of the class that day or to any agenda, students start to see the writing as part of school or the lesson, not as a chance to write whatever they want in whatever way they want. They may not really explore the topic we hope they will because they start to see our use of informal writing as a backdoor into something we want to accomplish, rather than just letting them write and make choices for their own purposes. In these situations, the writer's notebooks don't seem to belong to the student writer but to the course and the work of the course. I have found that much is lost when the informal writing becomes more about class and less about the writer.

I have recently found—and used—a new book about immigration that is useful for writer's notebooks. In every group, it seems to encourage writers to consider all sorts of issues, both personal and social, in interesting and personal ways. *Wishes* by Múón Thi Văn, includes images of people fleeing their home and enduring hardships as they make their journey to what they hope will be a safer, better place, but the words are poetic, giving the wind and water and sun and clock human feelings—wishes. The combination evokes some of the most poignant writing I have heard students share, but I can imagine that if I then used the lesson to set up a debate about immigration, it might seem heavy-handed to my students. The book would be useful for starting that discussion, but when we use books like this to invite informal writing, we have to think about context. Students are more willing to write about sensitive topics, I think, when they feel they can own the ideas rather than have them directly used as fodder for class.

Additionally, if the picturebook seems to invite sharing highly personal, even intimate, information, writers may feel reluctant to write or share. This is a tricky space. We want students to feel that the informal writing is their choice, but sometimes students believe that teachers are encouraging them to share personal information that they don't want to share. Some even feel that they will be judged if they don't write about highly personal experiences. In such situations, the purposes of informal writing will be strained because students see the activity more from a what-someone-else-wants-from-me perspective than from one where they can write freely. So I try to be sensitive to the content that a book might draw out from writers.

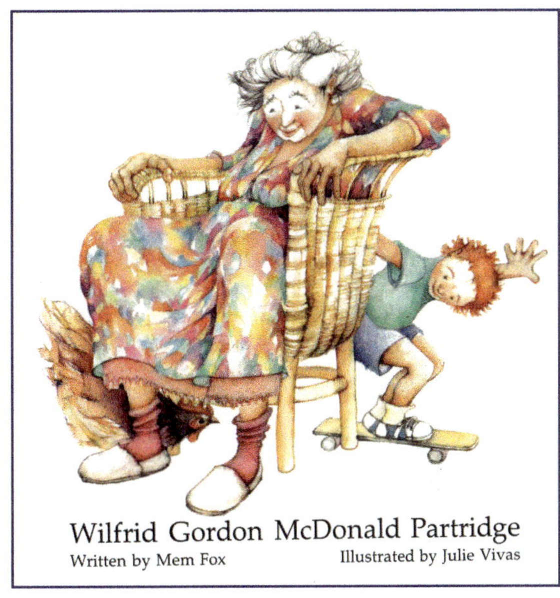

Wilfrid Gordon McDonald Partridge is a tender story by Mem Fox that is often a good one for getting students to write about memories. In the book, a small boy becomes friends with several elderly neighbors. When he hears that one of them is losing her memory, he wants to help. He asks the others what a memory is. Their responses—something warm, something funny, and so on—inspire him to collect objects that to him are warm, funny, etc. He takes the box of items to her, and his objects trigger her own, long-ago memories that are very different. As much as I like this book for its possibilities, it might cause some students to feel compelled to share personal information that they are unwilling or not ready to share.

Although I don't usually do anything after reading beyond saying, "Let's write!," one way I hope to avoid students feeling as though they must share what they are not ready to share is through a little intermediary activity. After reading the book together, we list the five elements of memory identified in the book: something warm, something from long ago, something that makes you cry, something that makes you laugh, something as precious as gold. Then each student lists a memory for each category with just a few words. My example: funny—Kate eating noodles for the first time. When everyone has had a chance to think about memories for a bit, each selects one to write about in greater detail. The listing gives writers a chance to consider multiple options for writing quickly and then have choice in which one they most want to develop. It offers students options besides the ones they might not be ready to share. The combination of choice and personal investment makes this invitation one that rarely fails to engage writers.

Sometimes books trigger emotional responses in students that we don't anticipate. It's good to know something about your students and what they are experiencing, if possible. But it's not always possible to know that a beloved grandparent just passed away or that a student just went through a breakup. Those are not always things we know in the moment, but life experiences like these might make students feel more tender about some topics. Even

months after my own father passed away, a presenter in a workshop I attended read a notebook invitation that had me leaving the room in tears, unable to write. I know the presenter had no idea—actually, I was a little surprised myself—but the experience made me more sensitive to this possibility. I now try to consider what I know is going on in my students' lives when I make choices for informal writing. And I will say that the year before my father's passing, when he was getting ill, I was also in a workshop when a presenter read Matt de la Peña's *Love* as the invitation. I wrote a lot—and tears flowed as I did—but it was a good experience. I remembered so many memories, and eventually I revised that piece of informal writing as a gift for my father before his passing. In that case, I was emotional, but not in a bad way. Teachers just need to be aware. Later I read some discussion about the appropriateness of de la Peña's book for children because it has an image representing some kind of family dysfunction (a child hiding under furniture). If a teacher knows this image could trigger someone in the class, they might want to reflect carefully about its use.

The first time I used *Perfect Square* by Michael Hall as an informal writing invitation was with older students. The book focuses on a square piece of paper that is rumpled and torn each day of the week, but each time chooses to make something beautiful from the tears and wrinkles. I find the book very moving, and the first time I wrote with my students after sharing it, I wrote about the way I was feeling that day, with too much on my plate to handle. I felt torn and tossed and wrinkled. Many of my students also wrote about this idea of what to do with ourselves when circumstances beyond us seem to be bent on making our lives difficult. The students who shared showed their vulnerability, and we all, I think, felt closer as a group because we understood how universal the feeling was even if the specifics in each life were different. I could see, though, that this book might not be a good one to use with all groups or ages.

When I shared the book with a group of teachers, I cautioned that it might not be appropriate for younger students, but one of the teachers decided to use it with her second graders anyway. She later shared her students' responses with me. They were very different from the way older students responded to the conceptual meaning of the book. Those second graders took the book literally, so they wrote about all the magical things that piece of paper could turn itself into! They shared creative and imaginative responses that the students obviously enjoyed writing. I tell this story to make the point that we often don't know how a picturebook might inspire students. With that in mind, we need to know our students and consider both structure and content in our choices for informal writing invitations.

4

Using Picturebooks to Teach about Reading and Writing Processes

In my early years of teaching, I was surprised to hear students ask me, "How is this going to help me in real life?," when we had writing lessons. I have to admit, as a person who loved writing and saw it as important to all aspects of my life, the question made me sad. Eventually, it did make me rethink what I was doing as a writing teacher. So you can imagine my excitement when I first saw *Click, Clack, Moo: Cows That Type* by Doreen Cronin, a picturebook about the value of writing. I loved that it showed writing as doing something, advocating for personal needs, and I talked to students and teachers alike about how this is a great way to think about writing as something useful, not just something we do in school. But this book also made me wonder whether picturebooks might have had an influence on my students' attitude toward writing—and whether they might change their attitude now.

What do our students think it means to be a reader? A writer? How do they see themselves in these roles? Their literacy identities are complex and fluid in many ways; readers might be avid readers at some times and reluctant ones at other times. Writers may be motivated to write in some genres and less inclined, even reluctant, to write in others. I know that feeling. I find my own reader and writer identities shifting in time and with different pressures. Scoggin and Schneewind identify five aspects of reading identity—aspects that can also be applied to writing: attitude, self-efficacy, habits, [book] choice, and process (77–78). When we look at picturebooks to help students consider reader and writer identities, we consider how those identities reflect these five aspects.

As we consider all of these aspects, we can see that students who self-identify as nonreaders or nonwriters, or "bad" writers or readers, might be considering only some of these aspects. After all, I tell my students, I feel competent reading and writing some genres and texts but less confident with others. My habits are to write and read some kinds of texts more than others—in fact, when I have been buried in academic texts for a long period, it is actually somewhat difficult to make the move to reading fiction for fun. I don't read long texts well online. I never read drama, and although I love poetry, I read it only rarely. I can write a letter of recommendation in a flash (lots of experience), but a sonnet makes me think I am not a writer after all.

My own life examples demonstrate that I have multiple literacy identities and they shift, depending on my life and what's going on in it. Research from Moje, Luke, and colleagues notes this important aspect of literacy identities: "[I]dentities are socially situated and mediated and are enactments of the self in particular time, spaces, and relationships" (433). Because of this, they encourage teachers to "include multiple text types and media into our curricula" as a way to give students a wider variety of experiences as they explore their literate lives (433). Picturebooks can certainly be considered part of that variety for secondary students.

Because literacies are socially situated, Merga looked at which social influences might affect readers beyond their early years. She found a variety, including indirect influences from a significant person such as a parent or teacher, an author, a companion, even social influencers. She concludes that "most avid readers will have been the recipient of positive influence from a social agent" (13). This causes me to wonder how part of those identities, the positions students claim, are defined by the ways they've been informally exposed to social ideas of what it means to be a reader and a writer—even inadvertently through picturebooks as young children.

Bronwyn Williams, in his writing about literacy and popular culture, identifies a challenge in the ways literacy is depicted in movies and television shows: it's often subliminal in nature, more behind the scenes than a real part of the action. Heroes and action figures don't do much reading or writing, usually relying on the brainy people back in the office, connected to the action figure through technology, which allows the action figure to bypass the reading and writing necessary to achieve their goals. Do such depictions diminish what it means to be a reader or a writer? It's a good question.

Because students might be exposed to the idea of being readers and writers in picturebooks as part of their early literacy experiences, I wondered what they might have learned. How do these books represent the complex processes involved in reading and writing—and how might they, as indirect influences, have shaped students' perceptions of what it means to be literate? What about the attitudes people have about reading different kinds of texts and writing in different genres? For instance, a book most students know, Dr. Seuss's *The Cat in the Hat*, follows two children at home alone on a rainy day with nothing to do. There are books in the house—we see them become part of the cat's messiness—but they don't seem to be a legitimate consideration for activity on this rainy day. Reading and books seem decorative, not an option for engagement on a quiet day at home. And there is no suggestion that writing is even an option of something to do on the boring, rainy day; nothing in the house indicates that anyone is a writer: no paper or writing utensils are visible in the illustrations. When such a widely read book, a classic of picturebooks, ignores writing and minimizes reading, is there an indirect effect on children and their view of reading and writing?

We can start the discussion of all the possible ways to be a reader and a writer with picturebooks that students—even readers and writers who don't identify in positive ways with those labels—could find appealing. Because students tend to find picturebooks more accessible than longer texts, these books could seem less threatening for students who might feel uncomfortable in these discussions. It will be important as we select books to be aware of the ways reading and writing are represented in the books we share. We want to present accurate ideas about what it means to be readers and writers, even expanding ideas of who we might consider to be readers and writers. We may want the picturebooks to acknowledge challenges that some students might find in those processes. As we share such picturebooks, we can have important discussions about the literate lives of our students, including in our classes and for their lives beyond the classroom. After all, "people's identities are mediated by the texts they read, write, and talk about" (Moje, Luke, et al. 416).

The Value of Reading

Many picturebooks about reading share the positive values of reading. From many such picturebooks, we learn that stories take us away to other times and worlds, that books inspire our imaginations and creativity. More currently, we see picturebooks about reading that contrast print texts with reading on screens, usually making the print text appear more positive: characters holding the book, snuggling with a reading buddy, getting comfy, becoming attached to a book so that it can be around—in other words, not at all like the reading students do with screens. This might be a good thing for students who don't identify as readers, as these books give us a chance to point out the reasons why they might want to consider reading from pages sometimes and not just on screens. But does it at the same time send a message that reading on a screen (or listening to an audiobook) is not really reading? Does it privilege one kind of literacy over another? These are some considerations we need to have in selecting our picturebooks—and in leading discussions after we read them.

To open a discussion about reading, I like to share Kwame Alexander's *How to Read a Book*. The images are bright and engaging while the text reads like a poem as it describes the process of reading. I read the book and its advice aloud—find a book, get comfy, wonder, never reach the end—and ask students to write whatever they want to in response. Most write about favorite books. Some have to reach back into their childhoods for that book, but the discussion after they write is rich with shared memories of favorite books. Some students pick an image from the poem and focus on that; I even have students write about reading messages from their friends from their phone but in a setting raised in the book (e.g., under a tree, on a rooftop). Even if that's all I did with this book—read it, have students write, and share that writing—it seems to me that we establish a positive feeling about reading in the classroom. For some students, that open discussion and reflection might begin to shape their attitude about reading that eventually develops a more positive reading identity.

The discussion can be extended with David Miles's *Book*, which begins with black print on a white page, until readers are zoomed in and see that the letters are literally filled with worlds and stories. In this book, we learn that reading is about stories and about learning, that it doesn't get viruses or need batteries; it is always *possible.* This book seems a perfect way to extend the discussion about where students do their reading and reinforces ideas they may have about what it means to read for pleasure. Research suggests that most students, when asked if they read for pleasure and say yes, mean that they read novels or stories (Moje, Overby, et al.). Does this book reinforce that idea? Should we raise that question as an assumption to be explored with students? *Book* also makes the case for reading in print text, but I can read books online too and still visit worlds and stories. Does this book, again, reinforce the idea that where we do our reading determines what counts as reading? If nothing else, this book should spark discussion of what counts as reading and if the mode matters. All of this talk can contribute to students' attitudes, habits, choices, and processes, helping them develop a fuller literacy identity.

Dealing with Challenges to Reading

One aspect of literacy identity involves process—the "work a student does independently to solve words, read fluently, and comprehend" (Scoggin and Schneewind 78). Again, considering the indirect influences that students' exposure to picturebooks might have had (or could now have) on their literacy identities, how do picturebooks represent reading processes? What messages might these books communicate to students about their own reading processes? Some picturebooks address the problem of having reading interrupted. In *Let Me Finish!* by Minh Le, a boy finds a quiet spot to read and is continually interrupted by animals commenting on his story, even after he looks for more and more remote areas to read in quiet. The same concept is addressed in David Ezra Stein's *Interrupting Chicken*, where a papa is trying to read stories to his chick, who keeps interrupting and telling the end of the story. Both stories are fun starters to a discussion of the conditions we prefer for reading and how we deal with reading when our preferences aren't met. Readers have preferences about reading—where they read, what they like in terms of sound and comfort, what kinds of books they like. Discussing what students can do when those preferences are unavailable may help them address some of the process and habit aspects of their reading identity.

In *The Good Little Book* by Kyo Maclear, a boy is sent to a library because of misbehavior—to give him "time to think." Instead, he finds a book that doesn't seem that inspiring from the cover but that entrances him anyway: "The good little book had been written especially for him." The boy reads the book and then reads it again. The text tells us that reading the book didn't turn him into a "bookish boy," but it did become a valued companion. This picturebook is full of potential links to students' literacy identities. First, what are the implications of assigning reading or writing as punishment? The attitude that might develop from such an action seems fairly straightforward—and negative for developing a literacy identity. In this book, that wasn't the case, but the potential is there. Can students consider what positive and negative influences have encouraged them to be readers (or not)? When the boy finds a book and reads it—twice!—he exhibits an attitude and a habit. The fact that the text clearly notes that he didn't become "bookish" seems to suggest an attitude about people who read—and maybe readers who reread books! Having a discussion with students about social attitudes toward people who identify as readers and writers can be a great way to have them reflect on how their literacy identities are shaped by social influences—the people and attitudes they experience.

We know that reading and writing are social practices. Merga identified shared experiences as important to reading; participants in her study identified "companionship in reading and enjoyment of reading together" as part of their reading identities (10). Becky Bloom's *Wolf!* tells the story of a wolf who is intrigued by a group of farm animals who read; he learns to read and works hard to get better at reading so that he can join the group. For him, acceptance into the group comes through his ability to read. Because we know that literacy identities are heavily influenced by social interactions and attitudes, this book allows students to consider the human world reality of this narrative. Do they have groups that are formed by literate interests (reading or writing)? Do they write fan fiction? Is that a group they join for literate activity? How do these social groups and situations shape their identities?

I love that most picturebooks about reading portray reading as a positive. Since I love to read nonfiction, though, I am a little dismayed that most picturebooks are about reading stories; however, I know that the love of all kinds of genres often grows from a seed of reading stories. Since book choice is an aspect of a reading identity, I like to read *A Child of Books* by Oliver Jeffers and Jeff Winston and ask students to write about the reading that has been most influential in their lives. I encourage them to consider books that were read to them as children and all the reading they do, not just books, so that students who don't currently read books still have some ideas for writing and sharing. As we share their lists, students find connections with other readers in the class (building community), and we begin to talk about the kinds of reading that are valued in our world and what kinds of reading don't get talked about as much. Because identity includes the kinds of reading choices students make, this discussion can validate that aspect of their identity.

I worried that all the positive books about reading might turn off students who don't see themselves as readers. A reading identity can include negative attitudes and low feelings of self-efficacy—but that isn't something often addressed since school is usually a place that values and rewards traditional literate behaviors. So I was pleased to find a book or two about people for whom reading isn't easy. *A Walk in the Words* by Hudson Talbott tells the story of a boy who draws and likes words but has trouble when the words get put into sentences. He notices that he isn't like the other students in his class and sees himself as "lost in a world of . . . words." He is afraid and wants to give up, but he loves stories, and his curiosity overcomes his fear. The book depicts some effective strategies the boy employs to learn to read: breaking big words into parts, looking for words he knows and using them to step around the words

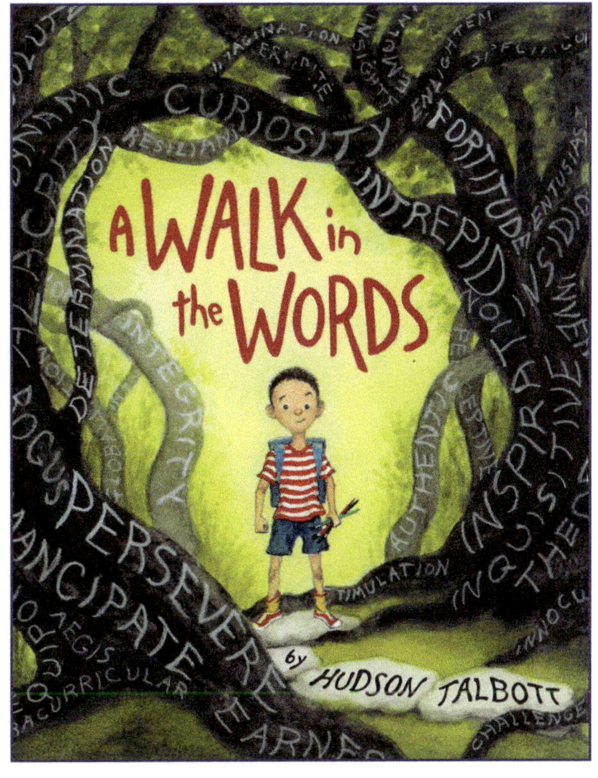

The Fantastic Flying Books of Mr. Morris Lessmore
by William Joyce

The Incredible Book Eating Boy
by Oliver Jeffers

Madeline Finn and the Library Dog
by Lisa Papp

Miss Brooks Loves Books! (and I Don't)
by Barbara Bottner

Open This Little Book
by Jesse Klausmeier

Wolf!
by Becky Bloom

he doesn't know, and drawing to help him understand. He eventually realizes that he can read—slowly—and that "slow readers savor the story." This book highlights a path toward developing a positive reading identity. The boy overcomes challenges to develop positive self-efficacy. In the peritextual matter, we find a page of famous people who were also slow readers, something I find appealing as it opens up a discussion of different ways of reading and shows that all of them have value. Students benefit from this discussion of different ways of reading, and this book helps some students feel seen as readers who read differently than other students in a class, a way to develop their self-efficacy.

Besides reading a book to the class as a discussion starter, teachers could also have a set of picturebooks (the ones described here and others listed in the text box) that students read in small groups with the direction to consider the key ideas the books are making about reading: What does each book say about attitudes, processes, and habits of readers? Do students see these as valid representations of reading? Why does it matter to think of these questions and processes as we develop identities as readers? After groups have had a chance to read the books and consider the questions, class discussion could address what literacy identities we see valued in the books. What books or stories do they think should be written so that a wider range of attitudes, habits, and processes are represented for future readers? This talk can be very helpful as students reflect on what their needs are as readers and what they feel about their own reader identities.

Writing and Writing Identity

Pew research reports that "among students, 'writing' continues to be defined as assignments they are required to do for school, as opposed to textual expression they engage in on their own time." When asked what writing is, students usually say school writing or stories. And they rarely consider digital writing as writing

(Pew Research Center). Students' writing identities, shaped by the same aspects as a reading identity—attitudes, self-efficacy, habits, choice, and process—may be even more socially constructed since writing is usually a dialogue with others in one way or another. Research suggests that writing identity is also a fluid and complex issue, with writers shifting efficacy beliefs, habits, and processes for writing different genres and for different purposes. As Bawarshi notes, writers are "written by . . . genres" (11), reflecting how writers' identities are shaped by many factors and not the same at all times. Williamson's research shows that genre and talk—both social aspects of writing—are significantly influential in a writer's identity. With this social influence, I wonder how students' exposure to picturebooks might have influenced some of their attitudes and habits—or might influence them now.

A number of picturebooks tell the stories of writers and even provide ideas for what people can do with writing. Many of these books posit writing essentially as "story," an idea common in the public sphere. Once I wore a T-shirt that said "I'm a writer. What's your superpower?" to the grocery store. A man stopped me and asked if I was a writer. I said yes, and he asked what I wrote. When I said that I wrote for teachers, he scoffed and told me that what I did wasn't "real" writing. In his world, only novels, poems, and maybe plays could count as real writing. This idea is supported by a lot of what we see in picturebooks: characters (human and animal) write stories and sometimes poems, but not much else. Andrew Larsen's *A Squiggly Story*, Alice Kuipers's *Violet and Victor Write the Best-Ever Bookworm Book*, Troy Wilson's *Little Red Reading Hood and the Misread Wolf*, Kate Banks's *Max's Words*, Peter H. Reynold's *The Word Collector*, and Corinna Luyken's *The Book of Mistakes* are all about writing stories and poems. Since one aspect of a literate identity has to do with choice, this limited perspective of what counts as writing needs to be addressed. When we know that genres shape writers and their identities, we need to ensure that students have a wide view of what we mean by "writing" and opportunities to write and read many genres.

For me, the value of these books to students is in the advice they give about the writing process—asking for help when we get stuck in writing and sharing writing with others—more than what they say about what we write. Since processes are an aspect of a literate identity, this aspect of these books could be useful to discuss: what do writers do when they are writing? We might have a romantic view of writers working alone, inspired to have the right words flow out of them without any effort, but that is rarely the case for writers. Using these books to help students discuss process options—and how those might shift for different writers writing different genres at different times in their lives—would be a helpful addition to students' writer identities.

To round out the ideas of what we can mean when we talk about writing, I

Thank You, Miss Doover
by Robin Pulver

Malala's Magic Pencil
by Malala Yousafzai

Dear Mrs. LaRue: Letters from Obedience School
by Mark Teague

Detective LaRue: Letters from the Investigation
by Mark Teague

LaRue for Mayor: Letters from the Campaign Trail
by Mark Teague

think we should make sure we also include books that show writing doing things in the world. Using the books listed in the text box, teachers can have students read the books to build a list of what writing can do in the world. After they list the purposes they gathered from the picturebooks into one list, they should add others that they can imagine. I like to follow this reading and listing activity by asking students in their groups to return to the book their group read and see what else it tells us about writing. After they list the informal messages about writing they have found in the picturebooks, I ask them to talk and then reflect in writing about whether they agree with the representations of writing in the book. As they do so, they are articulating and developing writer identities.

Written Anything Good Lately? by Susan Allen and Jane Lindaman is an alphabet book that includes an example of a different kind of writing for each letter of the alphabet. This clever book raises the point that we can—and do!—write lots of genres in the world. One of the most interesting questions I ask my students at the beginning of the year is which genres they are good at writing. They seem puzzled at first. When I say that I am a very good grocery list writer but a weak haiku writer, I can see lights going on. We aren't talking about writing like WRITING. We are talking about everyday writing, the kinds we all need to do all the time. After reading *Written Anything Good Lately?*, asking students to make their own ABC lists of writing is a great way to enlarge their ideas about what constitutes writing and helps them get ready to be writers for the year in my classroom. And it's fun to fill out an ABC chart. Also, since choice is an

aspect of writer identity, this discussion is an important consideration for their understanding of all the possible writing choices they have.

Attitudes and habits are aspects of literate identity, so developing a wider view of writing can influence students to see themselves and the writing they do differently. Picturebooks can also communicate the value of writing, and one of those values is that what we write can matter to an audience. Rufus, from *Rufus the Writer* by Elizabeth Bram, builds a story stand rather than a lemonade stand, and he gets lots of business from people wanting stories about themselves or stories as a gift for a friend, suggesting the value of writing to an audience. Following this reading with a discussion of how people see value in writing would have a significant impact on students' attitudes.

The Writing Process

Because process is part of a literate identity, reading picturebooks about the writing process can open up ideas for students so that they can see options in process they might not have considered before. A surprising number of books focus on aspects of the writing process, particularly about how to get ideas. Pamela Zagarenski's *The Whisper* is about inspiration when a girl carries a book home but has its words stolen on the way by a fox. The images spark stories the girl writes down. *Ideas Are All Around* by Philip C. Stead and *Ish* by Peter H. Reynolds both see art as inspiration for writing, while Rebecca Gardyn Levington's *Brainstorm!* suggests a more traditional method for generating ideas. Sometimes the writing process is shown in the details of a story, as in Larsen's *A Squiggly Story*, where a young writer seeks to imitate his older sister—a writer—and learns that stories start with what he knows. Having students read these books in small groups and then building a class list of ideas for how they might get ideas for writing (besides Googling a topic) is a good activity to enlarge understandings about process and develop writing identity further.

Some picturebooks address drafting and how to overcome challenges during writing, countering the idea some other books might suggest that writing is easy. In Mary Jane and Herm Auch's *The Plot Chickens*, Henrietta wants to write a book, goes through trials in the writing and publishing process—and then gets a bad review. Her sadness is smoothed away when it turns out that the children in the library enjoy her story despite the review, reminding writers that some of our writing might not be successful for one audience but may be just right for another. Two books—Luyken's *The Book of Mistakes* and *A Perfectly Messed Up Story* by Patrick McDonnell—suggest that sometimes writing might go in a different direction than originally intended—and that can be okay. Pulver's *Thank You, Miss Doover* is a rare book that addresses revision as a way to make writing more effective, countering a common impression that writing is easy, or should be. I like to share these books when we are writing so that the topic can match the part of the process students are engaged in at the moment. These books give us a chance to read a book and then talk about process beliefs and habits and how we might reconsider our processes as we write.

When students are developing writing identities, the kind of writing they do in school has a big influence. Genres matter to their developing identities (choice and process). And teacher comments on that writing have a big impact on student writers' self-efficacy (Ferris). Even a quick Google search shows hundreds of posts about positive and negative comments from teachers and the impact they had on student writers—they either became writers (my own experience) or they hate writing, sure they are horrible at it. I believe that some of those feelings also reflect the kind of writing students complete for school: mostly five-paragraph essays or literary analysis. Maybe a research paper. Most of these genres are not genres students read outside of school, so it would only make sense that they are unfamiliar with them and likely to resort to strategies to just "get it done." And then they get feedback that might not be very positive.

The Bear Report by Thyra Heder tells the story of a girl who is assigned to write a report about polar bears. We see some of her writer identity represented in the story and images, and in the process she chooses. She begins in the traditional way, with a handout where she has written three basic facts that people might assume about polar bears just from common knowledge. In fact, I have tucked inside my copy of the book a copy of one of my grandson's reports about bears from third grade that looks remarkably like Sophie's example in the book. She looks bored as she writes, opening up a possible discussion in class about how students feel when they are writing for school. Do their attitudes (their literate identities) change when they write for their own purposes? When Sophie goes to watch TV after she has filled in the three lines of her report, a polar bear shows up in her living room and takes her all around his world, showing her so much more about the life of a polar bear than the bare facts she had noted. The book is a delight and illustrates how important inquiry can be to writing, how much more it shows us about our topics,

and how we feel energized about writing when we know a lot. I often use this book to introduce the concept and value of inquiry. We discuss how our attitudes and processes change when we get to write something interesting, or about a topic we love and know a lot about, and how these changes also lead to higher self-efficacy.

Principles

- ✓ Share books that have expanded views of reading and writing.
- ✓ Find books that expand who is considered a reader and writer.
- ✓ Look for picturebooks that don't simplify the processes but instead provide possible solutions to potential issues.

Share Books That Have Expanded Views of Reading and Writing

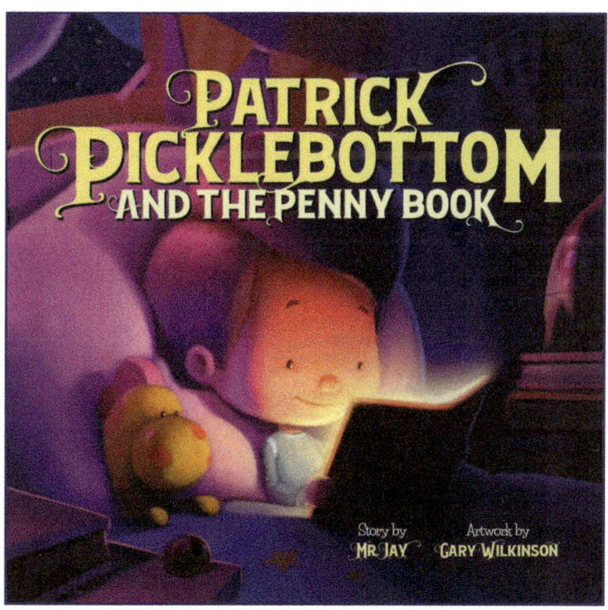

It isn't hard to find picturebooks that provide positive views of reading and writing—they are all around. What we might want to think about are books that expand what we mean by reading and writing. A new book, *Patrick Picklebottom and the Penny Book* by Mr. Jay, is a fun read that shows the joys of reading as the little boy carries his newly purchased book home, passing friends who are all playing with technology and touting its benefits. Patrick arrives home and finds that his book does everything his friends said their devices do—and more. In this picturebook, the author certainly favors print text, but the idea of digital texts is raised in positive ways too. The discussion after reading this book should engage students in thinking about all the places they might read and write—and the benefits and constraints of all the options. The rhyming text is bouncy and fun to read, emphasizing that reading can be fun. If we can find books like this, books that have the positive message but also tell it in an interesting and engaging way, we can make the point that reading and writing are skills and processes we want to engage with and get better at. Even more, as teachers, I think we want to make sure that the books we share are ones that open up ideas about how students see themselves as readers and writers, and we need to be aware if the choices we select are positive but still limit some aspects of what it means to be a writer or reader. In other words, do they suggest positive attitudes toward *story* writing or reading but never mention other kinds of reading and writing that might have value?

Find Books That Expand Who Is a Reader and a Writer

Most picturebooks represent reading and writing in ways that are positive—reading is good and writing is fun. But as I've mentioned, sometimes the representations of both processes can be seen as easy or limited to certain genres (stories). We should be sure to also find picturebooks that expand what it means to be a reader or writer, how to face the challenges of each, and what it means to read and write broadly, with all kinds of genres and audiences and responses. Christopher Myers's *My Pen* talks metaphorically about all the ways that writing can work in the world; it's a perfect text for older students who can discuss what the implications of each abstraction might mean as a writer in the world. Finding more books that open up what it means to be a writer and reader benefits our students, especially those who read only nonfiction, for instance, and often feel marginalized in an English class.

Look for Picturebooks That Don't Simplify Processes, but Instead Provide Possible Solutions to Potential Issues

Process and habits are part of what builds literacy identity. The book I find most useful to address the writing process is not even a book about writing. *The Most Magnificent Thing* by Ashley Spires tells the story of a girl who imagines making a magnificent thing, actually the *most* magnificent thing. With the help of her

assistant (a dog), she begins to make it, but as much as she tries, she can't seem to make it come out in the way she envisioned it. She fiddles with it and tries again and again. Even when onlookers admire her creation, she knows it isn't yet magnificent. She gets mad. She tries to force it to fit her ideas and explodes when it doesn't. Then she takes a break, calms down, reviews all the attempts she has made, and tries again. The magnificent thing she finally ends up with is not exactly what she had envisioned to begin with, but it *is* a magnificent thing. After we read the book as a class, we discuss how it relates to writing. Most students can identify with one or more aspects of the girl's story as it relates to their writing experiences—imagining the final product but being unable to make the writing match, getting frustrated, wanting to quit. When we talk about how the girl resolved her problem, we make similar connections to what they might do when they are writing or reading.

5

Using Picturebooks to Teach Reading and Literature

One of the earliest ways I tried using picturebooks in my classroom was to teach literary elements and devices. I was not quite prepared for how much my students needed to understand elements of literature and literary devices to get the most from our reading. I could teach them the way I was taught—and I tried that a bit too—by teaching the term, giving a definition, and then expecting my students to find the element in the literature. For example: *A symbol is the use of a person, place, or thing to represent some other idea in a piece of literature.* What symbols can we see in the story we just read? But I could see pretty quickly that that approach didn't engage my students, and I also quickly realized that it wasn't as effective for most of my students, even though it had been fine for me. After all, most of them didn't read literature much and few, if any, were planning to be English teachers. I needed a way to help my students understand these concepts in accessible and engaging ways before they considered those elements in the literature, so I thought first of picturebooks.

I had some picturebooks already in my classroom that included examples of some of the elements I knew I wanted to teach: similes, metaphors, alliteration, and so on. I could read the books, explain the concept under discussion (similes, for example), and have students find them in the books—and since these were fast reads, we could move beyond just identification to also discuss the *effect* of each element. Perfect. My problem was that I was just starting out. I didn't have a lot of books—and I didn't have a lot of time to explore more books for other elements that weren't as easy to find in picturebooks.

But in my search for ideas, I found a book by Susan Hall, *Using Picture Storybooks to Teach Literary Devices*, which listed literary devices and a whole string of picturebooks to use to teach each device. It was a treasure!

After that, when I knew I wanted to teach a particular device or two, I would visit the public library with Hall's book and find as many of the picturebooks she listed as I could. Now, instead of having one book and pulling out some examples to put on the screen, I could begin to help students understand a concept by first showing a concept in one picturebook to the whole class and then having them work in groups, each group with a different picturebook, to find more examples and be ready to share with the class—both the examples and the effect the concept had on the book. Because the books are short, this was a quick lesson, and I immediately knew whether students understood the concept and its effect. A sample lesson might be something like this:

- ✓ Read a book aloud to the whole class. I read *Duck, Death and the Tulip* by Wolf Erlbruch, but I would recommend that teachers of younger students consider whether this would be appropriate for them.
- ✓ Briefly discuss students' reactions to the story itself. What does it mean? How does it make them feel? What do they think the author's purpose was?
- ✓ Ask about the Tulip. It is mentioned in the title, but it is seen only briefly in Death's hands at the beginning of the book and then beside Duck at the end of the book. It must be more than decoration—we are alerted to that by its inclusion in the title. What is it supposed to mean? Let students generate possibilities, asking for each response an extending question: What would that meaning add to the story?

- ✓ Explain what symbols are in literature: they are objects, characters, places, or other concepts that represent important ideas in the story.
- ✓ Get into groups and look at a picturebook together. (A list of possible titles is in the text box.) See what symbols you can identify in the book and consider what each symbol adds to the idea of the story. Be ready to share with the class at the end of the allotted time.

Eventually I used picturebooks to teach other aspects of reading too: skills, strategies, and processes. Although there are so many books and so many strategies, elements, and techniques we could teach with picturebooks, I address here only a few as examples and a starting place for teachers. I hope the examples provide sparks for ways teachers might use picturebooks to meet other needs of their own student readers.

The Magic of Wonder
by Jenna Copper et al.

The Good Egg
by Jory John

Memory Jars
by Vera Brosgol

Grandfather's Journey
by Allen Say

Tar Beach
by Faith Ringgold

Tofu Takes Time
by Helen H. Wu

Vocabulary

Vocabulary development is one way picturebooks can help our students develop as readers—and in a fun way. Research shows that reading picturebooks aloud helps to develop vocabulary because students hear the words in engaging contexts (Layne 74), and this is true for all students, including MLL students. In choosing picturebooks for a variety of purposes for secondary students, we might want to also consider books that help to develop vocabulary—and many do. I like to try a few that define some abstract words. Bernard Waber's *Courage* (mentioned in Chapter 6, on writing) and *Serendipity* by Tobi Tobias are two of this kind of book. They both have a word in the title and then are composed of many concrete examples that help to clarify the word. After we read the books, I like to ask students to think of some of their own examples for the word—and then I can see how much students now know about the words from the examples they give. The same process can be applied to other abstract words we would like to discuss: *freedom, compassion, creativity.*

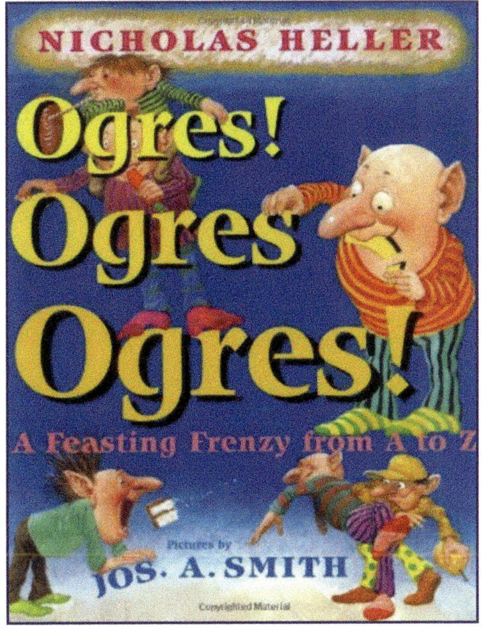

Nicholas Heller's *Ogres! Ogres! Ogres!* is a good book to use for a language lesson on alliteration, vivid verbs, and even basic sentence structures (basic transitive structures in simple, compound, and complex sentences). Because this is an ABC book, each page represents a letter of the alphabet, with an ogre whose name starts with the letter eating something that sometimes starts with the same letter. I mention the book here because, even though it's a fun one that can serve other language lesson purposes, it has some words that might not be as familiar to our students. The book's context will help them learn the words. For example, "Indolent Imogen imbibes juices" might have two words unfamiliar to students (*indolent* and *imbibes*). The images can help readers infer the meanings, and students can learn vocabulary in the context of using the book for other purposes. Because my students write their own ABC books, this is one we often include in our genre study before they write.

Reading Strategies

We can teach students a wide range of reading strategies to develop their overall skills as readers and specifically as readers of literature (often our concern). And we can practice these in a variety of ways with the literature we teach. So, for instance, when I taught *To Kill a Mockingbird* (Lee), I often stopped to ask students to describe Maycomb from the description in the book, to try to see it from the words on the page. This visualizing we do with students as we read helps them read with more meaning. We might pause to ask them to make connections to other books or stories we have read or to pose questions they have about what we might read next, even predicting from the title or from an event in the reading. All of these actions we can model as we read to help students learn and practice these strategies—and we can do that while we are reading the texts for our classes. But if our students need help with specific reading strategies, we might pull in picturebooks to help teach them prior to our reading so that students can activate them as needed for their independent reading.

Predicting and Inferring

So, for instance, to teach the difference between making predictions and making inferences, we might use *Last Stop on Market Street* by Matt de la Peña. We can look at the cover and read the first few pages before we stop to ask students to make predictions about the book: *What do you think the book will be about?* Students should be able to predict that the book will be about a bus ride with a woman and a little boy. As we continue to read, we can confirm our predictions and predict further events in the book: *What do you think might happen next? Why?*

Then, as we read, they can start to make inferences, opinions we might draw based on clues. For example, as we view the images, we can ask about where the characters are going and what in the images helps us understand this. Students might infer that parts of the town are less affluent than others. Since the book never specifically says this, we can only infer from the images and events in the story that it is so, but the predictions and inferences will be borne out with our further reading. I often ask about the abuela's character: *What kind of person is she? How do you know that?* As we work through questions that get at predicting and inferring in this one picturebook, I can help students see how the strategies can benefit them as readers, helping them understand and see more about what stories might mean. Then, when we read novels or short stories, I can remind them of these strategies. Clarifying these two reading strategies with the same picturebook can help students as readers going forward.

With older students, I like Julie Flett's *Birdsong* for teaching inference. Because the text is spare, students need to look deeply at a lot of clues to figure out what is really happening in the story, similar to the way they will use inference in more complex literary texts. When they see something curious in the text, maybe something that is outside the expected or something in the images that is not what the words communicate, I tell students to consider what they are meant to think from those items. Authors give us depth in unexpected ways, but we have to learn to observe and question and then infer. In most cases, our inferences should extend the story, but sometimes we are given clues that might actually contradict the text. Sprinkled through *Birdsong* are unfamiliar words (the author is Cree-Métis), with a short glossary for pronunciation and meaning in the front pages. These words and the images combined can be used to help students see how they can use both for inferring, a useful skill in today's world with so many genres that combine images and words.

Summarizing

Another strategy I like to teach with picturebooks is summarizing, a reading strategy that specialists encourage secondary readers to learn (McEwan) and one that also benefits students' writing development (Graham and Perin). When I first started my teaching career, I assumed students would have learned summarizing in elementary school. And they had. To a degree. With certain texts. In my desire to figure out how to help them improve their summarizing skills, I learned that summarizing stories is very different from summarizing informational texts—and that the complexity of texts can make summarizing more challenging as students move from elementary to secondary schools. As a teacher, I knew that summarizing information was useful to my students, but I didn't realize until the Graham and Perin report that summarizing is one of the most effective skills I can teach my students, essential to both reading and writing.

I started working with summarizing by using *The Important Book* by Margaret Wise Brown. Usually, I read the book all the way through and then I go back and ask students to look at the structure that is repeated on each page: "The important thing about ________ is ________. There is [this and that, other details about the thing], but the important thing about ________ is ________." Then we discuss: Would you say that the important thing about a daisy is that it is white? Or that the important thing about a spoon is that you eat with it? We talk about all the other possible important things we might have chosen for the objects in the book. Why did Brown choose as she did? Why might that have been important to her? We discuss the way the pattern allows us to see a few aspects of an object and what is important out of all the possible aspects that could have been chosen: *How do we tell about something big in a small way?* As oral practice, we can generate some ideas and examples as a class: The important thing about our school is. . . . The important thing about lunch is. . . . And so on.

I follow up this discussion by having students write a summary about a concept. For example, when we have just finished practicing several prewriting strategies in preparation for writing a movie review, I ask students to consider what they did to prepare to write, what strategies they used, and what effects those strategies had. Then I ask them to write a summary of what prewriting is—the important thing about prewriting. I remind them of the pattern in *The Important Book*—the important thing, the other things, but the important thing—and have them write. It's an interesting way to find out what students think because the pattern is, in a way, a form of metacognitive writing, but it also pushes them to consider what is most important—and that is key to good summarizing.

One thing teachers like Kissner know about developing writers learning to summarize is that they are often distracted by interesting or unusual facts and focus on those instead of the main idea or the most important idea. So giving students lots of practice with summarizing, especially with nonfiction texts, is important preparation for the kind of reading they need to do for writing in secondary schools. They will need to know the information, the main ideas, the details that support those ideas, and the other information that might be interesting but not essential to the ideas a reader needs to take away.

Fluency

Good readers need to develop fluency; it helps them read with accuracy and comprehension. We often assume readers develop fluency before they come to secondary school. I mention this in the chapter about using picturebooks with MLL students because it is a particular concern for them, but fluency seems to be more of a need for *all* students after the COVID shutdowns kept students from being exposed to direct instruction and modeling of effective reading strategies in the classroom. We are seeing that students of all ages and backgrounds need to become more fluent readers. And picturebooks are perfect for helping to build fluency.

One reason picturebooks help build fluency is that they can be read aloud with ease. I return to this practice for this objective because it matters so much here too. Oczkus points out that "over 10,000 studies . . . found that the most important activity for building the skills and background for eventual success in reading is reading aloud" (21). Gold and Gibson note some of the key benefits students gain from hearing texts read aloud: it can develop "the listener's interest in books and desire to be a reader" and "demonstrates the relationship between the printed word and meaning." As they note, because people can listen to language read aloud at a higher level than they can read themselves, reading aloud gives students access to ideas and vocabulary they might not otherwise access. And as we are using picturebooks for various purposes in our classes, we have the opportunity to read aloud from them regularly. Students can hear how texts should sound, how expression enhances comprehension, and how punctuation can influence the meaning of texts—all important elements of reading fluency.

Students, once they have practice hearing books read aloud, can further their fluency development by learning to read them aloud themselves. Finding books that have good rhythms and a high level of interest for students is an important consideration in choosing books to use for students to practice reading aloud, especially since students will usually read the books multiple times in practice. Books that have dialogue can help readers learn to read with expression; books

The Book with No Pictures by B. J. Novak: Lots of humor and expression are possible in this book.

If You Give a Mouse a Cookie by Laura Numerof: The repeated structure can benefit some readers who are learning to read aloud.

The Stinky Cheese Man and Other Fairly Stupid Tales by Jon Scieszka: Lots of variation in sentence styles and humor add to the readability of these fables.

Where the Wild Things Are by Maurice Sendak: Variety in sentence length and interesting rhythm create a lovely read-aloud feel in a story for students of all ages.

Alexander and the Terrible, Horrible, No Good, Very Bad Day by Judith Viorst: Good rhythm and sentence variation help create effective fluency.

Robo-Sauce by Adam Rubin: Bouncy sentence rhythms with parallel structure creates fun reading.

The Gruffalo by Julia Donaldson: The rhyme and repetition make this book fun to read and fun to hear.

Bedtime at the Swamp by Kristyn Crow: Lots of dialogue and a repeated refrain make for a fun read-aloud (with a funny ending).

I'm Not Afraid of This Haunted House by Laurie Friedman: A little more complex rhythm and rhyme fun for older students.

Three Little Ghosties by Pippa Goodhart: A read-aloud with rhythm, rhyme, and humor that just trips off the tongue.

Tomorrow Most Likely by Dave Eggers: A shorter text with very smooth sentence fluency and rhyme—and a squirrel.

Click, Clack, Moo: Cows That Type by Doreen Cronin: A book with sounds and rhyme that make the reading sound a little like a typewriter tapping.

with variations in punctuation help them learn to read the signals writers give readers for pauses and breaks. Syntactical variation helps readers learn to match tone with reading. Some recommended books for fluency are shown in the text box. Teachers may want to bring in a wide variety of picturebooks that might fit students' interests. After students select a book, they practice reading the book aloud multiple times and then record their readings. When those recordings are uploaded to a private class website to allow sharing inside the classroom, students can also develop fluency as they hear their classmates reading other books well too.

Activating Background Knowledge

I was surprised the first time I realized that my students didn't always have the requisite knowledge to understand the setting or context of a novel. Our department taught *Anne Frank: The Diary of a Young Girl* (Frank) in eighth grade, but many of my students had no real understanding of World War II or the Holocaust. Other schools may read *The Boy in the Striped Pajamas* (Boyne), *The Book Thief* (Zusak), *Number the Stars* (Lowry), or *Night* (Wiesel), which are also set during World War II and require background knowledge for understanding. I liked having picturebooks to provide background knowledge. My favorite is *The Butterfly* by Patricia Polacco, as it tells the story of a family who hid Jews who were trying to escape. Told from the perspective of a young girl, the book presents some of the terror and fears of that time and place. The story starts innocently enough as the hidden girl sneaks out at night to Monique's room, and they become friends. And then one night they are seen by a neighbor. Monique's mother's urgency in getting the family out before soldiers come is so palpable that even the young girls recognize the danger. This is a longer picturebook, with a lot of text on each page, so it isn't a quick read, but it is one that is useful for introducing the sense of hiding and fear that we see in many of the novels about this period that are commonly read in secondary schools.

Karen Hesse's *The Cats in Krasinski Square* is a shorter picturebook that tells the true story of the Jewish Resistance in Poland and the ways people found to undermine the soldiers trying to round them up and also help the Jews who were locked in the ghetto. It might raise some questions because it tells a story that has lots of room for inferring and questioning about the circumstances of the story; that can be good for teaching some reading strategies at the same time that it fills in background for older students.

Similarly, teachers across the country have found ways to use picturebooks to develop the initial understandings of the content for the literature their students will read. Nancy Roser reports on a teacher's use of picturebooks to prepare students to read Lowry's *Number the Stars*. The teacher shared Tom Feelings's wordless picturebook, *The Middle Passage: White Ships/Black Cargo*, with her whole class; she then briefly previewed related picturebooks on the topic of World War II before asking her students to read them in small groups and take notes, preparing them to be able to discuss the themes and ideas that would enhance their reading of the novel. This pairing—a picturebook the whole class reads together with small groups that read different books—can create a powerful connection and understanding to support students' reading of class or group novels.

Literary Elements

Literary elements, those aspects of literature that apply globally to most story-based writing, are an essential aspect of secondary English classes. These are what most of us learned about in our own education—plot, characters, setting, theme, and so on. We want students to learn about these elements so that we can help them enjoy stories and, we hope, want to read stories outside of school too. Sometimes, teaching these elements with the literature itself is most effective, but sometimes it helps when students understand these elements before we read the literature so that they can enjoy the longer story and see the elements as part of that enjoyment. My own children often told me that they didn't like it when teachers picked everything apart as they read. They just wanted to read. And enjoy. Picturebooks can help teachers teach literary elements ahead of reading longer texts so that students can experience the elements in their literature and just enjoy the novels they read.

Character

Mother ~~Goose~~ Bruce by Ryan T. Higgins is a fun book to use to teach the concept of character. When we were reading Dickens's *A Tale of Two Cities*, I particularly wanted my sophomores to pay attention to how a character changed. I wanted them to be able to describe the changes they noticed in the characters and find evidence in the text. We can teach this concept in a variety of ways, and I have used video clips from the beginning and end of accessible films like *Turner and Hooch*, but without context, the character changes can seem stark. When I found Higgins's book, it seemed a better fit. It's funny

and students enjoy it. At the beginning, Bruce (a bear) is a grump who likes to cook. We see evidence of these traits right off. But when the eggs he collects for his special recipe hatch, he finds himself unable to complete the recipe—the first clue that maybe there is more than grump to him. The rest of the book shows Bruce trying to get rid of the ducklings, finally raising them, trying to get them to understand migration, and finally settling into his new role, taking the ducklings south every winter and spending time in the sun with them. When I ask students what Bruce is like at the beginning of the story and what he is like at the end, I often get descriptions like "grouchy" and "nice," which is okay, but I ask them for details: How do they know? What evidence can they find for each position? This is the important part, and the book provides examples for students to cite. The book lends itself to a good, quick discussion about how characters develop from the events in a story and the evidence we can identify to explain the changes. This understanding helps us plan what to watch for as we read our literature—to see the character development and look for evidence of those changes.

Theme

I really like to introduce the concept of theme with picturebooks. Students, especially in junior high but even when I taught high school, often confused theme with main idea or even topic (the book is about . . .). With my ninth-grade classes, we used to memorize and even chant a definition of theme: "A complete sentence that makes a statement about life supported by the events in the story/book/poem." So, after reading a book like de la Peña's *Last Stop on Market Street* and discussing the differences between inferring and predicting as readers (strategies), I ask students to suggest some possible themes for the book as a way to practice identifying themes. And if students say something like "look on the positive side," I remind them of the difference between a moral and a theme: a moral is a life lesson we should learn, but a theme is a statement about life that the story supports. So we could change our moral to a theme by adding something: If we look on the positive side of things, we will be happier with life.

I always ask students to identify multiple themes for a book because I don't want them to think there is only one right answer. Either individually or in small groups, they generate more that we can list and discuss (what is the evidence for that theme?) before we go back to the main lesson. This repeated practice is useful when it comes time for them to consider themes of longer pieces of literature. Some other picturebooks I like for considering themes are found in the text box. I like these because they are interesting to secondary students and

> *Three Hens and a Peacock*
> by Lester L. Laminack
>
> *Black Dog*
> by Levi Pinfold
>
> *Watercress*
> by Andrea Wang
>
> *Sophie's Masterpiece*
> by Eileen Spinelli
>
> *Heroes*
> by Ken Mochizuki

have the potential for multiple themes. Once students have an idea of what a theme is, I give small groups a picturebook and have them practice finding themes before passing their book to another group. We compare the themes they develop at the end of the lesson to reinforce the learning.

I especially like *The Cello of Mr. O* by Jane Cutler as a book to teach theme with older students because its ideas are more complex—mostly inferred—and it has so many possibilities that work really well for clarifying the difference between the main idea, a moral, and a theme. The story is told from the perspective of a young girl learning to deal with living in a war-ravaged city, with all its dangers and privations. She and the other children in her neighborhood don't like—and taunt—an elderly neighbor who seems different and aloof. One day he brings his cello into the square and begins to play for people while they wait in long food lines. When the food trucks are bombed, he continues to play in the square to keep spirits up. One day he steps away from his cello to stretch just when it too is bombed. The children have begun to recognize the value of his music and think that now all is lost. The next day Mr. O shows up with a harmonica, and they are again fed by his music. There are so many themes in the book—and lessons to be learned too if teachers want to talk about those as well. Because of the richness of this picturebook, considering theme seems to come naturally from our discussion about the book.

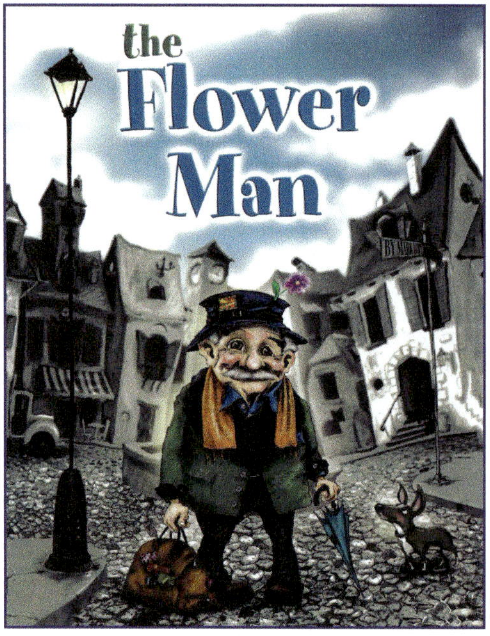

More recently with high school students, I have used two wordless picturebooks, *The Flower Man* by Mark Ludy and *Sidewalk Flowers* by JonArno Lawson and Sydney Smith, to discuss theme. Both books have more complex stories going on than many wordless picturebooks do and use color against black-and-white drawings with symbolic meaning as part of the story. Both would be useful for teaching theme. *Sidewalk Flowers* seems straightforward, but it has a more ambiguous ending, something younger students may find puzzling but that older students appreciate. *The Flower Man* has more potential for complexity because in addition to the main storyline there are many other stories going on with the townspeople. Asking students to combine and contrast summary and theme statements for these stories is a nice way to practice reading skills and identify literary elements with the same text. The wordless text means that all students are required to depend more on their visual literacy skills, a benefit for their learning.

Literary Techniques

Literary techniques might or might not be present in a piece of literature; they are sometimes referred to as those elements that work at the sentence level (e.g., similes and metaphors), but some techniques are really global, like allegory. Hall's book about teaching literary devices is a wonderful place to start to find picturebooks to use to teach literary techniques—but it's really only the place to start. Teachers will want to find their own books that show the devices they want to teach their students for the literature they are reading. Those will probably be the best books anyway.

Alliteration

I have collected ABC books for a long time, and *Animalia* by Graeme Base is one I had long before I used it for teaching. It's a perfect book for teaching alliteration as each page of lush art is accompanied by a phrase that is completely alliterative. So, for *A*, the text is "An armoured armadillo avoiding an angry alligator," and for *D*, the text is "Diabolical dragons daintily devouring delicious delicacies." When I used this in junior high, not only did we read the book to learn about alliteration (it takes only a few pages for students to be able to identify the concept), but we also created our own pages. Students (and I!) took the first letter of either our first or last name and wrote a phrase like the ones in the book, putting it on tagboard with an illustration to hang on the walls of our classroom. We noted the general pattern of the phrases (adjectives +

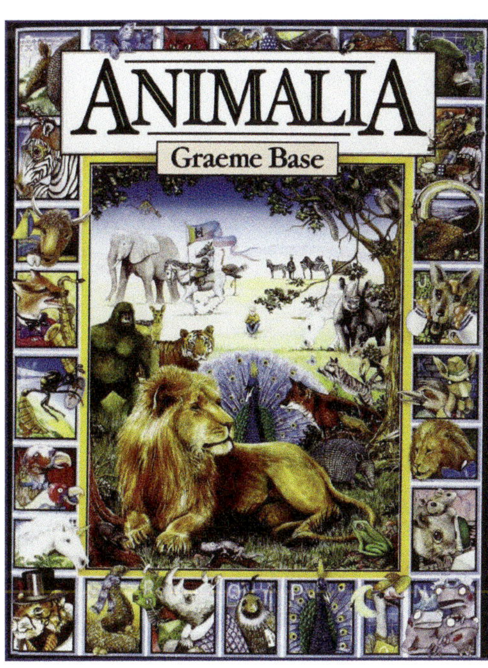

noun + *-ing* word + adjective + noun), allowing for additions of adverbs or other elements of language if students wanted to and could do it. A lot of students went overboard on this because they liked doing it so much. But for me, besides the way the text taught alliteration so easily, I got one more chance to talk to students about the difference between a sentence and a phrase, a concept I needed to teach multiple times. I could teach absolutes with this book—and it was a natural outcome. I simply told students that the -ing word needed a time marker to make it a sentence, the exact structure of absolutes. So my poster of "Dancing dogs deliberately designing dangerous distractions" could become a sentence by adding a simple time marker: "Dancing dogs **are** deliberately designing dangerous distractions." Voila! A complete sentence.

Foreshadowing

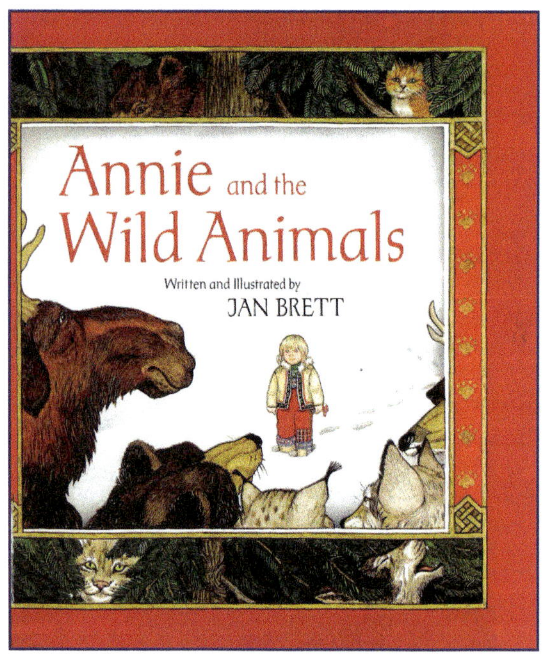

A favorite book for teaching foreshadowing is Jan Brett's *Annie and the Wild Animals. The Mitten* by Brett also works, telling a Ukrainian story about a boy's lost mitten. Both are gentle stories about boys and girls who live in snowy places. Each story follows the plot diagram we often use to help students understand stories—introduction, rising action, climax, resolution, and falling action—so they are good for setting foundations to build a story. But the illustrations are where we find foreshadowing. So the first time I read the books, when I get to the middle, I start asking students what they think is going to happen. If they don't have any ideas yet, I remind them to look at the pictures, especially those in the frame of the pages. There they can see what will happen on the next page (which animal will live in the mitten or which ones will come for the food Annie puts out to find a new pet). We can even answer the question of what happened to Taffy, Annie's cat, by looking at the images around the edges of the page. My eighth graders, in a narrative unit, were happy to write short picturebooks (I put the books together with tagboard covers and multiple pages inside, about four inches square) where they told a story using what they knew were the elements of narrative and drawing the illustrations to provide foreshadowing for readers. The days we read these were lots of fun—and decades later, I still have a few in my office.

Parody

I always thought parody was a challenge for students to understand. With junior high students, I like to use Jon Scieszka's *The True Story of the Three Little Pigs: By A. Wolf.* Students are familiar with the original story, so this exaggerated version that creates a comic effect is a good example of the literary technique. One challenge I've had is that some students just see that book as a "different perspective" rather than a parody, so we need to work through the clear exaggerations that are more than just the point of view of a different narrator. A good book that helps to make that distinction is *Goodnight, Goon* by Michael Rex. Imitating the childhood favorite of *Goodnight, Moon* by Margaret Wise Brown, this book uses a similar situation—going to bed at night—but when the little werewolf starts to say goodnight to his room, a goon comes in and begins to trash his room and all its décor—goo and mummies and bones and bats. At the end, the werewolf sends the goon away (to under his bed) so that all the characters can sleep. If students aren't familiar with Brown's classic original, it would be a good idea to have a copy in class so that students can read both of the texts and begin to articulate how Rex pokes fun at the original. When students confuse satire and parody, I like to have this book to refer to since satire sometimes uses exaggerations but to make a serious point, whereas parody pokes fun by imitating style and using exaggeration to amuse and entertain.

Teaching Literary Analysis

When I first started trying to teach literary analysis, I struggled. As an English major, it was a genre I was familiar with writing in my academic life. It was, I knew, the way most English teachers assessed students' understanding of the literature they read. But as a teacher, I couldn't find any mentor texts to help my students, still developing as writers, understand the expectations of the genre. It isn't, after all, one they would have read. And genre theory helps us understand that when we are not familiar with the community of a genre (as English majors and academics would be) or familiar with a genre through reading it, the complexity of writing that genre multiplies. Even reading a genre doesn't always mean we can write it effectively as there is a gap between being a reader and being a writer of a genre.

And yet, as a teacher, I thought analysis was a good thinking skill to develop. We need to learn to analyze all types of information to succeed in life, so I wanted to teach analysis, and I labored on the best I could. But once I had read 150 (or more) essays analyzing the same piece of literature, I wasn't sure I was up to the task. Because I saw my students' interest perk up when I used picturebooks for my lessons, I decided on a different approach to teaching analysis: students would use at least three picturebooks by the same author to write an analysis of that author's style. When my students heard this plan, that they were going to write about picturebooks, they were excited. They still had to learn what it meant to analyze (to take apart and draw conclusions) and to write up an analysis (providing examples as evidence), but I think they thought that writing about the books and authors they loved would be easy. It wasn't really, but writing about content they knew well and felt like they could master seemed to make the more complex aspects of the task seem accessible.

To begin, I had them reminisce about the picturebooks they loved as a child. We listed them on the board, amid lots of "Oh yeah! I loved that one too!" Because I wanted them to have access to the books and I wasn't sure that they would at home, I checked out sets from the library and brought them to class. I let them browse the authors for one class period, and then I asked them to list three authors they would like to write about, because I wanted students to have knowledge of at least one of the books in their set, but they didn't have to be familiar with all of them. The next class period I gave them the name of the author they would analyze and access to the books. The text box provides examples of some of the sets I used or have seen other teachers use.

> Dr. Seuss: *The Cat in the Hat*; *How the Grinch Stole Christmas*; *Horton Hears a Who*
>
> Eric Carle: *"Slowly, Slowly, Slowly," Said the Sloth*; *The Very Hungry Caterpillar*; *The Grouchy Ladybug*
>
> Mo Willems: *Don't Let the Pigeon Drive the Bus!*; *Pigeon Finds a Hot Dog!*; *Waiting Is Not Easy!*
>
> Kevin Henkes: *Lilly's Purple Plastic Purse*; *Wemberly Worried*; *Waiting*
>
> Karma Wilson: *Bear Snores On; The Cow Loves Cookies*; *Bear Feels Scared*
>
> Tomie dePaola: *Strega Nona*; *Big Anthony and the Magic Ring*; *Strega Nona Meets Her Match*

In class, we had mini-lessons on style: What does it mean? How does an author create a style? We learned about how some authors do things in similar ways even though their books are different: they may write about the same kind of topics, they may have tones that stay relatively the same despite changes in topics, they may use sentences or description or the images or literary devices similarly across texts. We learned that these moves are what writers do to create a style. As students settled on what they could see across the three books, we learned to make claim statements. And then we learned to find examples to support our claims. The short texts we were working with made it much more enjoyable to return to the texts again and again to look at our sources for examples and to further our claim.

Because students enjoyed the texts they were analyzing and felt that they could develop some expertise on these authors and books, they were more willing to engage in the challenging work of literary analysis. Their writing was more interesting because they saw themselves as knowledgeable, which was generally not the case when they wrote about literature. By using picturebooks in this way, students can engage in some of the complex thinking we hope for in our English classes but with texts that are accessible and interesting to them.

Principles

- ✓ Find the right book, not just a good book.
- ✓ Find books that clearly do the job of the objective.
- ✓ Consider using books that might address multiple purposes well.

Find the Right Book, Not Just a Good Book

Sometimes I find a book that I just *love*. I love it because it speaks to my heart or my experience or for some image–text aesthetic—and I would love to use it in my class. But I really have to stretch to find an academic objective it will meet. One such book is *The Last Dance* by Carmen Agra Deedy. I found it long ago, an anniversary gift for my husband, and I still weep over that book and its lovely language and message. But it is a book for people who understand the challenges of love and loss across years of experience, not so much for children or even young adults. And for teaching reading? As much as I love the book, I really can't find a strong enough reading objective that makes the work of overcoming the challenges of the book worth it. I leave it at home.

Another example. For some stories or novels we read, I want students to consider how characters deal with death and loss (e.g., *Lord of the Flies*, Golding; *Monster*, Myers; *Freak the Mighty*, Philbrick; *The Giver*, Lowry). I have several picturebooks to choose from as a way into these longer texts. I would recommend Glenn Ringtved's *Cry, Heart, but Never Break* over another, *Tear Soup* by Pat Schweibert and Chuck DeKlyen, even though *Tear Soup* was very helpful to me when a friend gave it to me after my father's death. That is the point of choosing for meeting objectives. *Tear Soup* helped me learn about my own grief and how to help family members (including my mother) deal with their grief. It taught me that grief is different for each person and the path through it is different. But it is not particularly literary, and its extended metaphor doesn't feel as useful in terms of application to literature. On the other hand, *Cry, Heart, but Never Break* is a book about learning how to let loved ones go, how to grieve and how to move on. The spare text with its lovely use of metaphor and simile, all as part of a dialogue with death, is easier to transfer over to the literature we are reading. For me, although I like both books, the contrast is what this principle is about. Finding books that we like is one thing; finding books that help our students meet the learning objectives can be something else.

Find Books That Clearly Do the Job of the Objective

We can find lots of books for lots of reading purposes in our classes—many can be useful for summarizing, for theme, for fluency building, for finding similes and imagery. But thinking through the objectives we want to achieve is important for our choices, and making sure that the books we use to achieve them are clearly going to do that job is important. Some are just better at doing some jobs than others or more appropriate for our students. A good picturebook for learning about allusion with older students is Ringgold's *Tar Beach* with its allusions to slavery, many of them subtle as the narrator recounts her dream of flying above Harlem and seeing her family's connection to all she sees, all she is a part of in the city, yet all she isn't able to claim as her own. It's a poignant book, with effective allusions that not all students will recognize or understand. That's not a reason to not use it if teachers want to help students become aware of issues related to slavery and racism. It's just a point that we need to consider in our selections.

On the other hand, Margie Palatini's *The Web Files* tells a farm detective story with ducks going after the criminals stealing all the vegetables. The story is told in the manner of *Dragnet*, the TV show from the 1960s—dum de dum

dum—an allusion most students will completely miss. However, the characters are familiar ones from nursery rhymes, so when the detectives say Jack Horner has an airtight alibi, even younger students can catch the allusion to sitting in the corner. And when Little Boy Blue is asked about witnesses to his sleeping under the haystack, we are told . . . the sheep were in the meadow and the cows were in the corn. Because younger students know these nursery rhymes, they are more likely to catch the allusions and the humor created through them. But if teachers have classes with lots of MLL students, they may find that this book isn't effective with them.

Both books are useful for teaching allusion, but, depending on the students in your classes and what they already know, one may be better than the other. Allusions depend somewhat on the reader's background knowledge—as do many other literary devices (such as similes, metaphors, allegory, symbolism, pun, satire, irony, parody)—so considerations of the text, the age of students, and their background knowledge all must be considered in selecting picturebooks to help them develop as readers.

Consider Using Books That Might Address Multiple Purposes Well

A reason I list this as a principle for reading probably starts with practicality: most of us have limits to the numbers of picturebooks we can purchase, and multiple trips to the library take up precious time. But, more important, I found that once I had taken the time to introduce a book to my students, especially if it was a good one, returning to it for another lesson was efficient. My students already knew the story, were already familiar with the way the book worked. If they liked it, then they were more than willing to listen to or read it again for a different purpose. I could take advantage of their engagement and interest in a more efficient way since introducing a new book takes extra time.

One of the first books I purchased for my class library after I found Hall's *Using Picture Storybooks to Teach Literary Devices* was *Through the Mickle Woods* by Valiska Gregory. Hall uses this book as an example of language that is "vividly lyrical with rich imagery, understated with precise simplicity, full of emotional allusions" (5). Then she lists the book under seven different categories of literary devices: aphorism, atmosphere, inference, metaphor, simile, symbol, and theme. I have used it also for reading strategies, for summarizing, and for considering character and setting, elements of reading beyond the literary devices plentiful in this text.

Gregory's book tells the story of a king in medieval times. He has lost his wife, and the story follows his coming to terms with his grief. His wife left him a note, instructing him to go to the Mickle Woods (a word of Scots origin meaning "great") and find the bear. Reluctantly he does, and the bear tells the king three stories, so one of the things I like about this book is its structure. Once my students knew the book, I often pulled the bear's stories out to read as stand-alones. I used them for many purposes, including language instruction to help students see that how the way sentences are structured can help them understand the text better and how precise verb and adjective choice can make a huge difference in creating tone and image. Each time I taught one of these pullout sections, we all remembered the original story, but we were able to have a different focus for our lesson in a way that used our prior knowledge of the text, also reflecting a good reading skill.

6

Using Picturebooks to Teach Global Traits of Writing

When I was first introduced to the six traits of writing (*Education Northwest*) as a fledgling teacher, I was excited. I loved that I now had a vocabulary for teaching writing, something I hadn't been given in my own teacher training or in the textbook I had been provided when I started teaching. In those spaces, I had learned the traditional terms of *coherence* and *unity* and *emphasis*—terms I understood as abstractions and had learned to identify in effective writing but had no idea how to teach. Now I could teach elements of writing through much more concrete terms: *ideas*, *organization*, *voice*, *sentence fluency*, *word choice*, and *conventions*. This felt like something I could do. But I didn't use picturebooks to teach them at first. Instead, I used the language on the rubrics, as my training in the traits had taught me.

It didn't take me long to realize, though, that even with these more concrete terms, students still needed examples of the traits, more than just criteria descriptors from a rubric. Once at a workshop, I was given a student revision checklist using the six traits provided to students that asked writers to evaluate their writing for different traits as they revised. For the first trait, ideas, the evaluative statement was this: "I have ideas." Hmm. I wondered what writing *doesn't* have some ideas. Every writer could check that off no matter how effective the writing was. Something similar was listed for each of the other traits. I realized that even though the six traits language is more concrete, students would still need a little more specificity to understand what constitutes each trait and what contributes to effective writing. And students need examples of what each trait looks like in actual writing. That's where picturebooks come in.

I could teach (and have taught) many of the traits with other kinds of texts (e.g., articles, books, even video clips), but the value of picturebooks for this purpose was obvious: (1) picturebooks are often familiar as a genre and therefore seen as accessible, and (2) the length allows us to see the concept in the context of the whole text, much easier than seeing the same concept in full-length novels or even short stories. And because of that length, picturebooks must be tightly crafted. Newkirk agrees, noting that we should see the "brevity of text not as a concession to young readers but as part of the consummate skill of writers" ("Reasoning" 13). Perfect for teaching writing!

Following is an example of what teaching writing concepts with picturebooks might look like when I want to teach students about having interesting ideas in their writing. I want to emphasize that the mini-lessons I describe here are meant to be taught while students are writing so that they can immediately apply the concepts to their own writing. Teachers can choose which concepts are needed for each kind of writing and when students might need those lessons.

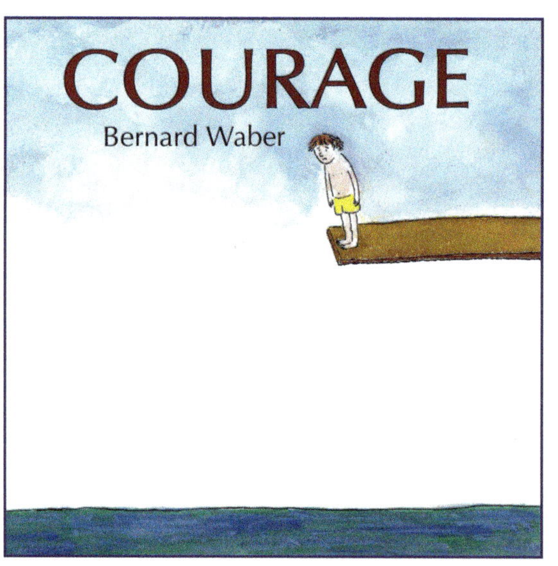

In one lesson for teaching ideas, I use Bernard Waber's *Courage*. The title tells us the concept. In class, I ask students what they think courage means, and we generate a lot of ideas. Then I read the book. Some of what we read is similar to what we anticipated—being brave or standing up for what we believe—but the book gets more specific (and thus more interesting) than our list usually is, which mostly stays at the abstract level. This contrast provides a good introduction to the concept of levels of abstraction (Hayakawa and Hayakawa), and students can begin to understand how moving between abstract and concrete details can make our writing more interesting to readers.

Then, as we read the book again, we begin to investigate how the unexpected examples of courage the author provides also make the book interesting, make us think more deeply about the idea of courage, and also entertain through appropriate surprises:

> Courage is two candy bars and saving one for tomorrow.
> Courage is deliberately stepping on sidewalk cracks.
> Courage is a blade of grass breaking through the icy snow.
> Courage is tasting the vegetable before making a face.

We discuss the examples in the book and consider how surprises can add interest to the ideas in our writing—something we can look for when we are conducting inquiry (what surprises do I find that will enhance my writing?) and during drafting and revision (what surprises have I included and do they make my writing more interesting to read?).

Here are some other ways to teach the global traits of ideas, organization, and voice with picturebooks.

Ideas

I wonder what developing writers think when teachers say that effective writing is based on good ideas, focused ideas, and interesting details. To them, any idea might be a good idea. The ideas they write about will probably be of interest to them, even if they are not particularly interesting to potential readers. In fact, I've had students tell me that: "I think it's interesting. I know what I'm talking about." And they are right—and that is great for writer-based writing. But when we write for readers, for an audience, we have to think of ideas from a different perspective.

I always think about a passage I read a long time ago from Wendy Bishop where she talked about the connection between inquiry and interesting ideas. She noted that "writers consume more than they produce" (v) to find the ideas that matter, the ideas that intrigue, the ideas that engage. She cited Kristina Emick's description of her inquiry into a topic most of us would think didn't require any research: hangnails.

> I researched the OED [Oxford English Dictionary] to find out how the word hangnail developed, how it gets used in idioms, and how its meaning changed over time. I searched beauty books for information on what causes hangnails and how to take care of them. I researched newspapers to find out if hangnails had shown up in recent news (they had, and both instances ended up in the essay). (qtd. in Bishop v–vi)

I explain the relationship of inquiry and ideas visually to my students; spreading my arms as wide as I can, I tell them, "You have to know this much," and then, bringing my hands in front of me about six inches apart, "to be able to write well about this much of your topic." I want students to know that ideas in writing aren't just about having a topic or knowing the same things everyone else knows about it. We have to dig deeper and think harder if we want our ideas to matter. To be interesting.

So how do we help students see what good writers do with ideas to create effective writing? As I think about effective writing of all kinds, I consider ideas from four aspects: interesting **content**; meaningful **details**; a clear, well-defined **focus**; and thoughtful, connected **support**, points that we see on the six traits rubric in one form or another. Good ideas can mean a lot of other things too, but this gives us a good place to start. I use the sliding scales I've included below to help students consider these aspects of ideas.

Focus

Vague 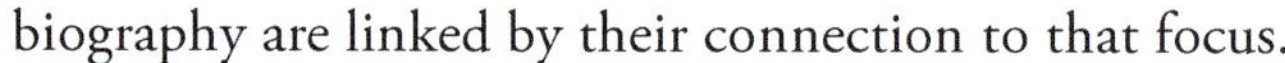 **Clear, well defined**

A clear focus does a lot to improve the ideas in a piece of writing. Writing about anything and everything, writing without a clear focus, usually doesn't move readers to want to read a piece of writing again, to share the writing, to linger and consider the ideas of the writing. M. T. Anderson, speaking in a conference session, talked about focus and referred to his picturebook biography of George Frideric Handel: *Handel, Who Knew What He Liked*. From the title, readers already have an idea of the focus of the book—and that focus gives us a connection to the composer and makes the book effective. The details that are chosen for a short biography are linked by their connection to that focus.

Once I watched a student teacher teach the idea of focus by having students look at a page from a Where's Waldo? book (by Martin Handford); her directions were to write for five minutes about everything they could see happening on the page. After they had finished, I watched one little seventh grader standing by his desk and shaking out his hand—he'd written like a maniac and his hand had cramped up. Then the teacher handed each student a quarter roll (paper circles the bank uses to collect quarters) and told them to find one place on the same picturebook page to see through the circle. For the next five minutes, they wrote only about what they could see through the circle. When they finished, students compared the two

Move!: Focuses on the different ways animals move and uses transitions related to the movements.

Never Smile at a Monkey: Focuses on different actions that cause aggression in animals.

What Do You Do with a Tail like This?: Focuses on amazing things that animal tails, noses, mouths, and eyes can do.

Time to Eat: Focuses on the different kinds of food animals eat and the ways they gather and store food.

Sisters and Brothers: Focuses on sibling relationships among animals—and which ones even have siblings.

pieces of writing, learning how a focus allows writers to go into interesting depth instead of skating across a surface. The student teacher said I could share her activity, as I noticed in subsequent visits how powerful the lesson on focus had been: students referred to it repeatedly throughout the year.

I also like to use Elizabeth Matthews's *Different Like Coco* to teach students about focus and how it works with ideas. The beginning sentences of the book are these: "At a time when France was the center of all that was wealthy, grandiose, and fashionable, Gabrielle 'Coco' Chanel was born poor and skinny. Coco was always different." From these two sentences and the title, I ask students to name the focus. Then, as we read the rest of the book together, I ask them to consider how each idea contributes to the focus the author established for the book. In this way, we begin to learn how we need to know a lot about a topic to find the focus, to know which details matter and which ones don't.

Just One Bite by Lola Schaefer is also a good book to help students consider focus, especially as it shows how focus might differ from our usual concept of it. We learn about how much different animals can eat in one bite. Students might think this book has no focus—after all, it shows different animals on every page—but the author chose to focus on one aspect of all those animals: what they can eat in just one bite. Asking students to consider how this author uses a wide range of animals but still has a unifying focus is a good way for them to consider how focus doesn't have to be a limiting factor in ideas for writing. And Steve Jenkins and Robin Page teach us about different kinds of focus in many of their books that seem to be about so much—but have a clear focus to make the texts effective (see the text box).

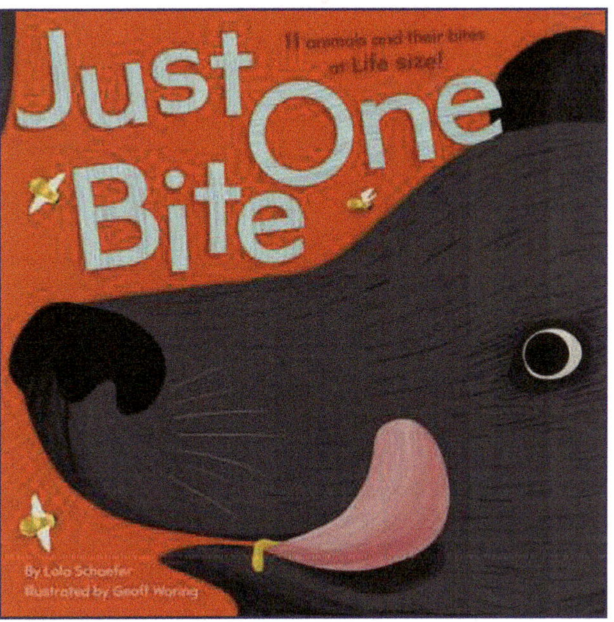

Content

Inaccurate, boring, predictable ⟷ Accurate, original, interesting

Feathers: Not Just for Flying by Melissa Stewart is a great picturebook for helping writers see beyond the obvious when they write about a topic. Taking something readers might be familiar with to one degree or another and then exploring aspects of the topic that readers may not know is a key feature of effective writing. If teachers have students write genres that provide information, this is a perfect concept text for showcasing the possibilities of moving beyond the known. We begin our class discussion before we read the book by naming what we know about feathers. After I read it, I ask students what new ideas they learned and which ones were the most interesting. I ask them if any of the new ideas made them interested in learning more—and usually the response is positive.

I like teaching what Womack calls the reversal essay. We find examples of this kind of writing in a variety of genres, particularly in online sites, where writers take a topic and, acknowledging what readers know, move beyond that to show information readers may not yet know. I share my teaching plan and some student examples in *Strategic Writing* (Dean). *Feathers* is a perfect book to help introduce the concept of moving beyond the known to take audiences more deeply into interesting aspects of a topic. Additionally, this book finds ways to make the new information relatable to the reader, a consideration of audience important for writers when they write about new ideas.

Details

Useless ⟷ Meaningful

In *Pablo Neruda, Poet of the People* by Monica Brown, readers can see the importance of choosing just the right details. The author effectively moves from general to specific—and, by choosing effectively, makes those specifics linger in the reader's mind, as is clear from this passage:

> Pablo wrote poems about the things he loved—things made by his artist friends, things found at the marketplace, and things he saw in nature. He wrote about scissors and thimbles and chairs and rings. He wrote about buttons and feathers and shoes and hats. He wrote about velvet cloth the color of the sea.

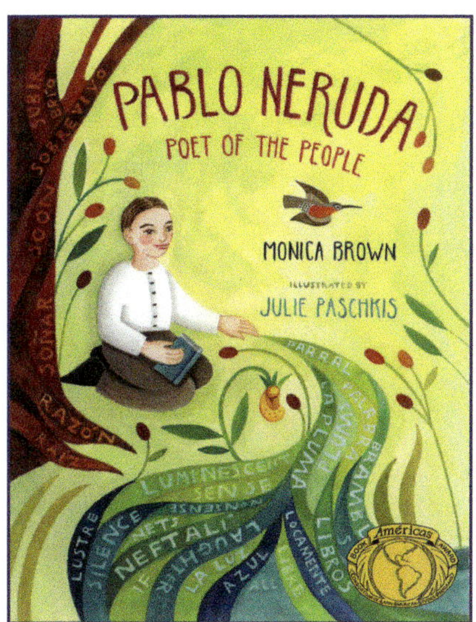

These details are all in Neruda's poems, so they demonstrate meaningful research by being included in the biography, but they are also examples of the everyday topics at the heart of Neruda's poetry. Although I often discourage student writers from using the word *things*, in this passage the word works because it is followed up with so many specific examples of what that word means in this context. And that's something my student writers can learn too. Students can go to their writing and decide what more specific details they can add to create more effective writing.

Support

Sporadic, tossed in, fragmented ⟷ Thoughtful, developed, connected

In Lane Smith's *John, Paul, George, and Ben*, the conclusion makes the point that the men most associated with American independence all brought something individual to a collective goal. To begin the book, the author chooses to tell a short history of each person. For each man, Smith begins with a statement of the trait he sees as valuable to the final outcome: American independence. We might anticipate the story for George Washington—the fable of chopping down the cherry tree, identified at the end of the book as untrue—to get at the trait of honesty. For others, though, we might not know the stories, but they are clearly tied to the key trait of each person. Thus, students can see that when we make an assertion, although there might be many facts or examples to develop it, we use only the ones that matter to the overall point we are making.

"Paul was a noisy lad" is followed by an explanation of how being a member of the bell ringing club at Boston's Old North Church caused hearing issues that resulted in his loud voice (and thus being able to cry warning). "Tom was an independent lad" is followed by the story of Tom ignoring the teacher's directions and doing his own thing repeatedly during art class. Despite the notes in the back of the book confirming that Paul was actually a member of the bell club and that the name of Tom's teacher is correct, I believe Smith took liberties with other story details. The point is still clear: evidence must directly support assertions. Asking students to identify the details and connect them directly to the main idea they support can help writers understand this concept of ideas.

All in Just One Cookie by Susan E. Goodman tells the story of a grandma and her pets as they make cookies to prepare for a visit. We don't know who is coming because the story starts with a phone call and ends with the doorbell chiming, but in between, the team has a good time making chocolate chip cookies. The interesting thing about this book is that as Grandma adds ingredients to the bowl, we learn about the ingredients—what each is, where it comes from, how it gets from its start to Grandma's kitchen. The two kinds of text—story and information—are in different fonts and spaces to help readers know how to read the text. Most important, I like to use this book to show my students how details need to connect. So, for example, we learn about eggs when Grandma is adding the eggs to the dough. I ask students, how would it affect us as readers if we learned about salt when she was adding the eggs? They acknowledge that the idea doesn't make sense, that readers would be confused. Then we can make the extension to their own writing. Do your details clearly connect to the bigger idea and at the right time? If they don't, how can you help readers see the connection? This is a concrete example that we refer to regularly: are you talking about salt when we are adding the eggs?

Organization

For me the hardest aspect of writing instruction is teaching organization. I can find ways to inspire curiosity and ways to teach how to inquire and expand thinking. I can help students learn craft. I can even help students understand the elusive concept of voice better than I can teach organization.

One of the challenges of teaching organization is that it is intricately connected to topic, purpose—and genre. As much as we might like to help students by providing pre-made forms, genres determine some aspects of structure—at least in the big sense—and therefore affect organization.

And it's true: when we write in a specific situation, we know that our readers will expect certain things in certain places. They know what to expect first, second, and last. For instance, if I write a letter of recommendation for a student, I know that the first paragraph is about how I know the student. The middle paragraphs address specific aspects of their character that matter for the scholarship/job/college, each with specific examples. At the end, I summarize and provide an overall assessment related to the specific requirements of the application. Done. I don't have to think about big structure stuff. I do have to think about little organizational stuff, though. About how one sentence flows into the next, about how I move from one paragraph to another, about how I know which character trait to address first, second, etc. Helping students to see the big organization is an important aspect of teaching genre.

Organization is also challenging to teach because it's hard to see. It's often almost invisible; at the least, it's pretty subtle. We have to learn to read intentions in order to read structure. That's tough. Bernabei and Hall's idea of text boxes helps somewhat. It makes the concept of reading structure concrete. Big structure, that is. But getting students to the point of reading that way is tricky.

So I like to begin with picturebooks that have some clear structures, some shapes that students can recognize and understand before we move into more subtle aspects of organization.

Z Is for Moose
by Kelly Bingham

A Call for a New Alphabet
by Jef Czekaj

K Is for Kick
by Brad Herzog

The Queen's Progress
by Celeste Davidson Mannis

Jazz A-B-Z
by Wynton Marsalis

Agent A to Agent Z
by Andy Rash

Gone Wild: An Endangered Animal Alphabet
by David McLimans

ABC books are good examples of big structure: a page for each letter of the alphabet on the topic of the book. I used examples like the ones in the text box to explain the structure to my students when they wrote about their reading of *To Kill a Mockingbird* in that structure. From there, I could help students understand the move from random, confusing shape of ideas to logical, purposeful paths of ideas that readers can follow with ease.

Flow

Random, confusing ⟷ Logical, purposeful

Mo Willems's *Because* uses its title word to build the structure of the story and makes a clear point that events follow prior events for a reason and events have results. The book tells the story of a young girl who attended a concert that changed her life so that she ended up on the concert stage herself. Set up at the beginning as a series of *because* clauses, the story builds from the creation of a piece of music to the moment the girl attends the concert: "Because someone's

uncle caught a cold—someone's aunt had an extra ticket for someone special." In the middle of the story, the turning point, we see the girl (unnamed so that she could be any child) at the concert. For a few pages there are no words, just images. And then the sentences are simple and straightforward—no dependent clauses to begin them, so they are stark and noticeable: "The girl was changed." From that point on, the story recounts what the girl does—because she is changed. And from this point on the story uses *because* clauses at the *end* of every sentence: "Soon, she started to write music, too—because, like Franz, the young woman had something to share."

This clever use of *because* clauses in these two ways sets up a structure that is clear to follow, one that also reinforces the theme of the book—that events are not singular, but they are linked and can have effects. Having students discuss the different ways this book sets up a clear structure, how it uses words and repeated ideas to reinforce the structure, and how that structure fits the main idea or theme can help students start to think about subtle ways they can consider structure and make clear the path readers need to take.

Those Rebels, John and Tom by Barbara Kerley provides interesting compare–contrast structures. The book begins by setting up the contrast: "When John Adams and Thomas Jefferson were young, they were very different." We can see from this beginning sentence that the author has hinted at the structure—we're going to learn about their differences. But implied in this sentence is that there will be more to these men than their differences; we will eventually see how they overcame their differences because of something they had in common. That ending is implied in the very first sentence, even though the author doesn't articulate it.

So the differences go back and forth in the first part of the book:

John skipped school to fly kites and shoot marbles. He loved swimming, hunting, wrestling—and the occasional boxing match, just for kicks.

Tom didn't skip school. He skipped recess—to study Greek grammar. He loved dancing, playing the violin, and reading all the books in his father's library.

This foundation helps to make the turning point—and the focus of the book—have even more impact: "John and Tom were indeed very different, but they did have two things in common: They both cared deeply about the American colonies, and neither of them cared much for George." From this point on, we see how both worked toward the common goal of solving common problems, even if the specifics differed.

This structure is particularly effective when we want to show purposeful comparison and contrast in ideas. The structure could be a model for informative writing—telling the story of a historical event or explaining processes—as well as for making an argument by explaining how two ideas relate to each other. The overall structure:

Difference . . . Difference . . . Difference . . . Commonality . . . Commonality . . . Commonality . . . Effect/Result

Connections

Lacking, reader is lost ⟷ Useful, guide the reader subtly

I'll admit it: I have taught connections by providing students with a list of transition words. When I read the results, I knew I had to try a different way to show connections.

I like to start with two picturebooks that make the use of transitions obvious but also show how they can be meaningful. The first is Jules Feiffer's *Meanwhile . . .*, which tells the story of a boy avoiding responding to his mom's call. Instead, he imagines himself having adventures in other places and times. The transition word, *meanwhile*, is written in a prominent font because it connects the adventures and gives clarity to the movement of the plot. The second book, *Previously* by Allan Ahlberg, cleverly uses the title adverb to tie multiple familiar nursery rhymes and fairy tales together while it moves backward through time. It starts at the end and then tells the first part of the story, ending with a word that ties to the end of the next story. So the book begins with Goldilocks coming home "all bothered and hot" from running through the forest. "Previously she had been sleeping in somebody else's bed, eating somebody else's porridge . . ." and "Previously she had bumped into a hurtling and older boy named . . . ." We turn the page and see the title of the next part: *Jack*. Then the story of Jack and the beanstalk is told, in reverse, until we see that previously he had "come tumbling down that high hill with his argumentative little sister. . . ." Readers can anticipate the name on the next page: Jill. This pattern continues until all of the stories join to end with the "once upon a time."

I ask students to discuss the use of transition words to make sense of stories. We often discuss how these are contrived for an effect—that writers rarely use the same transitional word repeatedly, as in these books. But students can clearly articulate the function of the transitions in these fun books.

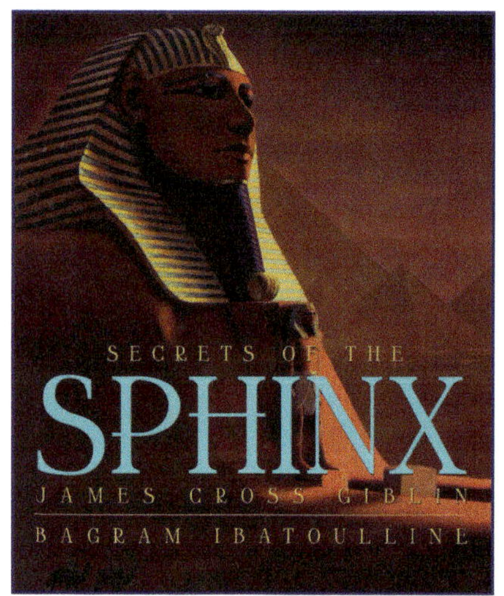

With high school students—and sometimes even with junior high students if they are ready—I use passages from a longer picturebook, James Cross Giblin's *Secrets of the Sphinx*, to teach a couple of mini-lessons about transitional devices, not just words. In a couple of passages, I want students to see how authors use synonyms, pronouns, and repetition to create connections. We read a couple of paragraphs together and discuss them, identifying other elements that contribute to connecting ideas. Then, with other paragraphs, I ask students to work together in pairs to identify words and phrases that they think help to cue the reader about flow and order, words that mark the trail for readers. Here is a sample paragraph:

> Religion was central to Egyptian life from the beginning, and the pharaoh played a key role in its rituals. In life, the ruler was thought to be the son of Ra, the all-powerful sun god. In death, he rejoined his father in the west, the place where the sun set. There, in the Egyptian afterworld, he would enjoy eternal life, but only if the earthy body was still intact.

When students have had a chance to work together on this challenging task, we review their findings together. They should notice the following; if they don't, I draw their attention to these devices:

- The use of a **synonym** to link to Pharaoh *ruler*;
- The **repetition** of two beginning phrases in a row to create a sequence: "in life" and "in death";
- The use of **phrases (appositives) that extend and explain** ideas: "the

all-powerful sun god," "the place where the sun set," "in the Egyptian afterworld"; and

- The use of an **adverb** to link one sentence to the next: "the place where the sun set. . . . There."

After we identify the transitional devices, we discuss the effects of these devices and why they might be more interesting than traditional word-variety transitions. We then immediately return to the writing they are working on to see where they could apply what they just learned.

Leading In and Out

Abrupt, without meaning ⟷ Effective, meaningful

With introductions and conclusions, mentor texts can help students learn to be meaningful and gentle instead of random and abrupt. Sometimes students start school writing with broad statements, so broad that there is no clear indication where the piece is going. Getting them to consider how to set a tone, indicate a focus, *and* engage a reader can be hard. That's a lot to do at once. Fortunately, because they have limited space, most picturebooks are really good at this. One example is Melissa Stewart's *Pipsqueaks, Slowpokes, and Stinkers: Celebrating Animal Underdogs*, where the title helps to establish the focus and tone at the same time. The introduction is one of the strongest I've found to help students see how they can establish the known with an audience and move to their own focus in an efficient and effective way:

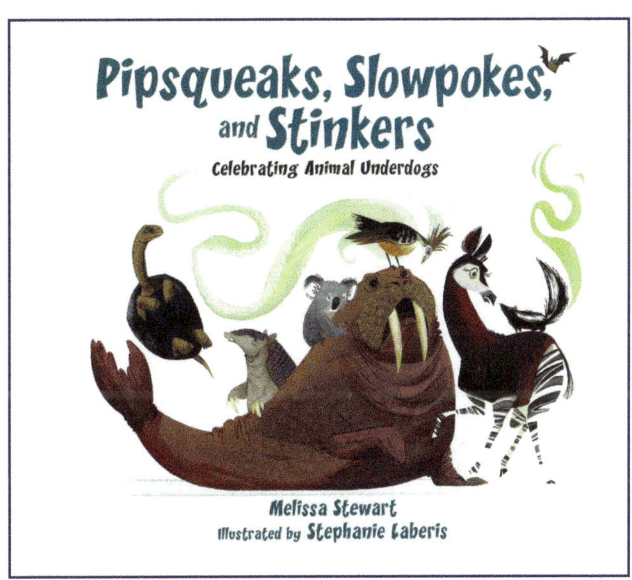

> Everyone loves elephants. They're so big and fierce.
> Everyone respects cheetahs. They're so fast and fierce.
> But this book isn't about animals we admire. It's about the unsung underdogs of the animal world. Don't you think it's time someone paid attention to them?

Sometimes a piece of student writing startles us with its abrupt ending, a sudden "The End" because the student doesn't know what else to do. I like

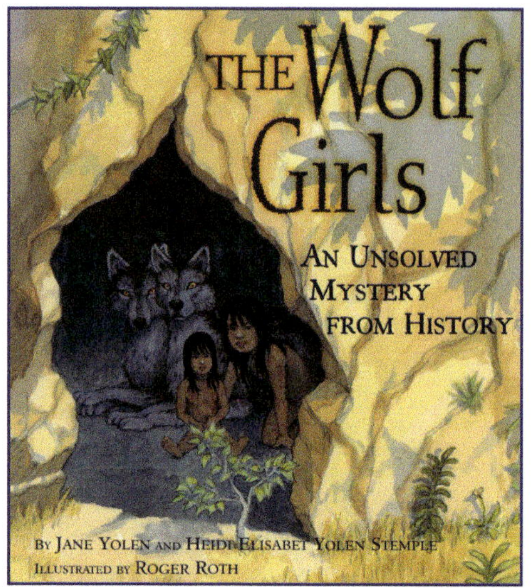

to have students explore a variety of ways to finish a piece of writing by looking at endings of picturebooks. One favorite is *The Wolf Girls* in which Jane Yolen and Heidi Elisabet Yolen Stemple end the mystery by listing four possible explanations and how evidence supports each—and leaving it up to the reader to decide the most plausible one. I often recommend this option for conclusions when it isn't clear that there is only one correct answer to a question. By learning from picturebooks effective options for starting out and meaningful ways to finish, students have options they can choose from for their own writing.

Pacing

Too much or too little content at times  **Spends just the right amount of time on content**

Finally, picturebooks are great for teaching pacing, for helping writers learn to identify when ideas need to be expanded or condensed, when it's better to spend time on an idea and when it's better to move on. The length of picturebooks makes them especially effective for teaching pacing, as writers with limited space must pay particular attention to this aspect of effective writing.

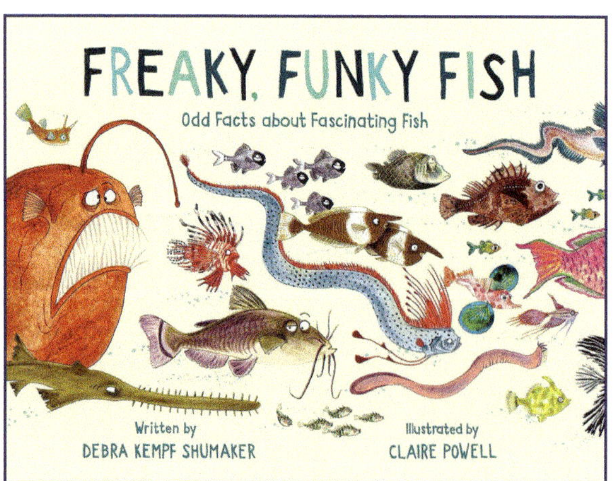

Freaky, Funky Fish: Odd Facts about Fascinating Fish by Debra Kempf Shumaker is a new favorite of mine for teaching pacing. When I want to teach pacing, I often turn to nonfiction picturebooks written in a literary style because the authors have made a choice about how much information they share in the main body of the text as a pacing decision. This book is a lively rhyming book providing generalizations about all kinds of fish, with fun images and informative labels (such as funky ratings): "One kind gives a shake and swat. One fish coats itself with snot. Some fish dance and some play dead. One fish sports a see-through head!" I can't imagine readers not wanting to know more about some of these interesting fish—but the author doesn't tell us all the information at once. I ask students: does that mean she doesn't know the information? Obviously not, as the ratings and images suggest. The back of the book tells us more about these freaky fish and lists sources the author used and sources the author recommends for interested readers to learn more. As we enjoy this book, I ask students why they imagine the author paced the book this way: *Why hold back some of the information for the end? Do you imagine the author knows more that didn't even make it into the information at the end?* This can be a good reminder that they need to know a lot about their topics.

Students have told me that one thing they don't like about inquiry-based writing is that they sometimes don't use all the notes they took. They see that as a waste of time; they want to include everything they learned. I want them to see that writers actually make great choices about pacing, about choosing what information matters most to the purposes of the writing and the interests of the readers. This is what pacing means. We need to look at our own writing, think about our readers, and then consider where they might need more information and where they might want us to move faster—and we should take out unnecessary details. That is pacing.

Voice

Many researchers and teachers have written about voice and the challenge of teaching it. Darsie Bowden even went so far as to challenge the concept of voice! Most of us understand the term to represent a kind of individualism that shows through in writing, an investment on the part of the writer, an honesty and a willingness to connect with the topic and audience that brings writing to life. The same writer may have a different voice in different pieces of writing, though, because, as Stewart and Correia note, tone is about the writer's feelings, but voice is about the reader: "An author crafts the experience they want the reader to have" (100). Voice involves the kind of writing we do, the stance we have about it, and the way we want our readers to experience that writing. It's HUGE! So how do we teach it?

I don't know.

I have, however, tried some things that I hope have helped to approach the concept for my students.

First, I try to have students consider a variety of texts that illustrate different ways authors approach topics and the ways they talk about them. For example, I show the following two passages about tarantulas from two different picturebooks. By comparing the passages, we can talk about the different approaches the writers took to the same subject. *What do we notice about the two voices? What about how those voices are created? Why did each writer choose to use the voice she did?*

- *One Day in the Desert* by Jean Craighead George

Near the coyote den dwelled a tarantula, a spider almost as big as a man's fist and covered with furlike hairs. She looked like a long-legged bear, and she was sitting near the top of her burrow, a shaft she had dug straight down into the ground. The hot desert air forced her to let go with all eight of her legs. She dropped to the bottom of her shaft, where the air was cooler. The spider survives the heat by digging underground and by hunting at night. The moist crickets and other insects she eats quench her thirst.

- *An Interview with Harry the Tarantula* by Leigh Ann Tyson

Q: What did you do?

A: I did what any tarantula would do. I leaned back on my hind legs, lifted my front ones up, and opened my fangs in horror. Then I reached around with my front legs and rubbed some hairs off my back and tried to fling them at her.

Q: Why did you do that?

A: Well, I'll tell you. It usually makes scary animals go away. I think my hair irritates them. Have you ever looked closely at tarantula hairs? They're really very nice. I'm quite proud of them.

Q: Could I look at one now?

A: You mean, like, take one out? No, I couldn't. I never know when I might need them. And I have shed my skin for the last time. So I won't have any more hair. I hardly have any left now.

My students wonder whether the difference in voice is purposeful, if writers think about these things. I think they do. It might not be the voice they use in everything they write, but it's a choice they made in a specific instance—for this topic, this genre. And they know how to do it partly from thinking about how language creates tones and reflects attitudes. I also have my students look at an encyclopedia entry for tarantulas, and we compare that voice. I explain that the encyclopedia isn't without voice; it just has a detached, objective one. We can discuss why encyclopedia and Wikipedia entries are written that way and how that objectivity is created, so that we can begin to consider how voice reflects the writer in a specific situation.

Another text my students learn about voice from is *Once Upon a Fairy Tale* by the Starbright Foundation. In this book, four familiar fairy tales are told from the perspectives of different characters—by actors who tell their stories from a particular stance and voice. The stories can be read or listened to since there is a CD with the book. As we listened to some of the stories, I asked students to comment on the ways the speakers chose to tell the stories. What did their choices do to the story? This helps us to understand something about voice. It's partly about attitude and perspective. Those shape the way we tell stories—what we choose to tell and what we leave out. The words we use and how we put them together.

After this lively discussion, I asked students to take one section of our disclosure document—written with a distinct teacher voice, right?—and rewrite it in some kind of student voice. Once, a concerned mom emailed to make sure her daughter wasn't going to be in trouble. She had rewritten my tardy policy in a pretty snarky student voice, and Mom was worried. I told her that her daughter was doing the task I had assigned and not to worry. And the next day in class we had a rich discussion about the choices students had made in order to revise the voice of a formal school genre.

By reading texts with interesting voices and considering what makes them interesting, students will begin to build their concept of voice.

Principles

- ✓ Find books with a clear focus on global traits.
- ✓ Find books that appeal to your students (age, interest, concept, style).

Find Books with a Clear Focus on Global Traits

When we are choosing picturebooks for the purposes of teaching the global traits of writing, we want to make sure that the books we select clearly exemplify one—or more—of the key aspects of the traits. By this, I don't mean that a picturebook should focus on only one trait; in fact, I think finding a book that is rich in conceptual examples can be very useful to our instruction. What I mean is that the examples for our instruction need to be clear so that students aren't distracted by other features or content. I once used an essay to try to teach an organizational concept. It was a disaster because the organization was subtle and the content was somewhat controversial, a wrinkle I hadn't anticipated. Students did *not* learn about organization from that essay. Picturebooks can present the same challenges if we are not intentional about our selections.

Dianna Hutts Aston's *An Egg Is Quiet* is a wonderful picturebook that could be used to teach about all three global traits: ideas (content, details, support), organization (flow), and voice. The book begins with a broad generalization, one we expect from the title. The first lines explain the generalization:

> An egg is quiet. It sits there,
> under its mother's feathers
> . . . on top of its father's feet
> . . . buried beneath the sand.
> Warm. Cozy.

Then the book chooses other details that we may not know about eggs. Each set of details is preceded by a broad statement: an egg is shapely (followed by images of many different shapes of eggs), an egg is colorful (on a page with many eggs shown in a variety of colors), and so on. I can only imagine Aston collecting all her research, looking at many kinds of eggs, and then choosing which details were the most interesting. These she grouped by category. She didn't talk about the eggs most of us know—white or brown, oval, smooth. She expands our understanding with facts most of us wouldn't ever know, facts that intrigue and linger, even if the topic might not initially seem that interesting. The contrast between the seemingly prosaic subject (after all, most of us might think, what is there to say about eggs?) and the text provides a good example of how choosing the right details, doing enough inquiry to find those details and knowing that they would be of interest, makes all the difference in effective writing.

This book is also useful for teaching organization and voice. The organizational element of pacing by choosing to identify characteristics of eggs and then expanding on them before introducing another characteristic is clear. I also like to ask students to consider the voice—objective, but also gentle and soft—and why that might be an appropriate voice for this book about something as fragile as eggs. I bring these other teaching options up to make the point: although I could teach a lot about writing with one text, I want to make sure that I can clearly identify the aspect of the trait I am using the book to teach.

Find Books That Appeal to Your Students

I've added this principle, as obvious as it seems, to make a point. Some books I've described are not necessarily on topics that many students will find interesting at first glance—Coco Chanel or eggs. But the way the authors write about them makes them appealing once students start looking at what the writer is doing. Once students know that they can trust that I have something of value to offer them from the books I choose, they are willing to give me some leeway, to go along for a bit, and then I can usually get them excited about the topic too. Or at least a little interested. But sometimes we have to consider whether the topic itself might help some students access the learning we want them to get. In this case, we want to find books that are also of interesting topics to our students—and do the other things we want them to do.

Surprising Sharks by Nicola Davies is a book that I think meets this principle well. First of all, many students have some background in studying sharks in elementary school. And let's face it, there is something inherently appealing in the topic: sharks frighten and intrigue. Too many movies set them up as the villain, so we just have to know more about them. We are attracted and repulsed simultaneously.

The book begins with an intriguing topic. It meets another requirement too; it does an admirable job with focus and in choosing effective details. In this case, the book doesn't give us everything about sharks—the title promises that it's going to tell us *surprising* things about sharks. Indeed, the introductory sentences are such an effective beginning that I often return to this text to teach introductions as well.

> You're swimming in the warm blue sea. What's the one word that turns your dream into a nightmare? What's the one word that makes you think of a giant man-eating killer? Shaaaaarrrkk!

We turn the page, and the text immediately shows a tiny shark, "just bigger than a chocolate bar," reversing the expected ideas about sharks: "Not a giant, certainly no man-eater, and a killer only if you happen to be a shrimp." The book continues with other interesting details about sharks: some have "built-in fairy lights . . . or blow up like a party balloon." This is a nice book for teaching ideas because of its interesting content, and it's a great example of finding details that intrigue and delight. It also serves well to teach elements of organization and voice, as both are clearly evident in the way the text develops.

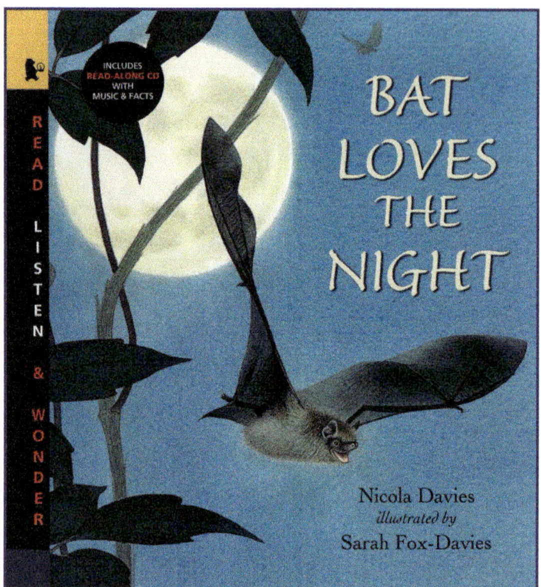

Nicola Davies's *Bat Loves the Night* is a lovely book that teaches readers about—you guessed it—bats. I shared this book with a teacher friend as a possible alternative to the traditional research assignment she was going to teach. As we explored the book together, we were able to identify ways she could teach about choosing interesting ideas and details to share about the animals to help guide students' inquiry. We noted the organizational structure—a day in the life of the animal—that could help writers pay attention to transitions when they choose an organization that fits the topic. And we also considered the lovely voice Davies has created for Bat so that readers engage with the information provided about the animal because it is written in a conversational tone (with a great use of word choice and sentence variety). This book does it all—and inspired my friend's students so much that they created amazing writing. Because it's such a great example of all the traits of writing, it really inspires students to write, and write effectively.

Another picturebook I have used to help teach the big ideas of organization is a counting book titled *One Leaf Rides the Wind* by Celeste Davidson Mannis. Like ABC books, counting books have a clear structure—following numbers, usually 1–10, with the content of each page related to the number. *One Leaf Rides the Wind* extends the structure a bit by combining haiku with short informative paragraphs about different aspects of Japanese gardens, each with a poem and paragraph related to it. Each page, 1–10, depicts an element of the garden. When students write their own counting books, they consider which subtopics align best to which numbers, if there can be a connection. Students consider what their topic is and what kind of poetry might best reflect that topic. One student, writing about his grandpa, wrote his poems in cowboy poetry. But all of the students had a big shape to use and a mentor for considering voice and idea development, which content went into an informative paragraph and which went into the poem.

7

Using Picturebooks to Teach Language

During all my years of teaching, at all levels of my teaching (junior high, senior high, and university), when people hear that I teach English, they say something about grammar, as if that is all I do as an English teacher: watch other people's language, correct language, teach rules. "Are you writing a book about semicolons yet?" my brother-in-law teases. I remind people that I do a lot more than teach grammar, but I have to admit, I do like teaching about language and style. I am convinced that my students gain power as readers and writers when they understand how local traits of writing—word choice, sentence fluency, and conventions—can help them read more effectively and write with authority and creativity.

When we use picturebooks to teach elements of language, we are using texts that students are comfortable with, but also ones that have been carefully crafted: writers have thirty-two pages of spare text to tell a story, make a point, inspire imagination. To do that, writers are particularly careful about words and sentences, and punctuation. A recent book by Penny Kittle makes the case for using micro mentor texts—including picturebooks—to teach writing and language because they are short, accessible, and beautifully crafted. We can teach language very effectively from shorter texts in ways that longer texts don't always make easy.

I have often used picturebooks to teach the *rules* of language—how to punctuate compound sentences, or when to use commas with introductory elements or in a series, or how to punctuate dialogue. I also use picturebooks to teach about style, about options writers have to create an effect with fluency, word choice, and punctuation. My process for either objective is fairly similar, whatever I am teaching: First I read a picturebook to students, either in whole or, if it works and is needed for time's sake, a pertinent part. After we talk about the shared book or section, I show students sentences I have selected from the book that serve as examples of the concept I am targeting in the mini-lesson. With a set of examples in front of them, students work in groups to identify what they notice: (1) what do the sentences have in common? (2) what is the effect? and (3) what we can learn as writers from those common elements? For some concepts, I use sets of examples and nonexamples to clarify a concept in more depth.

For example, to teach about commas before conjunctions in compound sentences (especially if I need to address it for the state test, let's say), we work with a set of examples and nonexamples from the book *Sitting Ducks* by Michael Bedard:

Nonexamples:

- It rolled off the assembly line and fell down, down, down into the shadowy darkness below.
- He just had to sneak away and explore the streets below.
- He rushed in and hopped up onto a stool.

Examples:

- The alligator acted friendly, but all the while he was thinking what a delicious meal the duck would make when properly fattened.
- At first, the alligator was bewildered by this weird welcome, but soon he joined in the crazy dance.
- They even tried going out together, but it proved to be very awkward.
- The alligator had warned him never to venture out alone, but the duck's curiosity got the best of him.

Based on their inquiry with these sets, students come up with some "rules" about when writers use commas in sentences, including these:

- It's not the word (*and* or *but*) that tells us to use a comma.
- It's what comes before and after it—a complete idea or sentence on either side of the word.
- We need BOTH the word (*and, but, or*) AND two whole sentences.

After we come to our conclusions, I acknowledge that published authors don't always use commas in compound constructions, even with this expectation. After all, my students will read many examples where the "rule" isn't followed. I ask students to look in a book they are currently reading (a class novel or independent reading) to find some examples and nonexamples that we can examine for an understanding of why this might be the case. Here are some examples from *The Chronicles of Narnia* (Lewis) like those that students might notice in the texts they are reading:

- He was very sad and he wasn't even sure all the time that he had done the right thing; but whenever he remembered the shining tears in Aslan's eyes he became sure. (95)
- Then suddenly they felt coats around them instead of branches and the next moment they were both standing outside the wardrobe in the empty room. (128)
- A broad river divided itself into two streams and on the island between them stood the city of Tashbaan, one of the wonders of the world. (228)

We discuss why writers (and editors) who know the expectations decide to do something else—use only a conjunction or only a comma. Why would they be intentional about that? My students have thought of answers that surprise me with their insight: because the two parts seem like they need to be closer than the comma-plus-conjunction would make them or that the writer needed to hurry into the next part of the sentence to create an effect in that part of the text. These are important insights—and help students see that writers use punctuation to *do* things, not just to follow rules.

At this point, we also talk about how test writers (or some teachers) might feel if they—eighth graders or juniors—punctuate in these alternate ways. Students recognize that sometimes they might need to follow the "rules," but at other times they might want to consider when it is in their best interest to create the effects they have seen when writers don't "follow the rules." In my class, I tell them, if they put a star by their alternate use, indicating that the choice was intentional, they can do it. I want them to start using punctuation to achieve effects, not just to follow expectations (but now they know them!).

We have heard for years that the best way to teach language (grammar) is in context, not from textbooks or worksheets. Instead, students learn language best through real-world texts, ones that students read in and outside of class, including picturebooks. Such texts show language doing things, not as rules or about correctness. Teaching language in context, with texts that students know or can come to know, shows them that language/grammar can do things for them: create a tone, draw attention to key ideas, cause words to linger in a reader's mind, make a point more emphatically, and more. Such use of language has power—and seeing language use its power in a text is magic.

When I create sentence sets for these language lessons, I try to choose my sentence examples thoughtfully, considering things like making sure that the sentences all show the concept I hope to teach but also exhibit variety in other ways so that students are not distracted from the concept. So, for instance, if I'm teaching appositives, I try to show appositives in different places in the sentences and punctuated in different ways so that students see options for their own understanding of how to use appositives. It never fails that students will see things I had not anticipated, but in general the practice is effective in getting students to perceive reader expectations of language—both style and rules—in authentic texts. As an added benefit, the sentences in picturebooks are usually very effective, so students are reading great sentences while they learn. I can teach rules and test prep through mini-lessons that are structured similarly, but I prefer to teach aspects of writers' craft that move beyond rules, writerly options that are more open to choice. For style. For rhetorical effect.

For these style elements, I use a process similar to the one for teaching the "rules," except that in these cases, as I collect examples, I look for patterns and then for examples that alter the pattern a bit but still exemplify the concept I want students to notice. I may use examples from multiple picturebooks when I'm teaching for style. Sometimes I bold aspects of the examples I want students to notice; other times I don't. Sometimes I show the example sets without bolding at first and then show the bolded set to focus attention. The choice depends on the concept and my students' knowledge. So, for example, one set I have shared with my students is the following:

> The **true** story of how **one** gentleman—**short and stout**—and another—**tall and lean**—formed a **surprising** alliance, committed treason, and helped launch a **new** nation. (*Those Rebels, John and Tom*, Barbara Kerley)
>
> On an **empty** beach, a **dark**, **silent** shape climbs out of the shallows. **Crashing** waves make the only sound. (*Tracks in the Sand*, Loreen Leedy)
>
> A secret, the eggs lie **hidden**. (*Tracks in the Sand*, Loreen Leedy)
>
> Across the way, another woman—also **well dressed**—extends her fishing pole over the water. (*Seurat and La Grande Jatte*, Robert Burleigh)

> In October the Acorn Moon comes **strong**, **yellow**. (*Long Night Moon*, Cynthia Rylant)
>
> Hippo watches as they honk and snort . . . until, finally, the **defeated** bull limps away. (*Hippos Are Huge*, Jonathan London)
>
> **Deep**, like the rumbling of mountains, the sound circled around him like a cloak. (*Through the Mickle Woods*, Valiska Gregory)

After students have time to study and discuss the examples in small groups, we combine our observations to help us learn craft. They usually notice that the words are adjectives (describers). I hope they will also make most of the following observations; if they don't, I use guiding questions to draw their attention to the ideas so that they can still come to the conclusion themselves:

- ✓ placement (some come before the nouns they modify but some come after—out of order)
- ✓ punctuation (some are separated by commas, others by dashes, and adjectives in a series sometimes have no punctuation—why?)
- ✓ type (some end in *-ing* or *-ed*, while others are nouns and others more traditional)

I ask students to hypothesize why each writer might have made the choices they did. For example, why might some authors choose to place adjectives after the noun they modify instead of in the expected spot, before the noun? Why might some of the authors use dashes instead of commas or parentheses (also options) to separate their adjectives? We might also notice that these writers use adjectives judiciously, depending on other parts of speech to do more meaningful work rather than using long lists of adjectives. When we draw attention to these craft elements, student writers can see that all writing moves beyond following expectations (rules) and into using what we know about language to become more effective, not simply correct. By contrasting the effect created by the choices the author makes with other options, students can begin to see that their choices with craft carry power.

Sentence Fluency

In Chapter 9, I share a way I use a picturebook, *My House Has Stars* by Megan McDonald, to have students write and make a class book. As part of that writing, we do a mini-lesson on sentence fluency that my students refer to again and again throughout the year. After we have read the book and identified its

- This sentence has five words. Here are five more words. Five-word sentences are fine. But several together become monotonous. Listen to what is happening. The writing is getting boring. The sound of it drones. It's like a stuck record. The ear demands some variety.
- Now listen. I vary the sentence length, and I create music. Music. The writing sings. It has a pleasant rhythm, a lilt, a harmony. I use short sentences. And I use sentences of medium length. And sometimes when I am certain the reader is rested, I will engage him with a sentence of considerable length, a sentence that burns with energy and builds with all the impetus of a crescendo, the roll of the drums, the crash of the cymbals—sounds that say listen to this, it is important.
- So write a combination of short, medium, and long sentences. Create a sound that pleases the reader's ear. Don't just write words. Write music. ~ Gary Provost (qtd. in Clark)

characteristics and they have conducted inquiry and started drafting, we look back at some of the pages in the *My House Has Stars* to consider sentence fluency specifically. I ask students to count the number of words in each sentence, and we make a list of the numbers for each page on the board. We notice strings of numbers like this: 7-8-7-6-7-5-11-8-13-7-12-11-29-18-8-4-3-12-1-1-4. Then I ask students to count the number of words in each sentence of their own writing and compare their numbers to the patterns we saw in McDonald's book. I share with students the Gary Provost quote in the text box, and we talk about the way we write compared to the way we speak. We often vary sentence length a lot more in speech, so, to make our writing sound like our mentor texts, we need to create a more conversational voice—meaning looking at sentence length variation.

I don't want students to just chop up or jam together sentences, though. We talk about the effect of long sentences (students know that these lull them) and short sentences (which draw attention). We talk about the effect when too many of each are next to each other (choppy or boring, they say). And we talk about when we put a short sentence before or after a long one—what is the effect? As we play with sentences on the board, moving them around, students start to see how choosing is about what they want to say, not about following a rule. I encourage them to start with the "punch" sentence in their writing. What can they do to make it knock out the reader? From that start, writers can rearrange or massage surrounding sentences to create the memorable rhythm they want. We count our sentence lengths multiple times, we read our writing aloud, and we revise for effect. It is amazing what students realize they can do when they understand the power of sentence fluency.

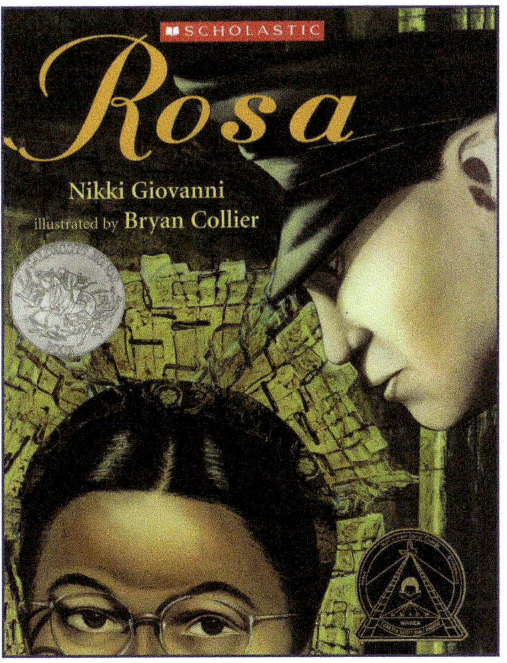

Another mini-lesson that sticks with my students is when I use a passage from Nikki Giovanni's *Rosa*. Because students are familiar with the experiences of Rosa Parks, if I am pressed for time I can use just one passage from that book to share with them for this lesson:

> She sighed as she realized she was tired. Not tired from work but tired of putting white people first. Tired of stepping off sidewalks to let white people pass, tired of eating at the separate lunch counters and learning at separate schools.

As we discuss this passage, we notice the effect of the repeated words, particularly *tired*. I note that I just feel tired from reading it, exactly what I imagine Giovanni wants readers to feel. We discuss the repetition but also the placement in a spot of emphasis—at the beginning of the phrases. I can also point out how Giovanni starts to repeat *separate* in the last part of this passage, a repetition she carries on in the next paragraph of the book.

As part of this mini-lesson, we must discuss why students might have been told to use different words—synonyms—and to not repeat words. If we have been told this, why might someone think it is good writing advice? We have to admit that repetition is not about saying a word again and again just because we can't think of a better one. We don't repeat filler words or insignificant ones. We have to pay attention to the words that repeat—they need to be words that matter.

And we have to talk, at least a little bit, about where in the sentence our words sit. This discussion is where sentence combining really pays off. When students regularly practice sentence combining, one of the primary skills they develop is a sense of how word order and word placement create different effects (Anderson and Dean). Words at ends of sentences get the most emphasis. Words at beginnings can be emphasized if we put a phrase (followed by a comma) before them, delaying their entrance and using punctuation to draw a pause—to make readers pay attention—to the word that comes after it. Looking at other sentences in this picturebook and in others will help students explore repetition as an aspect of sentence fluency. Hand out different picturebooks to different groups and have them look for examples to share with the class. Since I always teach this lesson during a writing project, students go back to their writing: Is there an idea they want to emphasize, a concept they want readers to focus on? If so, how can they use repetition and word order to create that emphasis and focus?

A favorite recent picturebook is *Courage Hats* by Kate Hoefler. I can use this book for so many purposes: I love it as an invitation for informal writing. I love it to talk about differences and how we deal with fears, even how we define courage, to get us started thinking about themes for literature. But I can't ignore that one of the ways this book could be especially useful is for teaching sentence fluency. This purpose would probably be better for older students and require teachers to read the book—or parts of it, at least—multiple times because the examples of sentence fluency are subtle. First, it would be an excellent book to talk about sentence length variety. The first three sentences are amazing for showing how a short (or two shorts) followed by a long sentence creates a great effect: "Not everyone loves a train. That's the world. But sometimes, you have to take one anyway."

Additionally, as the story details both Mae and Bear and their train journey, we see many parallel sentences, patterns for each of these characters that mirror each other (intentionally, to reinforce the point that despite being different, we are more alike underneath than we might know): "Mae wore a special hat so a bear would think she was just another bear. Bear wore a special hat so a person would think he was just another person." As students study these parallel sentences and discuss their importance in the book, they can consider the effect here as well as parallel patterns in other sentences. Have students look in other picturebooks you have selected for this purpose, such as *If You're Not from the Prairie . . .* by David Bouchard, to have students explore other texts with similarly patterned sentences to identify other options and determine effects. After they have explored and discussed these sentence patterns and parallelism in general, have them return to their writing to see where they might be able to build sentences of similar patterns to create the same unifying effect—or simply to check for parallel structure in their sentences.

Word Choice

Picturebooks with creative and effective word choice can help students see how choosing just the right word is important to writing—and knowing lots of words can help us choose just the right word. Mary Lyn Ray's *Mud* is a favorite of mine for teaching about just-right words. For one thing, the book begins with this short sentence: "One night it happens." I pause and ask students what they think "it" is. We have a brief talk about the effectiveness of raising curiosity in a reader by using a pronoun *before* we know the noun it stands for, something that isn't usual. We wonder about "it." Then I read the next page, where we see the "it" again without its antecedent. We make more predictions, this time from the images. Not until the fourth page spread do we get a hint, and then, instead of reading "spring" or "mud," we learn "earth comes unfrozen."

This is a lingering type of picturebook, inviting us to spend time on each page, so talk with students for a minute about being indirect (why not say "spring"?) and its effect—and challenges. Writers have to be careful when they use roundabout wording. The next pages have lovely sentences with vivid images and alliteration. When winter melts, we hear it with the words splattered across the page spread: *Squish, Slurp, Squck*. Then, for several pages we get to play in the mud with muddy-sounding words. After we finish our reading, we discuss some of the effective sentences in the book, and students in small groups rewrite them in "regular" language, not the rich, lively words we read. By reversing the goal and then comparing the sentences they invent with the ones in the book, we can see the power of word choice. We take a few minutes to go back to their writing and look for places that would come alive if students chose a better word here and there—not just to choose a big word or a different one, but to create images and sounds and feelings with the words we choose. I like to have students share their new choices in small groups when they are done.

Most of the time, published writing has language that sounds fancy or smart or like school or poetry. *The Adventures of Mark Twain by Huckleberry Finn* by Robert Burleigh is the story of Mark Twain as told by the character Twain created. The language in this book is not like school or poetry. In fact, the book

begins with a double-page spread warning the reader that Huckleberry Finn is not a writer but is instead a boy who "almost never went to school." The warning tells us that the editors want readers to be prepared for the language we will read in the book and provides some examples (dropping *g*'s and using old-fashioned words and idioms of the time). We are assured we will be able to figure it all out.

This book is a biography with more text on a page than is usual with picturebooks. Depending on the purpose for using the book, teachers may want to read only part of it to the whole class unless circumstances allow for an entire reading (which is enjoyable, just lengthy). I generally read the first part and selected pages, just to get the flavor of the text and set up a discussion about using language in our writing to match the situation. This discussion can be a great introduction to language of different time periods, contrasting passages from Twain's actual writing with passages from Dickens, Melville, Shakespeare, and some modern writers like Jason Reynolds. Again, having students rewrite passages in "other ways" of using language can help students see what is lost from this text, but they might also try rewriting one of their own stories in the language of this picturebook to see if it loses something. This is a good way for students to understand how word choice needs to fit the tone, situation, genre, and time of a piece of writing.

Conventions

The thing about conventions is that we usually teach them as rules (from definitions and dos and don'ts), but those don't really stick. At least in my experience they don't. When I teach conventions from examples and texts in the world, students see punctuation as tools that do things for them as writers and readers. I know I am a little nerdy about this, often stopping when we are reading something as a class to ask students to notice some way of punctuating a sentence or phrase in a way that draws my attention and makes me wonder about what the writer wants me to think from the choice. I always have quotes about punctuation around my room that emphasize the role that I see punctuation taking in our writing and reading (see a few in the text box).

- "Punctuation marks are the road signs placed along the highway of our communication—to control speeds, provide directions and prevent head-on collisions."
- "And no one scans a letter so closely as a lover, searching for its small print, straining to hear its nuances, its gasps, its sighs and hesitations, poring over the secret messages that lie in every cadence."
- "Punctuation establishes the relations between people using words."
- "Punctuation, in fact, is a labor of love."

—Pico Iyer, "In Praise of the Humble Comma"

When I teach punctuation, if I am teaching it as a concept, I usually start with a mini-lesson patterned in the way I shared at the beginning of the chapter: a set of examples or a set of examples and nonexamples. Both of these allow students to use inquiry to draw conclusions. That is much more effective for them as learners and writers. But I also sometimes want to make a point about something and will create a mini-lesson from a single picturebook, as in the following examples.

Over and Under the Snow by Kate Messner is a book I like to have students study when we are thinking about organization. It's obvious what Messner is talking about because she consistently orients readers with her use of initial prepositional phrases: "Over the snow I climb, digging in my edges so I don't slide back down." And "Over the snow, a deer has crossed our path." Even from these two examples, it can be easy to see the question a student might raise: why does she use a comma in one sentence and not in the other? That's a great question. Let's look at other examples in this book. I ask some students to list the examples we read that use a comma and the others to list the ones that don't. When we have the lists, perhaps we can come up with a theory. There is no "rule" I can find to answer the question, but I have a theory of my own. I am not going to voice it here—it's just my theory. For now, the point of the lesson is the discussion. We have explored a small punctuation mark that is clearly being used deliberately and we are trying to theorize why. I want my students to learn to

notice and wonder and question. I also want them to learn to live with ambiguity sometimes. That can be good for them.

I love Rylant's *Long Night Moon* for so many reasons, so I try to use it whenever I can. One of my favorite uses is to teach adjectives—and commas with them. The book is short enough to read multiple times, so after a first read to listen and think about what the book is doing, I ask students to notice the way the author uses descriptive words, what we might have heard called adjectives. I have two copies of the book, so I can pull the pages apart from one copy and hand a different page to different groups. They notice the adjectives on their pages and write them on the board so that we collect examples from the whole class and the entire book. From this collection, I ask students to work in their groups to see what they notice. They see a lot, but they usually notice that sometimes Rylant uses commas between adjectives and sometimes she doesn't: "in a cool, crackling breath" and "small green trees." From their observations, we are able to consider theories: *What makes the difference? Why use commas in some adjective phrases and not in others?* I don't (necessarily) want students to memorize the terms, but this is when I can introduce the difference between cumulative and coordinate adjectives: cumulative adjectives don't require commas but must come in a specific order; coordinate adjectives can be written in any order, but they need commas to separate them. Sometimes students ask why some adjectives must come in a specific order—this is a tricky question. Native English speakers learn this order like learning to walk; students who are learning English have to learn the order—and it's hard if you just memorize the list (opinion, size, physical quality, shape, age, color, etc.) and then have to think about leaving some adjectival elements out. Some classes move into discussions of Oxford comma use as part of this discussion, but I usually let that be organic. After the discussion, I ask students to go to today's writer's notebook and look for adjectives: where might they add adjectives to create a more visual effect—and do those adjectives need commas or not?

Another example of a picturebook for teaching an element of punctuation is *The Hair of Zoe Fleefenbacher Goes to School* by Laurie Halse Anderson. This fun picturebook is great for an informal writing invitation and for teaching sentence fluency. It's got great rhythms for a lively read. It is also a good example of the effective use of ellipses. This lesson works better if we have read the book for other purpose before we use it for this lesson, because for this lesson I like to remind students of the story and then focus on a few examples of ellipses in the book, like this one: "The class held its breath . . . it . . . worked!" We can discuss why the author might have used ellipses—twice—in this sentence. Students of all ages will notice the suspense created by them, so we can count that as an effect of using ellipses. Then students in groups look at other picturebooks that have examples of ellipses (and lots of picturebooks have them). Here are a few that teachers might want to consider: *This Story Is Not About a Kitten* by Randall de Sève and Carson Ellis; *Bella's Recipe for ~~Disaster~~ Success* by Ana Siqueira; *How to Eat Pizza* by Jon Burgerman. When they look at their picturebooks, groups gather examples and start to look for patterns that explain effects: why do writers use ellipses? With their newfound knowledge, they go back to their writer's notebooks and see where they can use ellipses to create one of the effects. Then I ask them to share with a partner, and some of them share them with the class.

Picturebooks with Language as Their Subject

While we can pull example sentences from picturebooks for study sets, some books address language elements as an essential aspect of the content. Teachers may want to have students study these entire books—and the point they are making—for discussion or as the content for mini-lessons.

- ✓ *Just Me and 6,000 Rats: An Adventure in Conjunctions* by Rick Walton. This fun story ends each page spread with a word that connects the ideas of that page to the ones that follow—*and*, *but*, or, *yet*, and other traditional conjunctions. It also uses some subordinate conjunctions so readers can learn about those too as ways to show relationships between ideas. Teachers might consider activities such as leaving out the conjunctions and having students generate ideas for how best to connect the ideas (or choose from a list) and then discuss why they made the choices they did as a way to consider how writers connect ideas—and why they make the choices they do.
- ✓ *Miss Alaineus: A Vocabulary Disaster* by Debra Frasier. In this disaster story, the narrator recounts her bad vocabulary learning experience using lots of synonyms. Besides defining words and names that have multiple meanings, this story can prompt a discussion about choosing the right word and the distinctions between words that mean, broadly, the same thing.
- ✓ *Max's Words* by Kate Banks. Max's brothers collect stamps and coins—but Max has nothing to collect, so he decides to collect words. He cuts them from newspapers and writes words he hears. He realizes that while the order of coins and stamps doesn't make much of a difference, the order of his words makes a *big* difference. That order helped him and his brothers create stories. Much like magnetic poetry sets, working with a set of words to see how many different things a person could say with those words, what stories they could tell, could help students see the value of syntax in creating meaning and effect.
- ✓ *The Boy Who Loved Words* by Roni Schotter. This story of a boy who loves words really appeals to me because it talks of liking the way words sound, the way they feel in your mouth, the way they move our thoughts and our emotions. Many students never think about words in this way. In this story, Selig is labeled an oddball because he collects all the words he likes until he has so many he must do something with them—and a djinn gives him a hint. As Selig goes forward, his words help a poet with writer's block, a baker whose pastries have been ignored, people who are arguing, and others who can't find the right words in the moment. The book's emphasis on the right word is enhanced by many synonyms (and definitions) that encourage readers to learn new words and use them. Students could choose one of the words from the book (one that feels good when they say it aloud, perhaps, or just one that interests them), learn about it, and write a short example on a note card of a situation in which that word would

be just the perfect word. The cards, which clarify the meaning of the word, could be put up on a bulletin board so that everyone can learn new words for just the right moment.

- ✓ *The Weighty Word Book* by Paul M. Levitt et al. This book actually does something similar to the teaching idea I presented for the previous book; it takes little-known words and writes a story that can help readers remember the words. These stories are longer and sometimes a little silly as they use the word to come up with story elements. Each story ends with a statement like this one for *nonconformity*: "So, whenever someone is out of step with others or out of line with other people's ideas, think of Mr. Fenderbender saying, 'None can form a T.' and you will remember the word *nonconformity*." Since these are longer, developed stories that match the sounds of the words and not just the meaning, I would encourage teachers to have students work in small groups to create these stories; generating ideas from the sound and meaning of the word to write a whole story could be challenging. Collaboration allows for lots of ideas and still encourages language learning and writing.
- ✓ *A Bunch of Punctuation* by Lee Bennet Hopkins. This book is actually a collection of poems about punctuation. The poems are fun to read (I especially like "Apostrophe" and wish more people would read it). Seriously, though, I have students read one or more, discuss what they learned, look online for memes that exemplify something the poem teaches, and share the memes with the class. Lots of learning potential.
- ✓ *Exclamation Mark* by Amy Krouse Rosenthal. Here is such a creative way to discuss the value of this one piece of punctuation—the exclamation mark (or exclamation point if you are American)—in a kind of "finding yourself" story. Using the punctuation as part of the story's text is essential. Students could see this as a mentor text and work in groups to write the stories of other punctuation marks coming to find themselves.
- ✓ *Punctuation Takes a Vacation* by Robin Pulver. A book that is probably familiar to many students imagines what would happen if, as the title states, punctuation took a vacation (at the teacher's request). Without punctuation, though, the teacher can't read the book anymore. Postcards from the different kinds of punctuation exemplify their function, so the students know who the postcards are from, but they can't write back without punctuation. With an overall point of the value of punctuation to reading and writing,

this book takes a fun look at the various ways we use different pieces of punctuation. Students enjoy trying to write postcards to and from punctuation as a way to show they understand the various uses.

Principles

- ✓ Find books with especially effective use of language or craft.
- ✓ Choose examples with clear connections to meaning making.
- ✓ Select books with engaging content.

Find Books with Especially Effective Use of Language or Craft

It seems obvious, so why is the first guiding principle about the effectiveness of the examples in a picturebook? Most picturebooks have effective writing and are grammatically correct; they wouldn't be published otherwise. What I mean by effective use of craft is **standout** language: phrases that linger in the mind after we've turned the page, sentences that beg to be read aloud repeatedly because they feel so good to our ear, punctuation that makes us rethink what we just read because it is just perfectly tied to meaning making. Many picturebooks tell great stories, but if the story is all there is, pass the book by for this purpose.

The Shoe Tree of Chagrin by J. Patrick Lewis provides multiple examples of language that lingers in the mind. In a folktale about a very tall woman in the West, readers find these lovely passages and words:

> Once long ago, so the elders tell, the tallest of the great plainswomen traveled the Ohio Valley in a two-wide wagon pulled by pluck and luck and a brute horse named Paw-Paw, thirty-two hands high. Susannah DeClare was as strong as a lockbox and as long as a good spit in a windstorm. . . . You'd often see her in the shut-eye towns of the back country, wearing old age like a gnarled oak. Was she sixty-eight? Or eighty-six? No one knew. She was at least as old as honesty, and as honey brown as the polish on her size 27 Tuesday boots.

These sentences, read aloud, roll off my tongue and please my ear. And they are full of many examples of craft that students can learn from and imitate: the use of effective similes, the use of long and short sentences in contrast to each other (even fragments), the use of participial phrases, and the use of the unexpected to draw attention, just to name a few. After reading the book aloud, share images of the pages with meaningful examples for students to review. They can identify effective words and phrases and then theorize about their effect to build a craft list to put on the wall and reference during our current writing project.

Another example of effective craft is Kate Hoefler's *Rabbit and the Motorbike*. In this book about friendship and courage and overcoming grief, the use of effective repetition combined with variation of sentence length creates a poignant tone that encourages reflective thinking.

> Long roads took him to where the giant redwoods were—where Rabbit was the wind that carried the leaves. And by the sea, where birdsong whirled—where all the birds wanted to fly like Rabbit. And through the Mojave Desert, where Rabbit howled at the moon—where he felt wide and wondrous—and full of stories.

A study of the sentences in this book yields a wealth of understanding about craft associated with sentence fluency and sentence construction. Early in the book, we see long and short sentences, a variety of complex, compound, and simple sentences to tell the story of Dog and Rabbit. In the center of the book, as Rabbit deals with his loss and fear, sentences tend to be more uniform in length—mostly medium-length sentences. Those choices create different tones. Other syntactical choices are used effectively and are worth exploring with students for options they might use in their own writing: repetition of where-clauses tie the three different locations together, and dashes create breaks in thought (as in the examples above). Also, two-word fragments create emphasis throughout the book: every night, every day, quite long. As we discuss these syntactical choices and their effects, I encourage students to return to their writing and look for places they could improve their writing's tone or rhythm or flow by trying out some of these same structures. They generally choose to use the elements that stood out for them—fragments, dashes, and where-clauses. I like the differentiation this study encourages in students' learning and application.

My favorite go-to picturebook for craft study is *Scarecrow* by Cynthia Rylant, and I have used it at all grade levels, seventh through university. The rhythm is particularly effective, but the text also contains memorable word choices and uses punctuation to enhance meaning.

I like to read the book aloud first, just to have students experience hearing it before they begin to look at how it works. It is really lovely to hear. After I read it aloud, I ask students to share any phrases or words that stuck in their minds. Usually they can give some examples, even though they might not be able to quote an entire passage, but sometimes I read the book a second time just for this purpose. I then show students the sentences of the book on a screen—each sentence on a different line so that students see them separately as well as in connection with the sentences around them. Then, with pages of a copy of the book that I've pulled apart, I ask them to work in groups to notice craft elements.

Students inevitably notice a couple of devices (although they don't know the names):

> *Polysyndeton:* "You can do this?" they ask. I remind them that they do it all the time when they want to emphasize the multiplicity of things they have to do, right? And I tell them how I used it once in an article for *English Journal*. When the editor sent the page proofs back, the *ands* were gone and the sentence read like a regular list of things teacher have to do, with one *and* before the last item. I wrote back, explaining the term and the effect I had hoped for—I wanted to emphasize all the things teachers do—and I asked for my *and*s back. The message I received in response? A smiley face and this note: "You can have your *ands* back."
>
> *Seeds are being planted, and inside them are ten-foot-tall sunflowers and mammoth pumpkins and beans that just go on forever.*
>
> *The earth has rained and snowed and blossomed and wilted and yellowed and greened and vined itself all around him.*

Epistrophe: This is not one that usually comes up first, but when they notice it, students are more willing to learn the name and discuss the effect. What does it do to repeat these phrases with the end part the same in each one? When we compare it to the subsequent sentence, where instead of "borrowed" we have a phrase that means the same thing, we really see the emphasis.

His hat is borrowed, his suit is borrowed, his hands are borrowed, even his head is borrowed.

Repetition: We have generally discussed effective repetition before students notice it in this book, but if not, this is a wonderful example of how effective repetition can create the perfect emphasis and sentence structure.

So he doesn't mind that there is always a smile on his face or that his eyes are always open. He doesn't mind being up high. He doesn't mind staying there.

Scarecrow includes many other examples of rhetorical devices, and some students will notice them too. We discuss the effects of these choices and how those effects might be useful in our own writing. I use this lesson when students have a piece of writing in process so that they can immediately consider which of the effects might be useful in their own writing and go straight to drafting new sentences with one of the elements they noticed.

Choose Examples with Clear Connections to Meaning Making

What we want the picturebooks we choose for this purpose to do is make clear connections between the language, syntax, punctuation . . . and meaning. That is, all the books have been carefully written, revised, and edited. They are going to use good words, effective sentences, and correct punctuation. What we need for this purpose is effective craft clearly connecting to meaning. One example is *When I Was Young in the Mountains* by Cynthia Rylant. The title, repeated at intervals throughout the book, creates a nostalgic tone that contributes to the meaning of the book, the idea of looking back fondly at childhood memories. The sentence structure also allows for setting up the details: that is, the adverbial clause demands a completer.

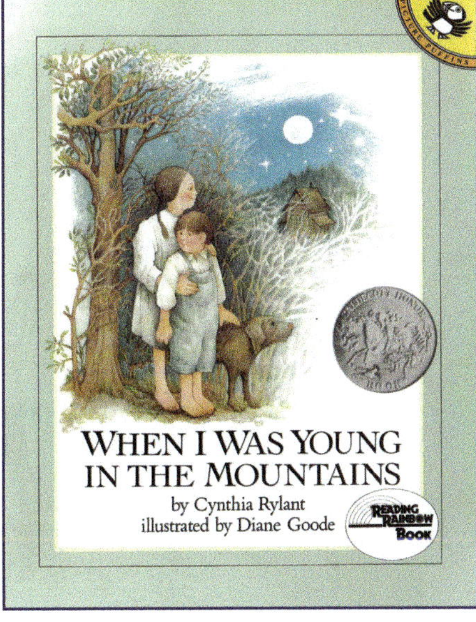

{When I was young in the mountains . . .}

Students can rearrange the sentences, move the completers to the start of the sentences, and then read them in the context of the rest of the text to test the power of the structure for the rhythmic pattern that feels soothing, nostalgic. Additionally, the repeated structure ties the book together—a series of memories that have power later in life. When my students use this text as a pattern for writing their own memory poems or stories, they can see how the construction creates a reflective tone for their own memories. Even when this impromptu writing is done as part of a lesson, it is some of the most powerful writing my students do.

In *Seurat and La Grande Jatte*, Burleigh uses punctuation to contribute to meaning through the use of dashes and parenthetical asides, as well as fragments. These elements create a conversational tone, for one thing, but they also parallel the artistic style of pointillism that Seurat is known for. I share these examples with students:

> A strange stillness. An almost eerie silence. A sense of mystery. Feelings like these hover over the entire painting, do they not? Nearly everyone appears to be quite alone. Alone. Quiet. Absorbed by something—but what that something is we cannot tell.
>
> And these dots—rather than lines or broad, flat sweeps of color—make up the people, the grass, the water, the trees.
>
> On the right, a fashionable couple (that's the woman with her sunshade and the man in his top hat) is on a promenade, or stroll. Across the way, another woman—also well dressed—extends her fishing pole over the water.

I ask students what they notice about the examples and draw their attention to the parallel between Burleigh's writing style and Seurat's art. Then I give them pages from the book to look at in small groups. Their groups identify other elements of craft, easier to do once we have done the first set as a class. We discuss the effects of the choices on the text and go back to our writing to see which of those options we might use in our own writing. Students share in pairs and explain the effect they were seeking when they applied the craft. When they can see multiple examples of craft's connection to meaning, they are more likely to want to learn the craft that will help them create meaning and tone in their own writing.

Select Books with Engaging Content

The final guiding principle is probably self-evident as well. We want to make sure the content of the picturebook is engaging. It's possible to find good examples of craft in many picturebooks, but if we don't pay attention to this principle, we miss an extra level of instructional power. For some students, the study of craft is confusing or, sadly, even a drudgery. After all, sentences that show good word choice or correct conventions or variety of syntactical choices are available in textbooks. And if we've ever tried using textbooks to help students learn craft, we know that they are not very effective. They can show correctness, but they don't move students to want to emulate the choices. That's the power that an effective and engaging picturebook can add to the study of craft.

In *Come on, Rain!*, Karen Hesse uses craft to slow the sentences down in the first part of the story about a hot day, and then uses sentence structure to show the relief and joy when the rain bursts and cools the air. The story is super engaging since most students have some experience dealing with some kind of unpleasant weather, even if they don't know the exact misery of such a hot day. Still, they can identify with wanting the weather to change.

Once we've read the book, I ask students to consider sentences from the first part and contrast them with the second part, as they usually notice how the book shifts tone with the weather change. The following passages exemplify this contrast and help students see how craft (different sentence types and constructions) can add meaning to an already engaging story:

> Up and down the block, cats pant, heat wavers off tar patches in the broiling alleyway. Miz Grace and Miz Vera bend, tending beds of drooping lupines.
>
> We twirl and sway them, tromping through puddles, romping and reeling in the moisty green air. We swing our wet and wild-haired mammas 'til we're all laughing under trinkets of silver rain.

We discuss as a class what word, syntactical, and punctuation choices contribute to the differences—and how those choices might apply to our own writing, even if we aren't writing about the exact same thing. How can craft contribute to mood?

8

Using Picturebooks to Teach about Multimodal Literacy and Genre

When I first found *Black and White* by David Macaulay, I was fascinated. I wanted to see what my students thought of it. I took my copy and the copies I could find at the local libraries to my ninth-grade class. I didn't really have a firm idea of what I was going to do with the book; I just wanted students to have some fun with it. Bad idea. I found the book fascinating and thought it would be of interest to my students—and thought maybe it could teach us something about reading. With hindsight I can see this probably wasn't the best way to introduce my students to postmodern picturebooks. I needed a better plan and a clear objective. I should have considered the potential problems.

I thought I had used some effective strategies. I previewed the text with students so they would know from the warning on the title page to prepare for an unexpected reading experience. I showed the double-page spread that comes next, with each half-page a different image, style, and title that introduces that same quadrant for the rest of the book. Then I put them in groups with directions to "read" the text and make meaning of it. I suggested that one person in the group could take responsibility for each quarter page, so there would be four readers, but I let them choose how to navigate it. When there weren't words, they should "read" the picture, I advised. The other people in the group were to watch and listen and see what they noticed. I wanted to know what they thought.

Many of my students did find the book intriguing. At first. It was the novelty, I suppose. Some groups had students who noticed how the stories overflowed into the other stories—cow spots and typewritten words and so on. Some students had fun with it, challenged by the differences from the books they usually read, especially picturebooks. But some of them also started to get frustrated with it. Some lost interest because it was "hard." It certainly isn't a story in the traditional sense—and if we try to read it with that frame, it can be difficult. The students' negative responses were partly my fault. I didn't prepare them well. But the book is also not like a lot of picturebooks students might have experienced in the past.

As I did research, I learned that my students' response is also the experience other teachers have had with what are now most frequently termed **postmodern picturebooks** in their classes (Bintz and Valerio; Madara). *Black and White* in particular has been the subject of many articles about how it differs from other picturebooks and the challenges it has raised since its publication—and since winning the Caldecott Medal in 1991 (Anstey; Pantaleo, "Everything"; Goldstone; Dresang; McClay). In fact, in his acceptance speech, Mccaulay explained that he didn't think this was the kind of book to win this award because "it tells readers, especially young ones, that it is essential to see, not merely to look, that words and pictures can support each other, that it isn't necessary to think in a straight line to make sense; and finally that risk can be rewarded." It is true that readers didn't know what to make of this book exactly—in my class or in other places—but it serves as a "prototype of Radical Change Theory (RCT)" (Dresang 45) and exemplifies several characteristics that help students become more skilled in the kind of reading they are likely to do in various online spaces.

We are really fortunate to have many picturebooks that help us accomplish a wide variety of learning goals in our classrooms. But for this purpose—to help develop students' multiliteracy skills (Farrar et al.)—we need to use specific picturebooks, those most often called postmodern. What characteristics set postmodern picturebooks apart? Different sources provide different lists, but they tend to be the same characteristics we might notice in reading digital texts. Silva-Díaz names these: "overlapping of narrative planes," narrators that step outside of traditional roles, ambiguity or unconventional narratives, parody, and play (73–76). Anstey adds "new and unusual design and layout, which challenge the reader's perspective of how to read a book," "intertextuality," and "the availability of multiple readings and meanings for a variety of audiences" (447). With so many characteristics—mostly about challenging expectations and boundaries—Pantaleo and Sipe recommend thinking of these picturebooks not as a binary—postmodern or not—but more along a continuum (4). This idea seems like a good one for teachers because then we can think of what we want to teach or how much boundary challenging our students can take when we choose the books we use to teach for the purpose of developing multiliteracies and the ability to read and interpret genres that move beyond printed text.

What do we hope to get from using these books? Because Goldstone asserts that "postmodern children's stories are more closely aligned to hypertext than they are to traditional picture books" (367) and Anstey explains that "multiliteracies focus on the many modes of representation and forms of texts that have been made available through multimedia and technological change" (446), we can be confident that we can use these books to help students improve their ability to navigate and interrogate online genres. In fact, Dresang has called postmodern picturebooks "handheld hypertexts" (45) for the ways they can put the "reader in the driver's seat" (46). As we help students read these texts, we will see them reread, choosing paths through a myriad of options, interacting with the books in a variety of ways (both mental and physical), and making judgments about reliability. We will also see them interpreting visual images in conjunction with words, whether they support or contradict each other, among other actions that resemble the way readers approach digital texts. We can use these interactions to develop students' ability to read digital texts more thoughtfully and intentionally by calling attention to the ways they interact with the postmodern picturebooks in our class and how these interactions can benefit their reading in other genres (Arizpe et al.).

But as I learned, reading these postmodern picturebooks is not easy. It takes some skill. It takes seeing, as Macaulay explained in his acceptance speech for the Caldecott Medal. He suggested that we would all be better off if we took time to draw because doing so can encourage curiosity. "Lack of curiosity," he said, "is the first step toward visual illiteracy—and by that I mean not really seeing what is going on around us." For Macaulay, postmodern picturebooks are about seeing more and seeing what isn't there as much as what is. Mackey reports what an early AI researcher had to say about reading—not just decoding, but knowing how to make sense of a book. Researchers had anticipated that for artificial intelligence, learning to play chess and things like that would be difficult. Instead, they found that "noticing what is important in a story turned out to be very, very hard" (104). What we do when we work with picturebooks, moving between images and words and making sense of them all together, helps students learn the hard things. What we do when we bring their attention to postmodern picturebooks might be even harder. What we know is that it is important and doable.

So how do we do this? Looking at the research conducted with students and postmodern picturebooks around the world, I see a few possibilities to consider. But first we have to consider the fun of these books. McClay noted that students reading

Black and White had fun, something she noticed diminished when she studied teachers reading the same text. Other researchers reported that students often noticed the jokes and puns that adults missed, especially when the humor was in the images. Since play is part of postmodern picturebooks and since collaboration is important in a postmodern world, thinking first of just enjoying the books together is a good starting point. After that, I use a modification of the multimodal strategy Schmidt and Kruger-Ross propose for investigating digital multimodal texts (9).

First, reading the books in small groups is important so that students can interact and notice what choices others make in interpreting and moving through the book. They will find that some readers notice images more readily than others, and some will be drawn to certain text types and fonts (as these elements often represent different modes of writing in the same text). When storylines have gaps or contradictions, students will be able to identify these and consider what to do with them. Watching students read the books is also a way for teachers to learn about their students. After reading, the first thing I like to do is ask students about content, the story: What is it about? How did it create meaning? Who is the intended audience? How do you know? When I first taught David Wisniewski's *Secret Knowledge of Grown-Ups*, that question began an interesting discussion as students started to notice the intertextuality (references and allusions only adults would understand) and puns that would not be recognizable to young children. Some noted that they hadn't thought about picturebooks being for grown-ups too until that question.

Next, we need to consider design options and how those impact the reading experience and what we understood from the picturebook. What color cues do we notice? How is font used to create meaning? Looking closely at images, what can we see beyond the text? How do the illustration choices affect our reading?

Finally, I ask students to reflect on the reading processes they used, maybe even contrasted to the processes they noticed others using. I remember the time I was reading a postmodern picturebook to one of my grandchildren. I had read it many times and to other grandchildren. But this time, Gabe stopped me and pointed out something in the images that contradicted the words I was reading. I was stunned. And unprepared for how that one detail made me rethink the story, a story I had thought was fairly straightforward. I share this story with students and explain that I have an affinity for the words—I gravitate to them and focus on them. I have to force myself to look at the images and then reconsider after the fact. I explain how this might work against me when I read online and some of the important information is found in the images and charts on the page. What I want students to think about for this question is how they are inclined to read multimodal texts and then imagine how they might revise their reading processes for online texts we read all the time.

Radical change theory is a way that Dresang found to explain aspects of contemporary society, particularly the ways that technology has changed the behaviors of users. She found it to encompass principles of interactivity, connectivity, and access, broad principles that encompass many of the postmodern characteristics mentioned above. In relation to postmodern picturebooks, Dresang sees RCT as a way to explain three broad types of change we see in these books: "changing forms and formats, changing perspectives, and changing boundaries" (41). Because Pantaleo sees this framework as a good way to approach reading experiences to "develop readers' abilities to critically analyze, construct, and deconstruct an array of texts and representational forms" ("Long, Long Way" 17), I use these broad categories derived from RCT to share some of the picturebooks I have introduced for various lessons about reading multimodal texts, but it will be clear very quickly that the books often fit more than one category—even better for teaching about multimodal texts.

Changing Forms and Formats

When looking for picturebooks that help students consider different ways to read varying forms and formats, we can choose books that show multiple layers of meaning, that are nonlinear, and that have unusual designs and layouts. I think of Dresang's "handheld hypertext" when I am looking for books that fit this aspect of multimodal picturebooks. Does the book require me to manipulate it? Interact with it in some way? Does it provide multiple reading paths through the book? Do the designs and fonts contribute to the meaning? Do the images do more than just explain the text—maybe add more to the story or even tell a contradictory story?

Some books have images that ***reinforce*** or ***explain*** the text. *An Egg Is Quiet* by Dianna Hutts Aston is one of these. The images help readers understand the meaning of the text as it explains all the different sizes, shapes, colors, and types of eggs. When students explore this book with the specific question of "what is the relationship of the images to the text?," they can see this idea clearly. The images help us better understand the text.

The images in some books actually ***contradict*** the words. John Burningham's *Come Away from the Water, Shirley* is a good example. On one side of each spread, the parents talk to Shirley about possible dangers she might encounter during a day at the beach: don't touch the dog, watch where you throw rocks, don't bring stinky seaweed home. On the other side of the spread, images tell a story of what is happening in Shirley's imagination, a very different story from the one that is happening with her parents (although there are fun connections between both stories).

Some books provide images that ***extend*** the text, telling part of the story that is not explained in the words. This is happening more and more as picturebook writers and illustrators expect readers to "read" both images and words in that way. I use *The Ghost Library* by David Melling to help students see this relationship between words and images. A little girl feels a tug on her book, grips it harder, and finds herself pulled into the ghost library—a place where ghosts go to read the stories they borrow. She reads a story to them (which is told only in pictures) and then encourages them to make up their own stories. This part of the book's plot is also told only in images, allowing readers to interpret these portions of the story (are ghosts real or imaginary?) themselves, thus extending the story in individual ways.

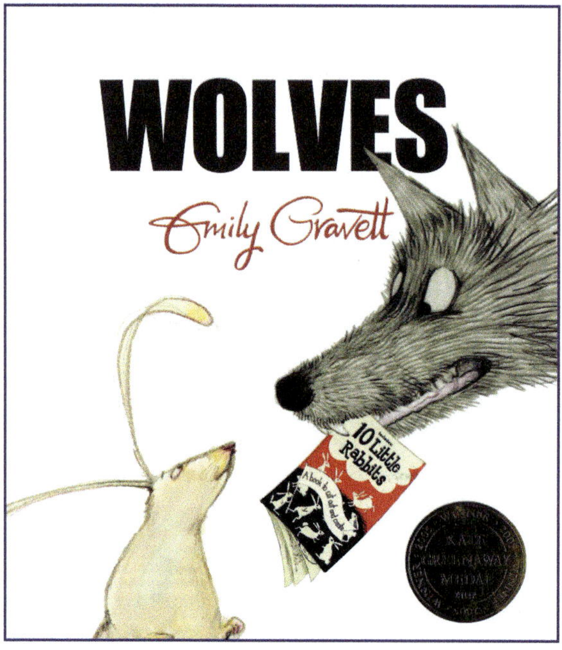

Since the publication of *The Ghost Library*, I have found other books that are good examples of this relationship. One of these is Emily Gravett's *Wolves*. The story—about a rabbit reading a book about wolves—seems fairly straightforward. But the book is set up so that readers don't just read about the rabbit reading a book; they read the book along with the rabbit. However, we are also aware of what is happening externally, which the rabbit is not: the wolf is stalking the rabbit. Changes in the illustration style give away changes in perspectives in the story.

Finally, sometimes images ***reinterpret*** the words, telling a different version of the story than might be expected. *Jabberwocky*, illustrated by Stéphane Jorisch, is one version of Lewis Carroll's poem with images that suggest a dystopian world with something like modern political ideas (and the failures they cause) as the foe rather than the dragon-like creature that is commonly envisioned. *Jabberwocky* illustrated by Christopher Myers is another example of reinterpreting because the illustrations tell the story of a basketball game against the words of this famous poem. Juxtaposed with different images, the poem seems to take on different meaning; readers are expected to rethink what the words say.

Some books require readers to interact with them physically, just as digital texts might require a click or a comment. For example, the almost wordless picturebook *Mommy?* by Arthur Yorinks is an elaborate pop-up book, in which the little boy, looking for his mommy, wanders into spaces inhabited by monsters. Pieces of the story pop out when a reader turns the pages; other parts are hidden behind flaps a reader can lift up to see more of the story, especially the little boy, clearly unafraid, helping or teasing the monsters.

Another way to reflect an interactive relationship between author and reader is through actual manipulation of the text in some way, allowing the reader to adjust the way the text works or the story it tells. Emily Gravett's *Spells* is one such book. In the middle of the story about a small green frog who finds a book of spells and decides he would like to be a handsome prince, pages are cut in half to contain parts of incantations that create different creatures, with each choice shifting the spell. Readers can mix and match the magic words to get different creatures, much like the frog might experiment with different spells. This interactive element encourages readers to take a more active part in creating the story.

Gravett's *Little Mouse's Big Book of Fears* is a different example of interacting with a picturebook. First, the cover suggests that Little Mouse has taken over

authorship of the book, as the author's name is crossed out, an example of changing perspectives. Inside, as Mouse tells readers of his fears, there is space on each page (which include allusions to familiar literature and scientific definitions of the fears being described) for the reader to make this their own book by writing in the open spaces about the fear (or another one, as the case may be). What I find interesting in this design is that, like an online site when a reader contributes to the text in a comment, the text is now a different reading experience for the next reader, changed by the contribution of the previous reader(s). When I explain this to students, I see their faces light up. They get it. And they better understand how different texts situate readers in different ways—and what they might do or not do in those different arrangements. Because I am aware of that in the *Mouse* book, we discuss who I would want to write in my book (do I feel the same about people commenting on my social media page?), why I might be thoughtful about what I write for future readers to read—and how that might relate to students and their online interactions.

Changing Perspectives

In this category, we look for picturebooks that show stories from perspectives other than those we might traditionally expect. That might be due to voices that don't usually get to speak, but it can also be from various narrators telling the same story. In these books, we sometimes see narrators talk to the audience or comment directly on the creation of the book, thus drawing attention to the process of bookmaking. We see intertextuality as references are made to other texts through allusions or parody. We also see a mixing of genres and discourse styles. An early book in this category that I share with students is *The Paper Bag Princess* by Robert N. Munsch. It is intertextual in the sense that the title and cover set up readers to expect a fairy tale—and for the first part of the book, the story follows expectations: dragon and magic. We are first warned of a shifting perspective when the prince instead of the princess is captured by the dragon. The princess goes to his rescue, but instead of using brute force, she outwits the dragon to save the prince, who is quite disdainful in his rescue, ending with one of the best conclusions I have ever read to my students. They all find it very satisfying, often even applauding when I read it. The story showcases intertextuality and unheard voices telling the story.

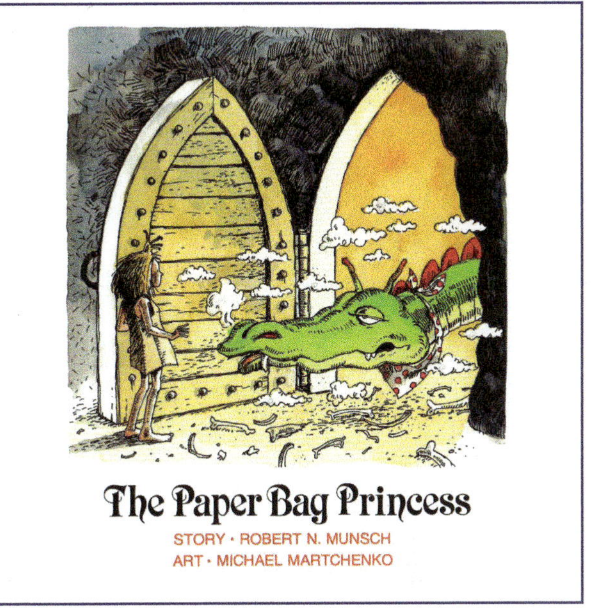

Ian Lendler's *An Undone Fairy Tale* is similar in that it depends on intertextual understanding of fairy tales, but this one adds the author, stepping out of the traditional role to openly acknowledge the reader. The author begins to speak to readers, explaining that the illustrator (Ned) needs more time to draw the illustrations and would like the readers to slow down a bit to give him time to draw them: "He's making all the pictures for this story. But you're reading so quickly that he hasn't finished the painting or costume for this page for you." Pleading with readers with increasing intensity as they move through the book, the narrator helps us realize that our continued reading forces the crown to be replaced with a donut, a suit of armor with a tutu, and so on, ultimately changing the story, supposedly because we (readers) are not acquiescing to the narrator's pleas. Even young children like my grandchildren see how the author giving control to the reader can create challenges.

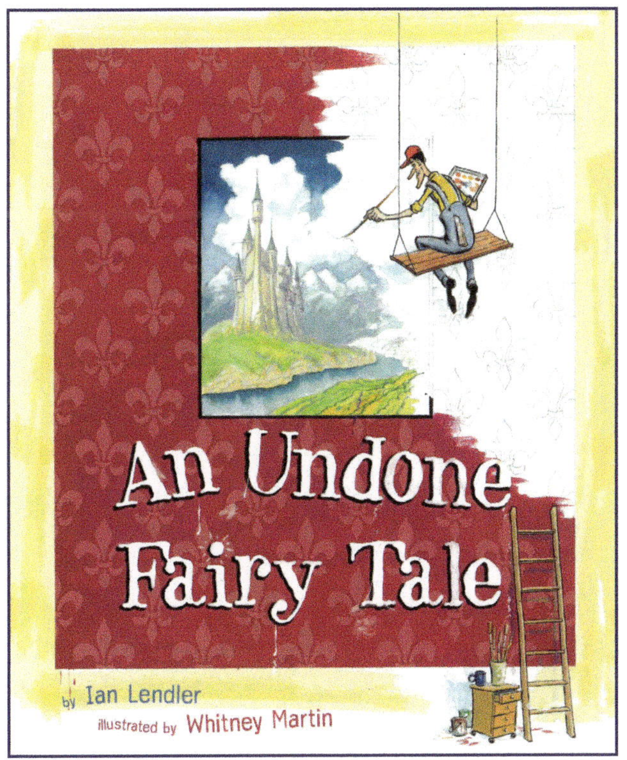

Too Many Pigs and One Big Bad Wolf by David Cali is another example of interactivity, where the reader's voice is in red font, asking the storyteller to make a longer story, a better story—and questioning the author's choices. The author keeps changing the story, never satisfying the reader. The book is a great example of reader participation, acknowledging that readers might want more from a writer and how they might—or might not—get it. *Too Many Pigs* definitely positions the reader more clearly in the text and represents what I often see in online sites.

Similarly, Mélanie Watt's *Chester* is a book about a cat who takes over authorship of the book. Chester doesn't like the story and takes a red pen to it, transforming it into the story he wants. This is extremely postmodern—readers having enough access to a text to be able to add their own perspectives, even if just in the comments. This draws attention to the composing process, to the nature of a genre—who gets to be the author?—and to the idea of multiple perspectives, the narrator's and the character's. The humor is irreverent, also something more common with postmodern literature.

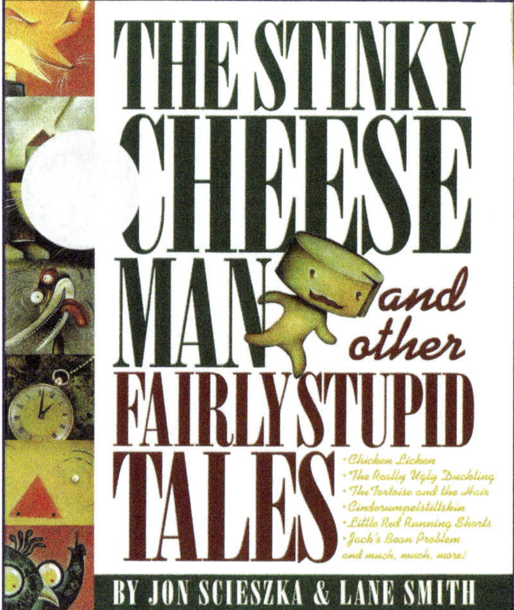

Jon Scieszka's *The Stinky Cheese Man* tells common fairy tales from other perspectives—letting other voices intrude into and have a say about the traditional stories. The book is definitely an example of changing forms, with its upside-down dedication page, which requires the reader to physically turn the book, and with an irreverent comment ("who reads it anyway?") that sets up the tone. The insincere dedication—"to our close, personal, special friend: (your name here)"—uses a digital design that replicates digital text, and then the introduction asks readers to stop reading, warning about what to expect—all attributes that shift perspective and allow for usually unheard voices to speak up. Loudly. In the introduction, the author sets up the concept of the book but then breaks the narrator role by speaking to readers—urging us to stop. Now. We see changing perspectives again with a warning stamped on the introduction page. And then the narrator steps into the story again because there was no table of contents, but the characters in the first story ignore that until the ToC enters the story by falling on and smashing them. The stories are highly intertextual, but they are disrupted by silliness, reinforcing the idea of play we often find in postmodern books—and in multimodal texts online.

Changing Boundaries

Picturebooks that fit this category deal with subjects and settings previously not considered appropriate for picturebooks. They may engage new types of communities or show unresolved endings rather than the tidy ones we tend to expect in traditional literature. Picturebooks have dealt with difficult subjects in the past; changing boundaries has to do with entering territories that Dresang calls "real and imaginary monsters" (49). She puts *Mommy?* (Yorinks) and even Maurice Sendak's *Where the Wild Things Are* in this category, as they deal with darker considerations of childhood and parenting. In Chapter 5, I write about Erlbruch's *Duck, Death, and the Tulip*, a book that definitely fits in this category of topics that have previously been considered outside the bounds of picturebooks. Michael Rosen's *Sad Book* also fits this category; I have it on my shelf, but I have never used it with a class. It recounts the author's grief at the loss of his son—and it could be triggering for some readers because at one point it refers obliquely to suicide as a way to deal with his grief. I have never felt that I knew enough about my students' life experiences to be comfortable sharing this book with the whole class.

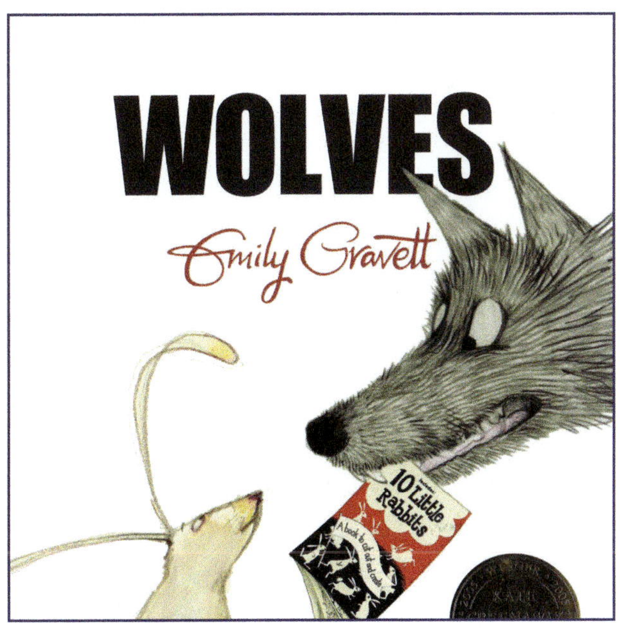

Wolves by Emily Gravett challenges boundaries in several ways. On the cover, the wolf carries a book titled *10 Little Rabbits: A Book to Cut Out and Create* in his teeth. We can find that exact book at the end of the book in our hands, complete with directions to cut the pages out and assemble it. Readers of this book inside the book can see that it tells the story of ten rabbits who die one by one until only one is left—and that rabbit goes to the library. We are aware, even from the cover, how this story will end, even if the rabbit seems not to be. Seeking knowledge is usually a good way to protect ourselves, but in this book, the opposite is true.

Changing perspectives are evident in the images, which move from traditional ones to a startling image of the wolf's face spilling out of the page, and the rabbit, suddenly aware of his plight, right between the wolf's eyes. The next pages show a damaged book, suggesting the end of the book and the rabbit. Then, a two-page spread shifts the ending, another boundary change that is typical of postmodern books. Here, the author speaks to readers, telling them that no rabbits were harmed in the making of the book and providing an alternate ending in which the rabbit and wolf take tea together. Readers will note the change in illustration style: created from scraps of images on other pages. As readers read on, they see another page spread filled with images of the rabbit's unopened mail, including an envelope from the library that readers can open and read. It is an overdue notice for the *Wolves* book, contradicting the soft alternate ending. This is a fun postmodern book that pushes boundaries and requires readers to get at the intended meanings through many of the elements of Radical Change Theory.

Woolvs in the Sitee by Margaret Wild also fits this changing boundaries category and is another text I have not shared with a whole class. It is creepy . . . and compelling. In dark-colored pages that suggest an apocalyptic setting, the narrator tells of "woolvs" in the streets and warns on the first page, "And soon they will kum. They will cum for me and for yoo and for yer bruthers and sisters." The narrator, Ben, has a neighbor who gives him food and encourages him to get out more—go back to school. She doesn't believe in the wolves, and she seems so sure that readers might be justified in thinking the wolves are just in Ben's mind. But he sees them, "prowling along pavments. Snarling up walls." In a foreshadowing event, Ben mistakenly thinks the sky is blue and runs outside, but the neighbor runs out and brings him back in. That is the last he sees of her, but her courage gives him the courage to go out looking for her, no longer willing to “scrooch.” The final page is white except for Ben’s face, looking directly at the reader, and his request, “Joyn me.” We don’t know how the story ends. The font and irregular spelling, the color tones, the fragments—all combine to create a book that isn’t for the faint of heart. I have shared it with some students individually, but its boundaries might not be for all students.

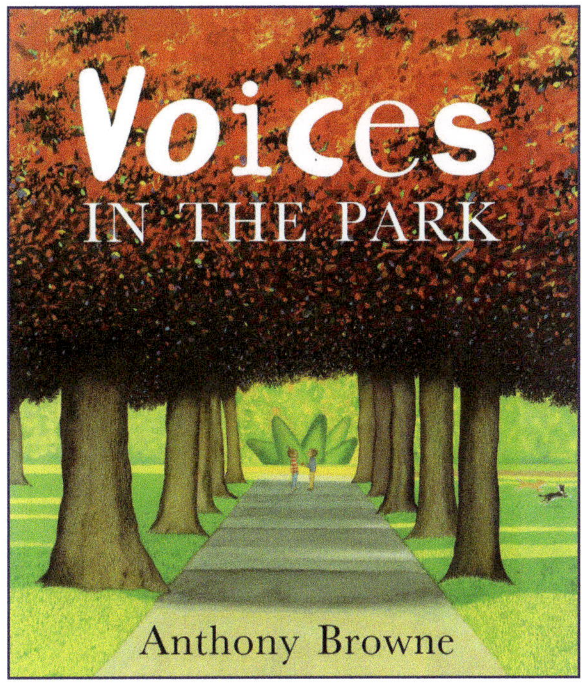

Anthony Browne’s *Voices in the Park* is another example of the changing boundaries aspect of RCT. It tells four stories of different groups of people who interact in the park. Each story has its own illustration style, its own font, and its own version of what happened in the park. As readers we are left to draw our own conclusions about what really happened (which students ask me after we read it). It’s interesting how readers can be swayed by one story or another, and I think that is part of the shifting boundaries of this text. We don’t know anything except four different ways of seeing the same interactions. It encourages us to consider multiple perspectives and maybe even hold more than one at that same time.

Postmodern Picturebooks to Teach Genre

As a result of these shifts in boundaries and perspectives, postmodern picturebooks often show up in different genres. I like to use picturebooks to help students envision how to write in different genres. Amy Devitt points out that we cannot teach all the genres students will need to write in their lives—as we know from observing all the new genres that have developed in our lifetimes. If I can’t teach students all the genres, I want to give them a way to approach new genres going forward. First, I look for picturebooks that can help students understand genre as a concept. Then I use some picturebooks as mentor texts for writing assignments that might (1) interest and engage students and (2) teach them something about genres and using mentor texts that they can take with them for all the future genres they may need to produce. Students are willing to engage with this approach because . . . these are picturebooks! They are accessible and interesting. They are not what students usually write in school—so it’s got to be better. But students can learn a lot about writing in a variety of styles and genres from this practice with writing in the style of picturebooks.

Concept of Genre

One of the best ways I found to help my students understand the concept of genre as a social construct is through the book *Dragonology* by Dugald A. Steer. To begin, I ask them to consider the title: what it means, what they think the book is about, and what other words they know that end in *-ology*. They list off *biology*, *geology*, *anthropology*, *archaeology*. A few even know *entomology*. When I ask what all these fields have in common, they usually say something about science, and I tell them that the suffix means "a study of," and the base is what they are studying. So *dragonology* is the study of dragons. I ask, with a title like this, what do they expect to read inside—and their guesses are pretty accurate: we will see the origins, the types, and other "scientific" information about dragons.

As we look through the book, I ask students to notice the elements that seem "sciency"—facets of the book that are similar to the ones they would find in science books: maps, pictures of specimens, a chart detailing different species, and even a flip chart of the biology and physiology of dragons with diagrams of muscle and skeletal structures. There are sections telling readers about tracking dragons, signs to look for, even a sample dragonologist's record book, to record sightings. Everything in this book makes it seem like an actual scientific study with actual science behind it. My students and I call it "truthiness," a way of seeming to be the truth but clearly, because of the subject, not.

The most interesting part of this lesson is the discussion that follows our exploration of the book. I ask students why the author would write about a myth using all these forms of writing that are like a science book, which we generally assume to be about true things. They are able to articulate, even though it's a new idea, that we have learned to trust information that is represented in these ways. The author is taking advantage of our association with the genres of science to make his fantastical subject seem like a real thing. I give them some examples of how we come to expect certain genres in certain places: If I am entering the theater and a person hands me a piece of paper, I assume it's a program. And it is! When I find a piece of paper under my windshield wiper after I return from shopping, I assume it's some kind of advertising flier (although it could be a note from someone who hit my car—that happened once: they left a note apologizing but not giving their name or contact information). Students come up with other places they have expectations of specific genres.

Since it can be a new concept for students, I try to get them to think of other times people might try to use a genre out of its normal "space" because they want to borrow some aspect of that genre. For example, when a hand-addressed envelope comes to my house, I usually expect a letter or a wedding announcement, something personal. Every so often, a business tricks me and it's a flier for an auto auction or an offer to buy my house. I feel a little irritated. We talk about our examples, about expectations, and about how people use or manipulate them. I want students to know before we look at genres in picturebooks that there is more to genre than form. There are lots of emotional expectations as well—and we have to consider those when we are reading and writing.

I also explain that sometimes writers borrow genre expectations as a way to be creative. Once, a former student wrote me a Christmas letter. She and her husband were both in PhD programs and had just had a baby. They wrote their letter in the genre of a research article, chronicling their lives with graphs and charts so that, in form at least, their information looked just like a research article—what they were spending their time writing. Other former students have written their Christmas letters as infographics or annotated maps. These writers all show that they understand genre and how creative writers can use a reader's understanding of genre to create another level of meaning.

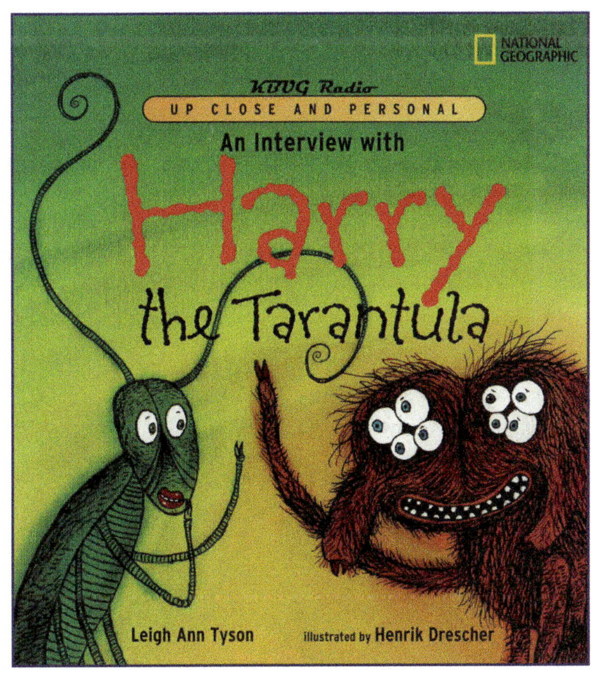

Lots of nonfiction picturebooks use this technique. I like using *An Interview with Harry the Tarantula* by Leigh Ann Tyson for showing students this aspect of genre. After we read it, we compare the style to interviews we discovered online. Each student finds an interview of a person they are interested in—usually an athlete or actor—and we compare the characteristics of those online versions to the one in the picturebook. With that understanding of genre, we conduct inquiry into other topics we choose and, borrowing from Tyson's model, write our own interviews (Dean, *Strategic Writing*). We found that we can use conversational language and share information about our topics in an interesting way.

Heather Lynn Miller's *This Is Your Life Cycle* has a similar strategy for presenting information in an interesting way, by imitating an old television series called "This Is Your Life."

One of the fun genres my students like to consider is wanted posters, and I have a couple of books I use to help us explore the genre and the messages it carries—and how authors have used those expectations in creative ways. *Watch Out for These Weirdos!* by Rufus Kline is the earliest one I used. The narrator warns newcomers to his neighborhood about the quirky children who live there—and then warns readers not to say anything bad about them because they are his friends. Each page has an intertextual connection, a wanted poster, something like the ones students might have seen in old books or Western movies. To begin, I usually show them some of the traditional ones so that students without the background knowledge of the genre will understand the humorous ways Kline moves away from the traditional expectations for his own purposes. We can see that certain aspects of the genre carry through: a picture, age, weight, height, hair color, aliases, what they are "wanted" for, and cautions. However, in this book, those are not always depicted as directly as they would be in the original genre—and thus, the humor and insight. So Tony's personality is reflected in his "Height: A foot shorter than he says it is. Hair: Always combed the way he says the bigshots do it." I have had my students make wanted posters about characters in a piece of literature we are reading—and the way they use these stretched elements of the genre shows me a lot about their insights into the characters. Another picturebook based on wanted posters is *Wanted! Criminals of the Animal Kingdom* by Heather Tekavec. Although the wanted posters in this book are also less traditional, the underlying concept of sharing information is there, accomplished in an entertaining way through the characteristics of the wanted poster genre.

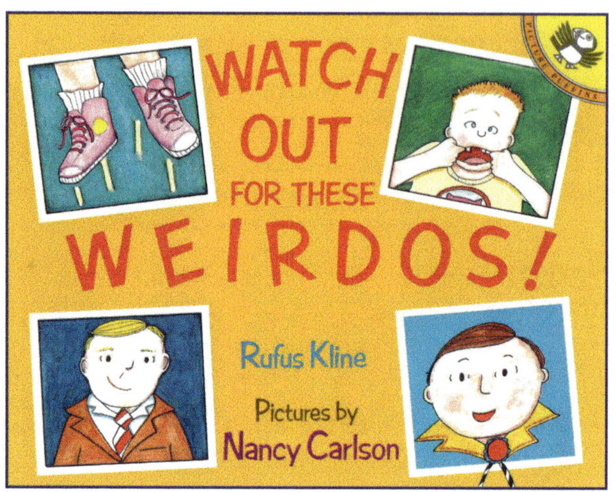

Lots of picturebooks use letters as a way to move a story forward or provide information in a more intimate way. When I first used Janet and Allan Ahlberg's *The Jolly Postman, or, Other People's Letters* with a ninth-grade class, several students were so interested that they asked their parents to buy them a copy. The book is a cute story with intertextual connections to characters readers know, including the Three Bears, the Giant (of beanstalk fame), the Wolf, Cinderella, and Goldilocks. Although the postman delivers a "letter" to each home, they differ in style and purpose; Goldilocks gets a birthday card (complete with Wonderland cash), Mr. Wolf gets a letter from Red Riding Hood's attorney, informing him he needs to vacate Grandma's house; and the Giant gets a postcard from Jack, who is traveling around the world. The book is interactive, each page containing an envelope that readers open to find the communication inside. When I used the book, we talked about the nature of letters, not a genre my students know as well today. How are they like and different from emails or texts or posts? What is gained and what is lost in each choice of communication? At the time, we were reading *Romeo and Juliet*, and I asked students to write a letter between any two characters in the play to show what they learned about communication in this genre from the examples in the book. I think if I did this now, I would also ask students to write other types of communication—a post or a text—and then reflect on the difference. It's an important aspect of genre understanding to consider what I call border genres—genres that do similar things but in different contexts—so that students develop sensitivity to genres and how they work beyond being a form.

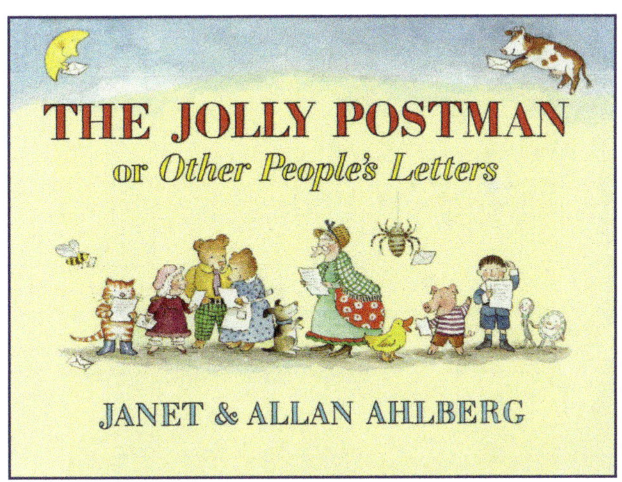

Other picturebooks also use letters to accomplish their purposes. *Dragon Post* by Emma Yarlett uses the letters between a boy and a number of people to help him solve some problems he has with a dragon in his house. He writes to friends, the World of Animal Welfare, even the fire brigade, and gets responses, including one that complicates the storyline—he gets a letter from his neighbor's attorney, complaining about the noise. Each letter is responsive to Alex, but they also vary depending on who they are and the purpose for their writing. This is a fun way to consider that even though the genre is a letter, the purposes and people involved can change its format and tone.

The Discovery of Dragons by Graeme Base tells readers in the introduction that this collection of letters from the original three explorers hunting for dragons is meant to address questions about the veracity of a previous book published about dragons. The author is certain that seeing the original letters as documentation of the explorations will prove the prior claims about dragons being real to be true. The letters then, in a variety of writing styles for each of the explorers, complete the rest of the book—and tell "information"

about dragons as it was discovered. *Around the World: Who's Been Here?* by Lindsay Barrett George also uses letters to share information. This book is set up as a series of letters from a teacher to her students as she travels around the world. Each letter describes a place and then gives clues about an animal (or two) she has seen in the place. The students (readers) are supposed to guess from the clues she has provided what the animals are. The pages between the letters show us the animals, and further information about them is found at the end of the book. What I hope students will consider from studying these books is a consideration of why the writers chose the genre of letters to meet their purposes. That understanding helps students clarify the way genres can be used intentionally outside of their original purpose to meet an author's needs.

Principles

- ✓ Have a clear purpose for the multimodal learning you want to achieve and choose books to accomplish those purposes.
- ✓ Choose books that students can access.
- ✓ Choose picturebooks that can add to students' understanding of genres they may interact with in their lives.

Have a Clear Purpose for the Multimodal Learning You Want to Achieve and Choose Books to Accomplish Those Purposes

Once we start looking, we will find many picturebooks that exhibit postmodern characteristics. We want to consider how the picturebooks we choose "provide a site for developing new literacies" (Pantaleo, "What" 11). I think *Beware of the Storybook Wolves* by Lauren Child is a great example of many of those characteristics. This book is about a boy whose mother reads him a book about wolves before he sleeps each night. Because of the warning on the back cover of the book, he asks her to take the book out of his room when she leaves each night, but one night she is distracted and the book is left in his room. He awakens to find the two wolves from the book—the Big Wolf and the Little Wolf—beside his bed and threatening to eat him. The rest of the story follows the boy as he uses other characters in other books to help him not get eaten. When he has gotten rid of the wolves and other characters, he piles all his books in a stack and puts his bed on top of them to keep any other characters from getting out, but the last page is a scene of the next time he reads *Red Riding Hood*—and the wolf is just a caterpillar, which he had been changed into in the nighttime escapade. So there is intertextuality, with all the references to other stories and fairy tales. There is indeterminacy with the ending, because we have the unsettled feeling that the events of the nighttime might have been only the start of something. Changing formats is also evidenced with the font—bigger for Big Wolf and smaller for Little Wolf, straight when Mom is reading the story to the boy, but wavy and wiggly in ways that fit with the images. Italics indicate emphasis in one place. The fairy godmother speaks in cursive font. The publishing information is found on the back cover of the book. So there's plenty of changing formats and changing perspectives and some changing boundaries—lots to work with when students explore the text. With a book like this, with so many options, teachers will want to focus on the characteristics that meet their objectives.

Choose Books That Students Can Access

I LOVE *The Last Resort* by J. Patrick Lewis. I can read it again and again and still not be sure I read it the same way or think it means the same thing each time, a true example of postmodernity in a text that is clearly ambiguous, intertextual, and participatory. The illustrations both explain and extend the text. But the references to literary characters require wider knowledge on the part of readers than most of my students have, which means that much of the meaning is lost to them. It's a challenging text, even for me, so as much as I love it, it's not a book I use in my classes. Choosing postmodern picturebooks means we also have to consider which aspects of RCT our students can access and which might not be suitable, as I mentioned earlier.

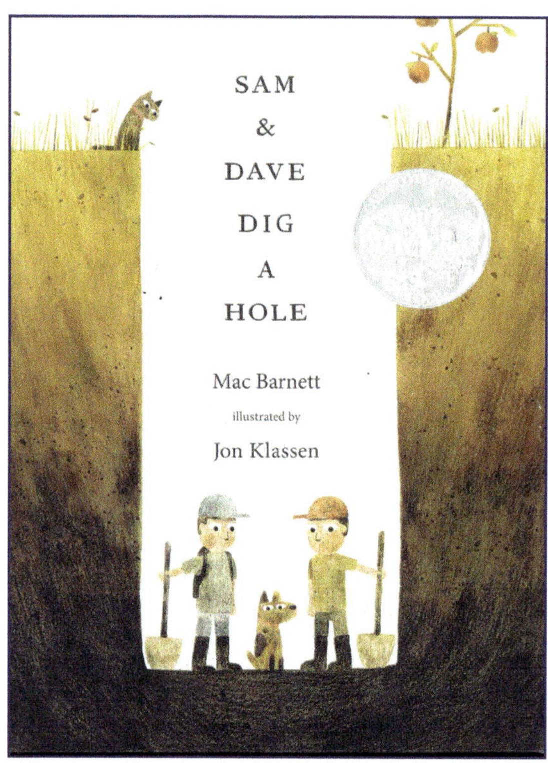

On the other hand, Mac Barnett's *Sam and Dave Dig a Hole* is an accessible book that reflects many of the elements of postmodern picturebooks and that connects the reading of print text with the reading we do online. The text relies heavily on the images to make meaning. The boys are looking for treasure and keep deciding to try a different direction just as the reader sees they are going to miss their treasure. The ending is ambiguous, not so much in the words but in the images if astute readers watch carefully from the beginning to the end. Even given the dependence on images for meaning making and the unresolved ending, this book is accessible to all students—and enjoyed by them too. Because of that accessibility, it can be easier for students to see how reading this text can help them consider their online reading practices as well.

Choose Picturebooks That Can Add to Students' Understanding of Genres They May Interact with in Their Lives

The concept of genre is easy to reduce to form. After all, genres form in social situations and the forms develop as part of the needs of a particular situation. What counts as a genre is often named because of its form. But form is not genre. When teachers share mentor text sets to help students write in a genre, be sure to use a range of texts to show this aspect of genre. Our students are unlikely to write picturebooks, but when we teach writing and are selecting mentor texts for students to learn from (Marchetti and O'Dell), it might benefit their learning to consider some picturebooks as part of those mentor text sets.

What are the genres our students might write—in school or outside, online or in other settings? It's hard to say. Here I mention one genre that is commonly taught in school and picturebooks that might be useful as part of the mentor text set for teaching this genre.

How-to writing: One of the mentor texts I have often used to help my students practice process, or how-to, writing is *How to Lose All Your Friends* by Nancy Carlson. It's a kind of informational writing students often write to learn about transitions and order. I like this book because it's short and direct, a clear example of how-to writing with an imperative statement followed by an explanation: "2. Never share. If you are eating cookies, hide them when your friends come over." My students are clearly able to see the characteristics in this text, which seems to work from the negative side to make a point about how we should treat friends. And when I read Vicki Spandel's use of this genre as a way to share information and summary of knowledge, I liked it even more.

But this isn't the only way to write about process, so when my students understand the basics, I want them to see more examples of the genre and how it might be expanded. We look at B. G. Hennessy's *The Scary Places Map Book*, with its overview of fake places and tours through them that were written in a way similar to the how-to pattern we have seen. So, for example, the Tour of the Wicked Woods and Witchfield Village begins like this:

> From Gingerbread Cottage (I6) take the Breadcrumb Trail northwest 10 broomsticks along the northern border of the Poison Apple Orchard.
>
> At Twin Trees, follow the Pebble Path west 7 broomsticks, then northwest 5 more broomsticks to Toad Pond.

Despite the difference in content—one is directions in space and the other is directions for relationships—there are some similarities in logical flow and clear details.

How to Build an Insect by Roberta Gibson states in the title that it is a how-to book, but it's structured differently. Instead of numbered steps, this book takes a

logical approach to the steps: "Let's build an insect. Where should we start? Humans have a head. Most animals have a head. Let's give our insect a head. What part should be next?" As the process develops, logic rather than numbers guides the organization. And we don't see imperatives as we might expect. Instead, questions and statements guide our path through the process. Yet this is still process writing, and sharing it with students as an example of genre helps them see that writing doesn't fit a template so much as it has elements in common to do a job that is determined by situation and purpose. That will help students write and read genres more effectively and also help them see where they might use genres in creative ways to do other jobs to meet their purposes.

9

Choosing Picturebooks

Mem Fox describes picturebooks this way:

> In my experience, the best-loved picture books are so well written that they leave a lasting impression on the reader. They have a passionate quality. By passionate, I mean a constant undercurrent of tension combined with compassion, which makes readers care desperately about the fate of the main characters. It's not easy to achieve, but I am convinced that writing without passion is writing for oblivion. . . . If we don't laugh, gasp, block our ears, sigh, vomit, giggle, curl our toes, empathize, sympathize, feel pain, weep or shiver during the reading of a picture book, then surely the writer has wasted our time, our money, and our precious, precious trees. (qtd. in Osborn 24)

Who could resist such a book? Certainly not our students. It is incumbent on us as their teachers to choose picturebooks that accomplish these responses.

Finding the Right Picturebooks

If it isn't clear by now, I'll just say it: I believe in the value of using picturebooks for secondary classrooms. I think they can help us teach pretty much anything. But teaching with picturebooks—and getting the results we want—begins with effective choices of picturebooks.

As the stories of my beginning practice with picturebooks in my classes demonstrate, I started mostly with the books I had on hand that I thought would serve a purpose in my classroom. As I saw the benefits, I spent time at the library, going through the shelves to see what options they had that might be useful for my classes. I didn't have the funding to buy a lot of books, so I had to be judicious when I purchased new ones. In the early days, I didn't always make the best choices and gradually started to develop the principles I have shared in this book so far. But at first, my selection was trial and error.

Whenever I talk to teachers on this topic, they always ask me about choosing books. I certainly don't expect them to choose only the books I share here. They will have their own preferences and student needs—and more and more books will be coming out in the years to come. Other advocates of using picturebooks in secondary classrooms have their own recommendations for choosing for different purposes—and I encourage readers to follow Ten Positive Picture Books (positivelyliteracy.com/blog) to see what teachers across the country recommend. So, in addition to the principles specific for the purposes I've expressed in the chapters of this book, this chapter offers principles and general thoughts about selecting picturebooks for your classroom library.

I had better say right at the start: I am kind of picky about my picturebooks—even the ones I buy for my personal library. And it's kind of idiosyncratic. For one thing, the look of the book has to work for me right off the bat. And that doesn't mean all the books have to be the same—I love a wide variety of image styles: bright, subdued, intricate, simple. But the images need a certain level of sophistication and connection to the words and mood of the book, a draw for me to pick up the book and open it. Then I need to see text that has a certain way with words. I need to see ideas that appeal and intrigue. When I pick up a picturebook, I want to connect and see pretty quickly a clear connection to my students and the purposes of our class. It's hard to explain why some books appeal to me, but I bring this personal connection up because I think it matters. If I don't like some aspect of a picturebook—the font style, what the images look like stylistically, the craft or style, the development or organization of ideas, how hard it is to read, even how the words are placed on the page—I tend to be not as enthusiastic in using it and students' responses are also cooler. I recently learned that my impression about this student reaction to the teacher's attitude was also recognized by librarian Mary Zdrojewski (Vercelletto): "My students will sit through much more 'childish' books than I'd expect if they can tell from my face and inflection that I really like that book." If I don't feel positive passion for a book, I will choose another for my purpose more often than not. So I guess to begin, I suggest finding books that you like and will want to share with students. If you do that, you start off in a good place.

However, if you don't have time to spend haunting the library or local bookstore (although I have to say it's a fun way to spend a few hours—or more), there are books and websites that suggest picturebooks to use in secondary classrooms. They don't often give suggestions for how to use the books and they might not list all the current books, but they can be a starting point for finding books for you, your classes, and the purposes you are trying to meet. Here are some places to begin:

- ✓ Culham, Ruth, James Blasingame, and Raymond Coutu. *Using Mentor Texts to Teach Writing with the Traits*. Scholastic, 2010.
- ✓ Hall, Susan. *Using Picture Storybooks to Teach Literary Devices: Recommended Books for Children and Young Adults*. Vol. 2, 2nd ed., Oryx Press, 1994.
- ✓ Tiedt, Iris McClellan. *Teaching with Picture Books in the Middle School.* International Reading Association, 2000.
- ✓ Picture Books Blogger: https://picturebooksblogger.wordpress.com/.
- ✓ Let's Talk Picture Books: https://www.letstalkpicturebooks.com/.

Another obvious consideration is to choose books that are age appropriate. Susan Hall talks about "all-age" picturebooks as a way to distinguish them from children's picturebooks. I don't recommend that we ignore all books for children, as some books seem to span age groups and might seem aimed at one level for children but also have a level for older readers. Sendak's *Where the Wild Things Are* is an example of this kind of picturebook that can be read on multiple levels. But we want to make sure we are using books that are age appropriate, that will appeal to our students. Books with simplistic language or concepts that are about learning language, like basic ABC books, might be less useful. For example, could I use Bill Martin Jr. and Eric Carle's *Brown Bear, Brown Bear, What Do You See?* in secondary schools? I might. If I had *lots* of students with very little English vocabulary, this simple text might be useful, but I would have to consider my learning objectives for the rest of the class. I might even make a case for using it for a language lesson (on parallelism or what part of speech is "looking at me") or to teach a direct sentence pattern. But could I find other picturebooks that might teach those same lessons with a little more sophistication and nuance, appropriate for secondary students? As much as I love to read *Brown Bear* to my grandchildren, it probably isn't one I would regularly use in a secondary classroom.

Here are a couple of more general principles I share about selecting picturebooks.

Principles

- ✓ Choose books that can serve multiple purposes.
- ✓ Choose books that address social-emotional needs.
- ✓ Choose books that represent a wide variety of students and lives.

Choose Books That Can Serve Multiple Purposes

One way we can make the best selections of picturebooks for our classroom, especially if we are beginning our collection, is to make sure at least some of our choices are useful for multiple purposes. Maybe the books would be useful for multiple purposes at the same time, but maybe introducing some books for one use and then bringing them back for another use later would be a good idea. Being able to do that—introduce the book once for one purpose and then repurpose it for another lesson later—is also efficient because it doesn't take so much class time the second (or third) time I use it. But we have to be very careful that the book is a really good one. If it isn't, students will groan and shut down when I bring the book up the second (or third) time. If it's a good one, students will welcome its return.

That means that when we are looking for books for our classes, we need to determine how many ways we might be able to use it. If I find a book that I can use for an informal writing invitation, and then again later for a mini-lesson about word choice, I'm happy to put it in my library. If I also think it might have an extra appeal for my MLL students or meet some other needs of students in my class, even better. What matters is that I can use a single picturebook to do lots of different things.

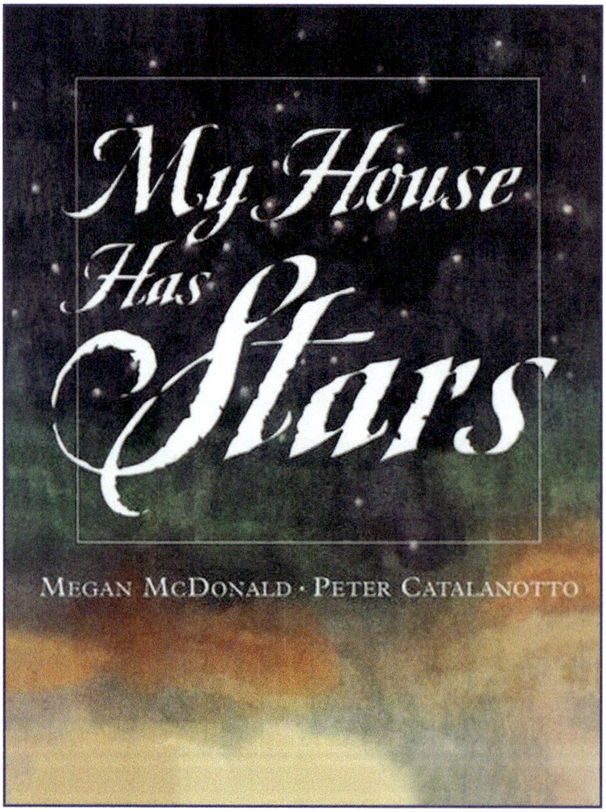

Besides serving multiple purposes, some picturebooks act as effective mentor texts for writing products—and then are available and useful for mini-lessons throughout the writing process. McDonald's *My House Has Stars* is a favorite picturebook that does this. As I mentioned in an earlier chapter, it's a text I use for a formal writing assignment—and I have used it with multiple grade levels (Dean, "Framing Texts"). The book is rich enough to supply an assignment that inspires and provides all the mini-lesson content I need. It is the one writing assignment that every student completes. Something about it appeals to all students, and one of my teacher friends with classes full of students who have lived in other places around the world said it was a game changer for the students in her class. The book has an overall frame about how night is falling on houses around the world, and they all have stars. Each page then tells of children in a different place in the world, describing their homes and families and cultures. All of the pages end with night falling and the line: "My house has stars." At the end of the book, the frame reappears, reminding us that the earth is home to us all, and the stars are the roof to our home.

My House Has Stars is a little long to read the whole thing at once. I like to read the opening frame first, then a couple of pages, followed by the closing frame. This way students can see how the book is set up in general. Then I ask them to read additional internal pages in small groups. I purchased several paperback copies and took them apart for this use and for future uses during mini-lessons. After they have all had a chance to read several pages, we discuss the point the book is making. I let students know we will each write our own page about a place we are familiar with and then create our own class book. Students brainstorm about the places they would like to write about and freewrite a bit about the one they are most inclined to use.

We spend a few days studying the way the book is written to prepare to write. We consider the kinds of ideas the author uses to develop each page. We make a list:

- ✓ Details about the **habitats** (houses)—what they look like and what they are made of
- ✓ **Sensory details**: the sounds, smells, tastes, and textures in the house and area
- ✓ Details about the **people** (number and kind) who live in the house—and maybe the neighbors—and what they do for play and work
- ✓ Details about the weather and **geography** of the area
- ✓ Details about the culture/folklore/religion—what **stories** the people tell and what **objects** reflecting their cultural beliefs are evident in or around the house

Once we have developed this list and students have selected a place for their own page, they are ready to conduct inquiry and know the kinds of ideas they need to seek. As students notice, not every page of *My House Has Stars* has everything from the list, so they don't need to worry if they can't find everything on the list. Instead, the ideas in the mentor text provide them with starting places for their own inquiry and writing—and I always add another category: anything they learn that strikes them as particularly interesting, something that most people wouldn't know. They never know when those interesting, new ideas will be useful when it's time to write!

Then we look at McDonald's book for other global traits of writing: organization and voice. We build a general frame for our pages, noting that, somehow, we all need to end up at night with the line "My house has stars" so that the book has coherence. We can discuss different options of order: outside to inside, inside to outside, morning to night, and other variations. We also discuss how the voice is created. I mostly want them to feel that the voice is personal and engaged—not just that it is young, but that it is one of the features of this book that students find appealing. I think they think this writing will be easier than academic writing, but it is really quite nuanced.

When students have drafts, we hold mini-lessons on sentence fluency (a key trait that contributes to the readability and voice of the text) and similes and metaphors, additional key features on each page. With older students, I have also had lessons on infinitives and vivid verbs. With younger students, I teach a lesson on weaving in words from other places and languages. The book is full of possibilities for language and craft lessons.

Students polish their writing, they add an image of some type, and I bind the pages together into a class book that students check out to take home and read through. During the COVID pandemic, I made the class book a digital one, but I went back to the hard copy afterward. Students preferred it. They like having a physical copy they can hold in their hands and share at home and with friends. Whatever form we choose, the writing from this picturebook teaches students a lot about writing (using mentor texts, genre, inquiry, and process), about language and craft, and about community. Learning about places that matter to all of us is especially good for building community, and MLL students are particularly engaged in this writing.

The process described here with *My House Has Stars* can be adapted for other picturebooks to serve as mentors for class books. I like to imagine a classroom or school library showcasing these student-generated books based on picturebooks. The following titles are potential options for this process:

- ✓ *The Scary Places Map Book: Seven Terrifying Tours* by B. G. Hennessy
- ✓ *One Leaf Rides the Wind* by Celeste Mannis
- ✓ *Don't Touch That Toad and Other Strange Things Adults Tell You* by Catherine Rondina

Choose Books That Address Social-Emotional Needs

The Important Thing about Margaret Wise Brown by Mac Barnett is a picturebook biography of Margaret Wise Brown, author of many picturebooks students probably know: *The Important Book*, *The Runaway Bunny*, and *Goodnight Moon*. Written in a style similar to Brown's, the biography reveals how her life didn't turn out as expected. How her books were not accepted—how she was not accepted. Told in the same number of pages as years in her life (forty-two), the style is postmodern—Barnett addresses the reader directly and refers to the process of writing the book—so it will be different from the picturebooks students are familiar with. But most important is the conclusion of this book:

> Lives are funny and sad,
> scary and comforting,
> beautiful and ugly,
> but not when they're supposed to be,
> and sometimes all at the same time.
> There are patterns in life,
> and patterns in a story,
> but in real lives and good stories,
> the patterns are hard to see,
> because the truth is never made of straight lines.
> Lives are strange.
> And there are people who do not like strange stories,
> especially in books for children.
> But sometimes you find a book that feels as strange as life does.
> Those books feel true.
> Those books are important.
> Margaret Wise Brown wrote books like this,
> and she wrote them for children,
> because she believed children deserve important books.

It's important for us, when we are choosing books, to consider all the important things that picturebooks can bring to the classroom beyond writing and reading and language. Picturebooks deal with important things that are part of our students' lives and can also be chosen for this purpose. Many teachers who use picturebooks in the classroom note the impact they can make in other aspects of our classroom. For example, Massey notes: "Children's picture books stimulate the imagination and serve as a receptacle for coping with psychosocial issues" (45). We might not be sure why this happens, but there is something tangible about the way using picturebooks in our classes helps us all relax, settle in, feel comfortable, feel better. We can choose books to accomplish the purposes of ELA classrooms—developing reading, writing, and language—but we might also consider, as one of the aspects of our choice, whether they could accomplish another purpose too: encouraging community building, acceptance, resilience, perseverance, and other traits we value. The following books might be ones we can use not only for multiple educational purposes but also for the less tangible outcomes we might want to address. With each title, I list the educational possibilities, but I also try to show the other benefits that might be felt from sharing the book in our classes. I don't usually voice the other thing I am hoping students will take from the books—I just read them for the primary purpose and see what happens with the talk or writing that follows.

Nerdy Birdy by Aaron Reynolds is about friends and cliques and how birds get categorized into groups. It's fun and clever and can be used to help students discuss what it means to "fit in" and who they fit in with. This book would be useful to introduce that concept before reading a novel like *The Outsiders* (Hinton) or *Lord of the Flies* (Golding). It is also a good text for inferring and for thinking about the way images and text build on each other. Because there is a lot of dialogue, another use might be gleaning examples for teaching punctuation, particularly dialogue. This text is also short enough that it could be used to prompt informal writing.

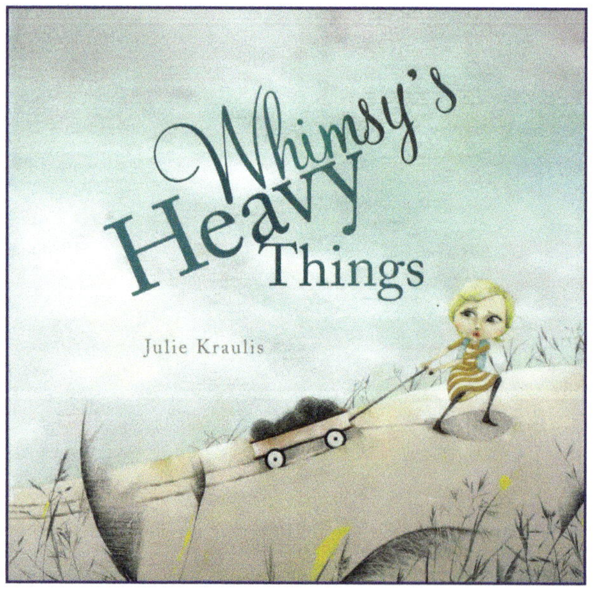

Whimsy's Heavy Things by Julie Kraulis shows how Whimsy tries to avoid dealing with her "heavy things" but eventually learns how to not only manage her heavy things but also turn them into advantages. Although the book is a great example of metaphor, with the heavy things and solutions more symbolic than real, it can be a great way to model how to deal with challenges of all kinds in our lives. I have used it for a prompt for informal writing (it's a quick read), and again, it's also a great example of metaphor. Its message of hope and perseverance might resonate with some literature discussions: how might Romeo and Juliet have handled their "heavy things" better? Finally, the use of font size to emphasize key words presents a great example for discussions of visual literacy.

Dan Santat's *After the Fall* makes use of the familiar childhood poem of Humpty Dumpty. It depicts Humpty after he has been put back together and is dealing with his fears of high places (like the wall). The storyline follows Humpty's attempts to first displace and then finally overcome his fears. Students will see his persistence and feel the difficulty of overcoming a fear—and then, I think, be surprised by the ending, which suggests we become something new when we push through our fears. The book is short enough to use for informal writing, but it would also be a good one to consider as we discuss characters in the literature we read—those who give up and those who push through. This book is also a good example of how color can establish mood in visual literacy.

Since most students know and enjoy Dr. Seuss, they like it when I pull out *Hooray for Diffendoofer Day!*, although they may not be familiar with it. In true Seussian style, it tells of a special school and all the teachers there. They have a lot of fun in that school, until the principal announces that students must take a test to keep their school open; the consequences of not passing are horrific (being moved to the school in Flobbertown, a dismal place). But the students have been taught "to think" in nontraditional ways and pass the test, thus creating the celebration day memorialized in the title. First, this book is just fun—and it can help students think about upcoming standardized tests, assuring them they have what they need to pass. But we can also discuss words—real ones and made-up ones—and how words shift from one part of speech to another, how sound matters in word choice, and how

surprising word choices can contribute to tone. One thing many readers may not know about this book is that it was left unfinished by Dr. Seuss; the back of the book describes his editor's process of getting Jack Prelutsky and Lane Smith to finish it so that we could have one more book from many children's favorite picturebook author. I like to use the back of the book (after we enjoy the actual story and discuss what we enjoy about it) to share about writing process, about collaboration, and about style (since both helpers had to try to match Seuss's style). My students like to consider how they might write in this style, so even a close study of style can follow reading this book.

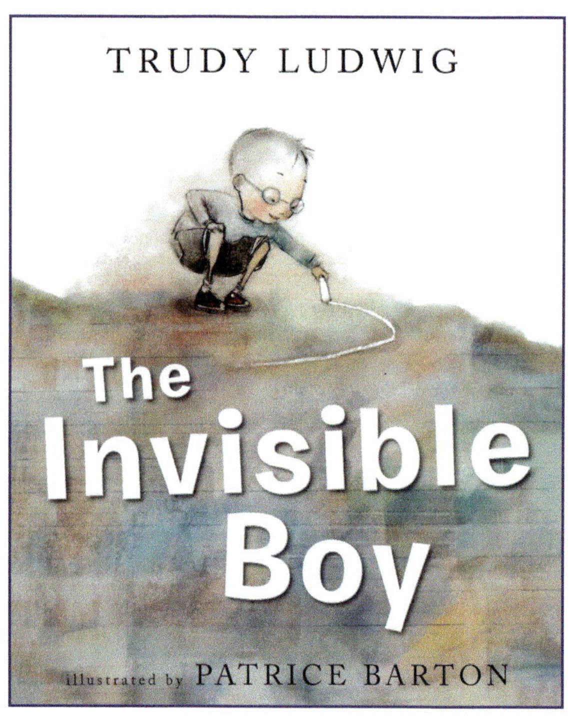

Trudy Ludwig's *The Invisible Boy*, a book about a boy who is an outsider in his classroom and thus metaphorically invisible, explores the social practices common in school: choosing partners for groups, eating lunch in the cafeteria, selecting team members for playing ball at recess. Brian is left out of all the events until a new boy comes to school. At first we think the new boy, who has some differences, won't be accepted either. Brian makes a quiet overture toward him, but, surprisingly, at least one other boy in the class accepts the new boy. However, the new boy draws Brian in until he too is accepted—and no longer invisible. Moments in this book are painful as we empathize with Brian's embarrassment, and students might discuss how our "normal" ways of school might be hurtful to those we don't notice regularly. It could start a conversation about awareness of our interactions and common practices and how they might appear to others around us, about how simple, gentle kindnesses have their own power. Another way this book can be used is for a study in visual literacy, because the pictures of Brian are gray until he is accepted—prompting us to consider why the author chose to use color this way and if we can name other places where we have seen image and color used to create tone or message. Again, the book is short enough to be used to prompt informal writing. It has some good examples of how sentence length variety can emphasize key ideas, which could contribute to a language or writing lesson.

Holler Loudly by Cynthia Leitich Smith is a fun book about a boy who has a VERY loud voice that gets him kicked out of everything—school, the movie theater, even his grandpa's fishing boat. Finally, at the state fair, he learns to listen and when to use his loud voice to save the town. The book employs humor and exaggeration to show that talents are best used in appropriate times and places—and uses font style to emphasize key words (e.g., *Loud* and *Hush*) and ALL the words Holler says. The book's language can serve as good examples of matching tone with word choice.

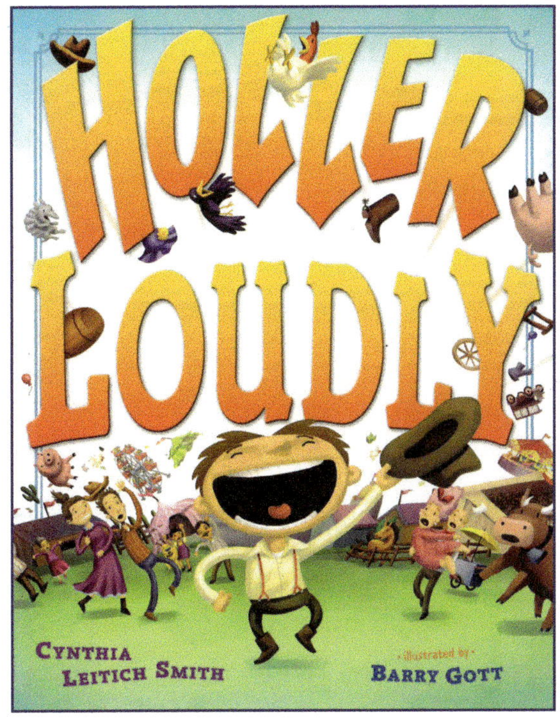

This Story Is Not About a Kitten by Randall de Sève and Carson Ellis is patterned after the style of "The House That Jack Built" and tells the story of a compassionate community of people (and a dog) who work together to help a kitten find a home. The final sentence tells us what this book is really about: "This story is about the stopping and listening, the holding and bringing, the offering and asking and *working together* it takes, sometimes, to get there." This idea of working together to accomplish a task is important to building classroom community. At the same time, the book is a great example of grammatical principles such as using adjectives out of order and dependent clauses to create sentences that grow and grow.

Sophie Blackall's *Farmhouse* is about a farmhouse (no surprise), the people who lived there, and the person who found the house after it had been abandoned—told in one winding, cumulative sentence. The story of the book is one of the passage of time and the rise and fall of the things people build as they look toward the future. It features a family from the past (farming and painting their own wallpaper) but with some traditions that may be familiar to students. It speaks to the idea of things that last and things that don't, something that might resonate with older students as they look to the end of their public school experience. *Farmhouse* could be interesting to consider for setting and background in preparation for books like *My Ántonia* (Cather).

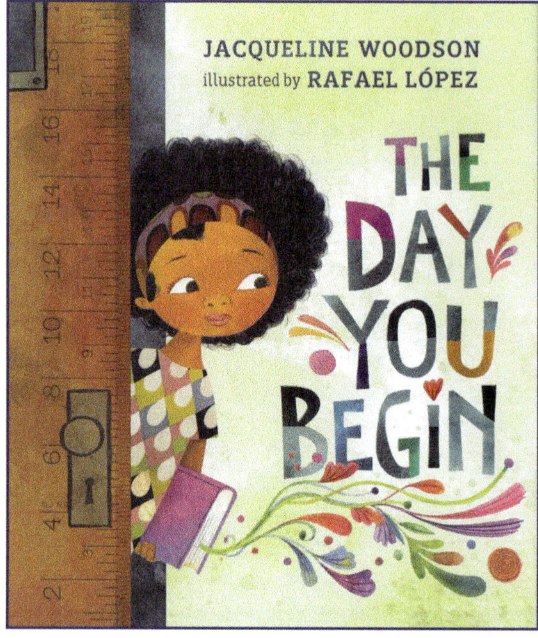

Although the story—and its telling in one long winding sentence that seems to mimic the passage of time—is interesting in itself, the author's note is fascinating; she explains how she came to find the farmhouse and, using the scraps and remnants she found in the rubble along with research in the valley, was able to tell the story of the house and its inhabitants. The process the writer goes through is a compelling study of writing process that, along with the story of the past and the possibilities for grammar teaching, means this book could be used for multiple lessons.

This lovely book, *The Day You Begin* by Jacqueline Woodson, addresses the myriad ways we might feel different in a new setting and how those feelings might make us feel alone—until we start to share our stories and find that we all have things we share and things that are unique to us. But we all belong. Woodson's prose is so lovely and could also be used to teach language and writing lessons: similes and metaphors, fragments and long sentences, repetition and parallelism. Lots of lovely language lessons are possible with this text and its positive message about belonging.

Red by Michael Hall is a quick read that tells the story of a blue crayon with a red paper covering naming his color: red. However, the actual crayon is blue. People expect him to color red, but he can't. Everyone makes excuses ("He's got to press harder.") or tries to help ("The scissors thought his label was too tight. One snip should do it."). But when a purple crayon asks Red to draw the ocean for his boat, despite initial resistance ("I can't. I'm red."), Red finds his true color and success. Clearly, the book serves a great purpose in helping readers consider that labels and names might not accurately represent the inner person. It's short so it would be perfect as an invitation for informal writing, but it's also a good book for examining digital and visual literacy as there are different font types to represent different voices and the disconnect between the crayon's name and the color that comes out—very postmodern to have the images contradict the words.

Matt de la Peña's *Milo Imagines the World* focuses on a young boy on a monthly train ride with his sister. As he travels, we don't know where he is going, but he is nervous: "a shook-up soda." As he rides, he watches others on the train and imagines their lives, which he draws in his notebook. The picturebook alternates double-spread pages of the reality, the train ride, with spreads that look like Milo's notebook drawings. This pattern breaks briefly when Milo's eyes meet another boy's, another train rider whose life Milo has already imagined. He starts to wonder what people imagine about his life, and when he gets to his destination and sees the boy in the same line, he starts to wonder about his imaginings and whether we can really tell who people are from their outsides. This book has a little more text than usual, but the flow is rhythmic. It could be used to invite informal writing, where it will undoubtedly prompt some writers to consider the same question. Also, the book would be great for a lesson on inferring in literature (Where are they going? Why isn't an adult with them?) or a lesson on sentence structure and fluency.

The first sentence puts the train as the subject of the sentence, with Milo and his sister in the dependent clause, when we might expect the opposite. The next three sentences are somewhat parallel in structure: a __________ has a __________ face (or something similar). Having students consider this choice (and others in the book) for fluency would help them think about the choices writers make to create flowing text. The peritextual elements (endpapers, title page, and back cover) would be a good focus for a lesson on visual literacy.

Choose Books That Represent a Wide Variety of Students and Lives

Since this should be obvious, what do I mean by this principle? It's not that we have to have a book to represent every aspect of our students' lives. Let me explain.

Mostly, I mean to raise awareness of what the totality of our books might say about the people in the world and the people in our classes. Beyond considerations of academics, aesthetics, and emotional support should be an awareness of the people our books represent. It used to be harder to address this principle, but more and more book illustrators and publishers are helping to make the current books more representative of our students and their experiences.

If we take this principle to its extreme, we will probably never be completely successful. One obvious reason is that the variety of students may change from year to year; trying to represent each of the varying lives would be a big job. But even more likely, some of our students' challenges might not have representation in picturebooks—or at least in picturebooks that have academic or other value to share in class. And although I know people want to be seen, some students don't want to have attention drawn to what might be special to them. I have two grandchildren with hearing loss, both of whom wear hearing aids. I have found very few books that specifically represent their lives and challenges, and none has met the other needs for using picturebooks in my secondary classroom. I suspect that if a teacher found one and used it in class, thinking they were doing a good thing, my grandson might appreciate it. My granddaughter would not. She wouldn't want the attention drawn to her and her specific challenges. This is another consideration; when we choose to share a book that represents specific students in our classes, they might wish that we hadn't. So it's tricky to honor this principle with all these other considerations.

Instead, I try to think of it this way: if we have options to meet the learning objectives we are seeking to achieve, choose picturebooks that represent widely. When I recently read *The Thing Lou Couldn't Do* by Ashley Spires as an invitation to write, a student approached me afterward to thank me. I had thought the book would be inspiring, maybe encourage students to think and write about how they handle difficulties. Instead, this Navajo student said thank you because it was the first time she had seen someone in a picturebook who looked like her. That is what I mean: There can be several books about overcoming challenges, but I can also consider who in my class might need to see themselves in some way in a book I share. I can choose for that too.

When I advise teachers to choose books that represent widely, I think it is more important to be sure we have a wide range of people represented in the books we use than that we find a book for each student. Do our books have characters of different cultural and ethnic backgrounds? If half my class is Latinx, I would definitely want to have books with students from Spanish-speaking countries in them, but I might also have books with characters from the Middle East, the Pacific Islands, and so on, even if I don't currently have students from those areas in my classroom. It's just good to think of showing the world broadly, no matter the current makeup of our classes.

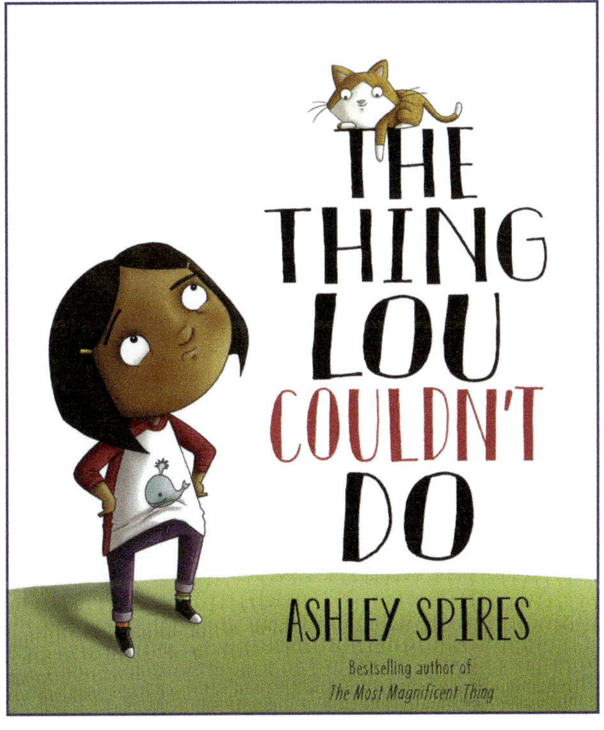

Our students may have lots of challenges in their lives. Choosing books that deal with challenges broadly might be more appropriate than books that focus on a single specific problem or challenge. Our students can all appreciate picturebooks that could apply to all the challenges they might face instead of zeroing in on one specific challenge. Again, *The Thing Lou Couldn't Do* is a good example of what I mean. Lou loves adventures with her friends, but when it comes time to climb a tree, she finds that she just can't make herself do it. At first she tries to avoid her fear; then she tries to find a way around it—all the things we all do no matter what our fears are. Eventually she tries to climb the tree—and fails. But the book ends with the positive anticipation that she'll try again. This is what I mean by choosing widely: this book addresses a challenge in such a general way that it could apply to many challenges people face. Students will see their own challenges in Lou's challenge. This book could be used for an invitation to informal writing, or it could be useful for a mini-lesson on sentence fluency—so it could serve other purposes besides this one of helping students consider ways to overcome their challenges.

Other titles that might represent widely include the following:

> *A Different Pond* by Bao Phi tells the story of a Vietnamese father and son on a short fishing trip and encourages thinking of heritage, family, and traditions. Academically, this book would be useful for examining visual literacy (its style is similar to a graphic novel in places), but it also has a variety of compound sentences without commas before the conjunction, useful for having students explore for that stylistic choice.

Nigel and the Moon by Antwan Eady is a charming story about a boy with big dreams who fears sharing his dreams aloud. His parents teach him to be proud of his dreams—and of who he is. This would be a good invitation for informal writing, but it could also be useful in mini-lessons on fragments and sentence variety.

Hair Story by NoNieqa Ramos tells the stories of two girls who play hair salon and, in the process, learn about the stories of hair in their different cultures (Black and Puerto Rican). This book is a lively rhyming text that would be wonderful to teach about word choice and rhythm, especially as it combines languages.

Choosing effective picturebooks for secondary classrooms isn't as rule-bound as it might seem. I use these as a guide, but sometimes I just discover a book I love so much that I find a way to make it work. And sometimes I watch teachers use other books that I would never use in my classes—and their students respond positively. A lot of it has to do with being the right book in the right teacher's hands. But beyond that, these guidelines might help other teachers focus their search for effective picturebooks. And more than anything, I hope teachers have a lot of fun when they are looking. That is a great place to start.

Recommended Picturebooks

Ahlberg, Allan. *Previously.* Illustrated by Bruce Ingman. Candlewick Press, 2007.

Ahlberg, Janet, and Allan Ahlberg. *The Jolly Postman, or, Other People's Letters.* Little, Brown, 1986.

Al Abdullah, Queen Rania, with Kelly DiPucchio. *The Sandwich Swap.* Illustrated by Tricia Tusa. Disney Hyperion Books, 2010.

Alexander, Kwame. *How to Read a Book.* Illustrated by Melissa Sweet. HarperCollins, 2019.

Aliki. *Marianthe's Story: Painted Words, Spoken Memories.* Greenwillow Books, 1998.

Allen, Susan, and Jane Lindaman. *Written Anything Good Lately?* Illustrated by Vicky Enright. Millbrook Press, 2006.

Anderson, Laurie Halse. *The Hair of Zoe Fleefenbacher Goes to School.* Illustrated by Ard Hoyt. Simon & Schuster, 2009.

Anderson, M. T. *Handel, Who Knew What He Liked.* Illustrated by Kevin Hawkes. Candlewick Press, 2001.

Argueta, Jorge Tetl. *Tierra, Tierrita* = Earth, Little Earth: Tal, Talchin. Illustrated by Felipe Ugalde Alcántara and translated by Elizabeth Bell. Piñata Books, 2023.

Arnosky, Jim. *Wild Tracks! A Guide to Nature's Footprints.* Sterling Children's Book, 2008.

Aston, Dianna Hutts. *An Egg Is Quiet.* Illustrated by Sylvia Long. Chronicle Books, 2014.

Atherton, David. *Bake, Make, and Learn to Cook Vegetarian: Healthy and Green Recipes for Young Cooks.* Illustrated by Alice Bowsher. Candlewick Press, 2021.

Auch, Mary Jane, and Herm Auch. *The Plot Chickens.* Holiday House, 2009.

Banks, Kate. *Max's Words.* Illustrated by Boris Kulikov. Frances Foster Books, 2006.

Banyai, Istvan. *Zoom.* Puffin Books, 1998.

Barnett, Mac. *The Important Thing about Margaret Wise Brown.* Illustrated by Sarah Jacoby. Balzar + Bray, 2019.

———. *Sam and Dave Dig a Hole.* Illustrated by Jon Klassen. Candlewick Press, 2014.

Base, Graeme. *Animalia.* Harry N. Abrams, 1986.

———. *The Discovery of Dragons.* Harry A. Abrams, 1996.

Bedard, Michael. *Sitting Ducks.* Walker Books, 2001.

Berger, Carin. *A Perfect Day.* Greenwillow Books, 2012.

Bingham, Caroline. *Coral Reef: Around the Clock with the Animals of the Ocean.* DK Publishing, 2005.

Bingham, Kelly. *Z Is for Moose.* Illustrated by Paul O. Zelinsky. Greenwillow Books, 2012.

Black, Michael Ian. *A Pig Parade Is a Terrible Idea.* Illustrated by Kevin Hawkes. Simon & Schuster, 2010.

Blackall, Sophie. *Farmhouse.* Hachette Book Group, 2022.

Blake, Quentin. *Clown.* Henry Holt, 1995.

Bloom, Becky. *Wolf!* Illustrated by Pascal Biet. Scholastic, 1999.

Bottner, Barbara. *Miss Brooks Loves Books! (and I Don't).* Illustrated by Michael Emberly. Dragonfly Books, 2018.

Bouchard, David. *If You're Not from the Prairie. . . .* Illustrated by Henry Ripplinger. Aladdin Books, 1995.

Bradby, Marie. *Momma, Where Are You From?* Illustrated by Chris K. Soentpiet. Orchard Books, 2000.

Bram, Elizabeth. *Rufus the Writer.* Illustrated by Chuck Groenink. Schwartz & Wade Books, 2015.

Brett, Jan. *Annie and the Wild Animals.* Houghton Mifflin, 1985.

———. *The Mitten.* Hodder Wayland, 2000.

Briggs, Raymond. *The Snowman.* Random House, 1978.

Brosgol, Vera. *Memory Jars.* Roaring Brook Press, 2021.

Brown, Margaret Wise. *Goodnight Moon.* 1947. Illustrated by Clement Hurd. Rev. ed., HarperCollins, 2007.

———. *The Important Book.* Illustrated by Leonard Weisgard. HarperCollins, 1949.

———. *The Runaway Bunny.* Illustrated by Clement Hurd. HarperFestival, 2017.

Brown, Monica. *Marisol McDonald Doesn't Match/Marisol McDonald No Combina.* Illustrated by Sara Palacios. Children's Book Press, 2011.

———. *Pablo Neruda: Poet of the People/Poeta del Pueblo.* Illustrated by Julie Paschkis and translated by Adriana Domínguez. Henry Holt, 2022.

Browne, Anthony. *Voices in the Park.* DK Publishing, 1998.

Burgerman, Jon. *How to Eat Pizza.* Dial Books, 2018.

Burleigh, Robert. *The Adventures of Mark Twain by Huckleberry Finn.* Illustrated by Barry Blitt. Atheneum, 2011.

———. *Seurat and La Grande Jatte: Connecting the Dots.* Harry N. Abrams, 2004.

Burningham, John. *Come Away from the Water, Shirley.* Red Fox, 1992.

Calì, David. *Too Many Pigs and One Big Bad Wolf.* Illustrated by Marianna Balducci. Tundra Books, 2022.

Carle, Eric. *The Grouchy Ladybug.* HarperCollins, 1996.

———. *"Slowly, Slowly, Slowly," Said the Sloth.* World of Eric Carle, 2007.

———. *The Very Hungry Caterpillar.* World of Eric Carle, 1994.

Carlson, Nancy. *How to Lose All Your Friends.* Viking, 1994.

Carroll, Lewis. *Jabberwocky.* Illustrated by Stéphane Jorisch. KCP Poetry, 2004.

———. *Jabberwocky.* Illustrated by Christopher Myers. Scholastic, 2007.

Charlip, Remy. *Fortunately.* Simon & Schuster, 1993.

Child, Lauren. *Beware of the Storybook Wolves.* Orchard Books, 2012.

———. *Slightly Invisible.* Candlewick, 2010.

Choi, Yangsook. *The Name Jar.* Dragonfly Books, 2003.

Cisneros, Sandra. *Hairs/Pelitos.* 1984. Illustrated by Terry Ybáñez and translated by Liliana Valenzuela. Dragonfly Books, 1994.

Cole, Henry. *Jack's Garden.* Greenwillow Books, 1995.

Copeland, Misty. *Firebird.* Illustrated by Christopher Myers. G. P. Putnam's Sons, 2014.

Copper, Jenna, et al. *The Magic of Wonder.* Illustrated by Madeline B. Shearer. Dave Burgess Consulting, 2022.

Cronin, Doreen. *Click, Clack, Moo: Cows That Type.* Illustrated by Betsy Lewin. Little Simon, Simon & Schuster, 2010.

Crow, Kristyn. *Bedtime at the Swamp.* Illustrated by Macky Pamintuan. HarperCollins, 2008.

Cutler, Jane. *The Cello of Mr. O.* Illustrated by Greg Couch. Dutton Children's Books, 1999.

Cuyler, Margery. *That's Good! That's Bad!* Illustrated by David Catrow. Henry Holt, 1991.

Czekaj, Jef. *A Call for a New Alphabet.* Charlesbridge, 2011.

Davies, Nicola. *Bat Loves the Night.* Illustrated by Sarah Fox-Davies. Candlewick Press, 2001.

———. *Ice Bear: In the Steps of the Polar Bear.* Illustrated by Gary Blythe. Candlewick Press, 2005.

———. *Surprising Sharks.* Illustrated by James Croft. Candlewick Press, 2005.

Day, Alexandra. *Good Dog, Carl.* Little Simon, Simon & Schuster, 1996.

Deedy, Carmen Agra. *The Last Dance.* Illustrated by Debrah Santini. Peachtree, 1995.

de la Peña, Matt. *Last Stop on Market Street.* Illustrated by Christian Robinson. Scholastic, 2016.

———. *Love.* Illustrated by Loren Long. G. P. Putnam's Sons, 2018.

———. *Milo Imagines the World.* Illustrated by Christian Robinson. G. P. Putnam's Sons, 2021.

dePaola, Tomie. *Big Anthony and the Magic Ring.* Harcourt Brace Jovanovich, 1979.

———. *Strega Nona.* Simon & Schuster, 1975.

———. *Strega Nona Meets Her Match.* Putnam, 1993.

de Sève, Randall, and Carson Ellis. *This Story Is Not About a Kitten.* Random House, 2022.

Donaldson, Julia. *The Gruffalo.* Illustrated by Axel Scheffler. Macmillan Children's Books, 2010.

Dunklee, Annika. *My Name Is Elizabeth!* Illustrated by Matthew Forsythe. Kids Can Press, 2011.

Eady, Antwan. *Nigel and the Moon.* Illustrated by Gracey Zhang. HarperCollins, 2022.

Eggers, Dave. *Tomorrow Most Likely.* Illustrated by Lane Smith. Chronicle Books, 2019.

Empson, Jo. *Rabbityness.* Child's Play, 2012.

Erlbruch, Wolf. *Duck, Death and the Tulip.* Translated by Catherine Chidgey. Gecko Press, 2008.

Feelings, Tom. *The Middle Passage: White Ships/Black Cargo.* Dial Books, 2018.

Feiffer, Jules. *Meanwhile.* HarperCollins, 1999.

Flett, Julie. *Birdsong.* Greystone Books, 2019.

Flournoy, Valerie. *The Patchwork Quilt.* Illustrated by Jerry Pinkney. Dial Books, 1985.

Fox, Mem. *Wilfrid Gordon McDonald Partridge.* Illustrated by Julie Vivas. Kane Miller, 1989.

Frasier, Debra. *Miss Alaineus: A Vocabulary Disaster.* Clarion Books, 2007.

Friedman, Laurie. *I'm Not Afraid of This Haunted House.* Illustrated by Teresa Murfin. Carolrhoda Books, 2005.

———. *The Wolves in the Walls.* Illustrated by Dave McKean. HarperCollins, 2005.

Garland, Sherry. *The Lotus Seed.* Illustrated by Tatsuro Kiuchi. Houghton Mifflin, 1993.

George, Jean Craighead. *One Day in the Desert.* Illustrated by Fred Brenner. HarperCollins, 1996.

George, Lindsay Barrett. *Around the World: Who's Been Here?* Greenwillow Books, 1999.

Giblin, James Cross. *Secrets of the Sphinx.* Illustrated by Bagram Ibatoulline. Scholastic, 2004.

Gibson, Roberta. *How to Build an Insect.* Illustrated by Anne Lambelet. Millbrook Press, 2021.

Giovanni, Nikki. *Rosa.* Illustrated by Bryan Collier. Scholastic, 2005.

Goodhart, Pippa. *Three Little Ghosties.* Illustrated by AnnaLaura Cantone. Bloomsbury Children's Books, 2007.

Goodman, Susan E. *All in Just One Cookie.* Illustrated by Timothy Bush. Greenwillow Books, 2006.

Gravett, Emily. *Little Mouse's Big Book of Fears.* Simon & Schuster, 2007.

———. *Spells.* Simon & Schuster, 2009.

———. *Wolf Won't Bite!* Macmillan, 2011.

———. *Wolves.* Pan Childrens, 2006.

Gregory, Valiska. *Through the Mickle Woods.* Illustrated by Barry Moser. Little, Brown, 1992.

Haldar, Raj, and Chris Carpenter. *P Is for Pterodactyl: The Worst Alphabet Book Ever.* Illustrated by Maria Tina Beddia. Sourcebooks, 2018.

Hall, Michael. *Perfect Square.* Greenwillow Books, 2011.

———. *Red: A Crayon's Story.* Greenwillow Books, 2015.

Handford, Martin. *Where's Waldo Now?* Candlewick Press, 2019.

Harmony, Cynthia. *Mi Ciudad Sings.* Illustrated by Teresa Martinez. Penguin, 2022.

Heder, Thyra. *The Bear Report.* Abrams, 2015.

Heller, Nicholas. *Ogres! Ogres! Ogres! A Feasting Frenzy from A to Z.* Illustrated by Jos. A. Smith. Greenwillow Books, 1999.

Henkes, Kevin. *Chrysanthemum.* Greenwillow Books, 2020.

———. *Lilly's Purple Plastic Purse.* Greenwillow Books, 2006.

———. *Waiting.* Greenwillow Books, 2015.

———. *Wemberly Worried.* Greenwillow Books, 2010.

Hennessy, B. G. *The Scary Places Map Book: Seven Terrifying Tours.* Illustrated by Erwin Madrid. Candlewick Press, 2012.

Herzog, Brad. *K Is for Kick: A Soccer Alphabet.* Illustrated by Melanie Rose. Sleeping Bear Press, 2006.

Hesse, Karen. *The Cats in Krasinski Square.* Illustrated by Wendy Watson. Scholastic, 2004.

———. *Come On, Rain!* Illustrated by Jon J. Muth. Scholastic, 1999.

Higgins, Ryan T. *Mother ~~Goose~~ Bruce.* Disney, 2015.

Hoefler, Kate. *Courage Hats.* Illustrated by Jessixa Bagley. Chronicle Books, 2022.

———. *Rabbit and the Motorbike.* Illustrated by Sarah Jacoby. Chronicle Books, 2019.

Holub, Joan. *Little Red Writing.* Illustrated by Melissa Sweet. Chronicle Books, 2013.

Hopkins, Lee Bennet. *A Bunch of Punctuation.* Illustrated by Serge Bloch. Highlights, 2018.

Jeffers, Oliver. *A Child of Books.* Illustrated by Sam Winston. Candlewick Press, 2016.

———. *The Heart and the Bottle.* Philomel Books, 2010.

———. *The Incredible Book Eating Boy.* Philomel Books, 2007.

———. *Stuck.* Philomel Books, 2011.

Jenkins, Steve. *Never Smile at a Monkey.* Clarion Books, 2014.

———. *Sisters and Brothers: Sibling Relationships in the Animal World.* Clarion Books, 2012.

———. *Time to Eat.* Clarion Books, 2011.

———. *What Do You Do with a Tail like This?* Scholastic, 2003

———, and Robin Page. *Move!* Houghton Mifflin, 2006.

John, Jory. *The Good Egg.* Illustrated by Pete Oswald. HarperCollins, 2019.

Johnston, Tony. *Levi Strauss Gets a Bright Idea: A Fairly Fabricated Story of a Pair of Pants.* Illustrated by Stacy Innerst. Harcourt, 2011.

Joyce, William. *The Fantastic Flying Books of Mr. Morris Lessmore.* Illustrated by William Joyce and Joe Bluhm. Atheneum, 2012.

Kerley, Barbara. *Those Rebels, John and Tom.* Illustrated by Edward Fotheringham. Scholastic, 2012.

Klassen, Jon. *I Want My Hat Back.* Candlewick Press, 2011.

Klausmeier, Jesse. *Open This Little Book.* Illustrated by Suzy Lee. Chronicle Books, 2013.

Kline, Rufus. *Watch Out for These Weirdos!* Illustrated by Nancy Carlson. Puffin Books, 1990.

Kraulis, Julie. *Whimsy's Heavy Things.* Tundra Books, 2013.

Kuipers, Alice. *Violet and Victor Write the Best-Ever Bookworm Book.* Illustrated by Bethanie Deeney Murguia. Little, Brown, 2014.

Kunkel, Angela Burke. *Digging for Words: José Alberto Gutiérrez and the Library He Built.* Illustrated by Paola Escobar. Random House, 2020.

Laminack, Lester L. *Three Hens and a Peacock.* Illustrated by Henry Cole. Peachtree, 2011.

Larsen, Andrew. *A Squiggly Story.* Illustrated by Mike Lowery. Kids Can Press, 2016.

Lawson, JonArno, and Sydney Smith. *Sidewalk Flowers.* Groundwood Books, 2015.

Le, Minh. *Let Me Finish!* Illustrated by Isabel Roxas. Little, Brown, 2016.

Leedy, Loreen. *Tracks in the Sand.* Doubleday, 1993.

Lehman, Barbara. *Rainstorm.* Houghton Mifflin, 2007.

Lendler, Ian. *An Undone Fairy Tale.* Illustrated by Whitney Martin. Simon & Schuster, 2005.

Levington, Rebecca Gardyn. *Brainstorm!* Illustrated by Kate Kronreif. Sleeping Bear Press, 2022.

Levitt, Paul M., et al. *The Weighty Word Book.* Illustrated by Janet Stevens. U of New Mexico P, 2009.

Lewis, J. Patrick. *The Last Resort.* Illustrated by Roberto Innocenti. Creative Editions, 2002.

———. *The Shoe Tree of Chagrin.* Illustrated by Chris Sheban. Creative Editions, 2001.

London, Jonathan. *Hippos Are Huge!* Illustrated by Matthew Trueman. Candlewick Press, 2017.

Ludwig, Trudy. *The Invisible Boy.* Illustrated by Patrice Barton. Alfred A. Knopf, 2013.

Ludy, Mark. *The Flower Man.* Green Pastures, 2005.

Luyken, Corinna. *The Book of Mistakes.* Dial Books, 2017.

Macaulay, David. *Black and White.* Houghton Mifflin, 1990.

MacLachlan, Patricia. *All the Places to Love.* Illustrated by Mike Wimmer. HarperCollins, 1994.

Maclear, Kyo. *The Good Little Book.* Illustrated by Marion Arbona. Tundra Books, 2015.

Maillard, Kevin Noble. *Fry Bread: A Native American Family Story.* Illustrated by Juana Martinez-Neal. Roaring Brook Press, 2019.

Mannis, Celeste Davidson. *One Leaf Rides the Wind: Counting in a Japanese Garden.* Illustrated by Susan Kathleen Hartung. Puffin Books, 2005.

———. *The Queen's Progress: An Elizabethan Alphabet.* Illustrated by Bagram Ibatoulline. Viking, 2003.

Marsalis, Wynton, with Paul Schaap. *Jazz A-B-Z: An A to Z Collection of Jazz Portraits.* Illustrated by Paul Rogers. Candlewick Press, 2005.

Martin, Bill Jr., and Eric Carle. *Brown Bear, Brown Bear, What Do You See?* Henry Holt, 1996.

Matthews, Elizabeth. *Different like Coco.* Candlewick Press, 2007.

McClements, George. *Night of the Veggie Monster.* Bloomsbury, 2008.

McDonald, Megan. *My House Has Stars.* Illustrated by Peter Catalanotto. Orchard Books, 1996.

McDonnell, Patrick. *A Perfectly Messed-Up Story.* Little, Brown, 2014.

McLimans, David. *Gone Wild: An Endangered Animal Alphabet.* Walker, 2006.

Melling, David. *The Ghost Library.* Barron's, 2004.

Messner, Kate. *Over and under the Snow.* Illustrated by Christopher Silas Neal. Chronicle Books, 2011.

Miles, David. *Book.* Illustrated by Natalie Hoopes. Familius, 2015.

Miletsky, Jay. *Patrick Picklebottom and the Penny Book.* Illustrated by Gary Wilkinson. New Paige Press, 2020.

Miller, Heather Lynn. *This Is Your Life Cycle.* Illustrated by Michael Chesworth. Clarion Books, 2008.

Mochizuki, Ken. *Heroes.* Illustrated by Dom Lee. Lee & Low, 1995.

Morales, Areli. *Areli Is a Dreamer: A True Story.* Illustrated by Luisa Uribe. Random House, 2022.

Munsch, Robert N. *The Paper Bag Princess.* Illustrated by Michael Martchenko. Annick Press, 1981.

Myers, Christopher. *My Pen.* Disney Hyperion Books, 2015.

Novak, B. J. *The Book with No Pictures.* Dial Books, 2014.

Numeroff, Laura. *If You Give a Mouse a Cookie.* Illustrated by Felicia Bond. HarperCollins, 2015.

Nuño, Fran. *The Map of Good Memories.* Illustrated by Zuzanna Celej. Cuento de Luz, 2016.

Offill, Jenny. *17 Things I'm Not Allowed to Do Anymore.* Illustrated by Nancy Carpenter. Dragonfly Books, 2011.

Palatini, Margie. *The Web Files.* Illustrated by Richard Egielski. Little, Brown, 2001.

Pallotta, Jerry. *The Skull Alphabet Book.* Illustrated by Ralph Masiello. Charlesbridge, 2002.

Papp, Lisa. *Madeline Finn and the Library Dog.* Old Barn Books, 2018.

Phi, Bao. *A Different Pond.* Illustrated by Thi Bui. Capstone Young Readers, 2017.

Pinfold, Levi. *Black Dog.* Templar Books, 2011.

Polacco, Patricia. *The Butterfly.* Scholastic, 2001.

———. *The Keeping Quilt.* Simon & Schuster, 1988.

Pulver, Robin. *Punctuation Takes a Vacation.* Illustrated by Lynn Rowe Reed. Holiday House, 2004.

———. *Thank You, Miss Doover.* Illustrated by Stephanie Roth Sisson. Holiday House, 2010.

Ramos, NoNieqa. *Hair Story.* Illustrated by Keisha Morris. Carolrhoda Books, 2021.

Rash, Andy. *Agent A to Agent Z.* Arthur A. Levine Books, 2004.

Ray, Mary Lyn. *Mud.* Illustrated by Lauren Stringer. HarperCollins, 1996.

Rex, Michael. *Goodnight Goon: A Petrifying Parody.* G. P. Putnam's Sons, 2008.

Reynolds, Aaron. *Nerdy Birdy.* Illustrated by Matt Davies. Roaring Brook Press, 2015.

Reynolds, Peter H. *Ish.* Candlewick Press, 2004.

———. *The Word Collector.* Orchard Books, 2018.

Ringgold, Faith. *Tar Beach.* Dragonfly Books, 1996.

Ringtved, Glenn. *Cry, Heart, but Never Break.* Illustrated by Charlotte Pardi and translated by Robert Moulthrop. Enchanted Lion Books, 2016.

Rondina, Catherine. *Don't Touch That Toad and Other Strange Things Adults Tell You.* Illustrated by Kevin Sylvester. Kids Can Press, 2010.

Rosen, Michael. *Michael Rosen's Sad Book.* Illustrated by Quentin Blake. Candlewick Press, 2004.

Rosenthal, Amy Krouse. *Exclamation Mark.* Illustrated by Tom Lichtenheld. Scholastic, 2013.

———. *One of Those Days.* Illustrated by Rebecca Doughty. G. P. Putnam's Sons, 2006.

Rubin, Adam. *Robo-Sauce.* Illustrated by Daniel Salmieri. Dial Books, 2015.

Ryan, Pam Muñoz. *Nacho and Lolita.* Illustrated by Claudia Rueda. Scholastic, 2005.

Rylant, Cynthia. *Long Night Moon.* Illustrated by Mark Siegel. Simon & Schuster, 2004.

———. *Scarecrow.* Illustrated by Lauren Stringer. Harcourt Brace, 1998.

———. *When I Was Young in the Mountains.* Illustrated by Diane Goode. Puffin Books, 1985.

Santat, Dan. *After the Fall: How Humpty Dumpty Got Back Up Again.* Roaring Brook Press, 2017.

Say, Allen. *Grandfather's Journey.* Houghton Mifflin, 1993.

Schaefer, Lola. *Just One Bite.* Illustrated by Geoff Waring. Chronicle Books, 2010.

Scheller, Melanie. *My Grandfather's Hat.* Illustrated by Keiko Narahashi. Macmillan, 1992.

Schotter, Roni. *The Boy Who Loved Words.* Illustrated by Giselle Potter. Schwartz & Wade Books, 2006

Schweibert, Pat, and Chuck DeKlyen. *Tear Soup: A Recipe for Healing after Loss.* Illustrated by Taylor Bills. Grief Watch, 2005.

Scieszka, Jon. *Squids Will Be Squids: Fresh Morals, Beastly Fables.* Illustrated by Lane Smith. Puffin Books, 1998.

———. *The Stinky Cheese Man and Other Fairly Stupid Fairy Tales.* Illustrated by Lane Smith. Viking Press, 1992.

———. *The True Story of the Three Little Pigs: By A. Wolf.* Illustrated by Lane Smith. Puffin Books, 1996.

———, and Mac Barnett. *Battle Bunny.* Illustrated by Matt Myers. Simon & Schuster, 2013.

Sendak, Maurice. *Where the Wild Things Are.* HarperCollins, 1963.

Seuss, Dr. *The Cat in the Hat.* Random House, 1957.

———. *Horton Hears a Who.* Random House, 1954.

———. *How the Grinch Stole Christmas.* Random House, 1957.

———, with help from Jack Prelutsky and Lane Smith. *Hooray for Diffendoofer Day!* Knopf, 1998.

Shirtliffe, Leanne. *The Change Your Name Store.* Illustrated by Tina Kügler. Sky Pony Press, 2014.

Shumaker, Debra Kempf. *Freaky, Funky Fish: Odd Facts about Fascinating Fish.* Illustrated by Claire Powell. Hachette, 2021.

Siqueira, Ana. *Bella's Recipe for ~~Disaster~~ Success.* Illustrated by Geraldine Rodríguez. Beaming Books, 2021.

Smith, Cynthia Leitich. *Holler Loudly.* Illustrated by Barry Gott. Dutton, 2010.

———. *Jingle Dancer.* Illustrated by Cornelius Van Wright and Ying-Hwa Hu. HarperCollins, 2000.

Smith, Lane. *John, Paul, George, and Ben.* Hyperion, 2006.

Spinelli, Eileen. *Sophie's Masterpiece: A Spider's Tale.* Illustrated by Jan Dyer. Aladdin, 2001.

Spires, Ashley. *The Most Magnificent Thing.* Kids Can Press, 2014.

———. *The Thing Lou Couldn't Do.* Kids Can Press, 2020.

Starbright Foundation. *Once upon a Fairy Tale.* Viking, 2001.

Stead, Philip C. *Ideas Are All Around.* Roaring Brook Press, 2016.

Steer, Dugald A., editor. *Dr. Ernest Drake's Dragonology: The Complete Book of Dragons.* Candlewick Press, 2003.

Stein, David Ezra. *Interrupting Chicken.* Candlewick Press, 2010.

Stewart, Melissa. *Feathers: Not Just for Flying.* Illustrated by Sarah S. Brannen. Charlesbridge, 2014.

———. *Pipsqueaks, Slowpokes, and Stinkers: Celebrating Animal Underdogs.* Illustrated by Stephanie Laberis. Peachtree, 2018.

Stone, Jon. *The Monster at the End of This Book: Starring Lovable, Furry Old Grover.* Illustrated by Mike Smollin. Golden Books, 2004.

Taback, Simms. *Kibitzers and Fools: Tales My Zayda Told Me.* Viking, 2005.

Talbott, Hudson. *A Walk in the Words.* Penguin Random House, 2021.

Tan, Shaun. *The Arrival.* Arthur A. Levine, 2006.

Teague, Mark. *Dear Mrs. LaRue: Letters from Obedience School.* Scholastic, 2003.

———. *Detective LaRue: Letters from the Investigation.* Scholastic, 2007.

———. *LaRue for Mayor: Letters from the Campaign Trail.* Blue Sky Press, 2008.

Tekavec, Heather. *Wanted! Criminals of the Animal Kingdom.* Illustrated by Susan Batori. Kids Can Press, 2020.

Thaler, Mike. *The Teacher from the Black Lagoon.* Illustrated by Jared Lee. Cartwheel Books, 2008.

Tobias, Tobi. *Serendipity.* Illustrated by Peter Reynolds. Simon & Schuster, 2000.

Tyson, Leigh Ann. *An Interview with Harry the Tarantula.* Illustrated by Henrik Drescher. National Geographic, 2003.

Underwood, Deborah. *The Loud Book!* Illustrated by Renata Liwska. Clarion Books, 2015.

———. *The Quiet Book.* Illustrated by Renata Liwska. Clarion Books, 2013.

Văn, Múón Thi. *Wishes.* Illustrated by Victo Ngai. Orchard Books, 2021.

Van Allsburg, Chris. *The Mysteries of Harris Burdick.* Houghton Mifflin, 1984.

Viorst, Judith. *Alexander and the Terrible, Horrible, No Good, Very Bad Day.* Illustrated by Ray Cruz. Atheneum, 1987.

Waber, Bernard. *Courage.* Houghton Mifflin, 2002.

Walton, Rick. *Just Me and 6,000 Rats: An Adventure in Conjunctions.* Illustrated by Mike Gordon and Carl Gordon. Gibbs Smith, 2011.

Wang, Andrea. *Watercress.* Illustrated by Jason Chin. Holiday House, 2021.

Watt, Mélanie. *Chester.* Kids Can Press, 2009.

Weitzman, Jacqueline Preiss. Y*ou Can't Take a Balloon into the Metropolitan Museum.* Illustrated by Robin Priess Glasser. Dial Books, 1998.

Wiesner, David. *The Three Pigs.* Clarion Books, 2001.

Wild, Margaret. *Woolvs in the Sitee.* Illustrated by Anne Spudvilas. Boyd Mills Press, 2007.

Willems, Mo. *Because.* Illustrated by Amber Ren. Hyperion, 2019.

———. *Don't Let the Pigeon Drive the Bus!* Hyperion, 2003.

———. *The Pigeon Finds a Hot Dog!* Hyperion, 2004.

———. *Waiting Is Not Easy!* Hyperion, 2014.

Wilson, Karma. *Bear Feels Scared.* Illustrated by Jane Chapman. Simon & Schuster, 2008.

———. *Bear Snores On.* Illustrated by Jane Chapman. Simon & Schuster, 2002.

———. *The Cow Loves Cookies.* Illustrated by Marcellus Hall. Simon & Schuster, 2010.

Wilson, Troy. *Little Red Reading Hood and the Misread Wolf.* Illustrated by Ilaria Campana. Running Press Kids, 2019.

Wisniewski, David. *The Secret Knowledge of Grown-Ups.* Scholastic, 1999.

Woodson, Jacqueline. *The Day You Begin.* Illustrated by Rafael López. Penguin, 2018.

Wu, Helen H. *Tofu Takes Time.* Illustrated by Julie Jarema. Beaming Books, 2022.

Yarlett, Emma. *Dragon Post.* Walker Books, 2018.

Yolen, Jane, and Heidi Elisabet Yolen Stemple. *The Mary Celeste: An Unsolved Mystery from History.* Illustrated by Roger Roth. Simon & Schuster, 2002.

———. *The Wolf Girls: An Unsolved Mystery from History.* Illustrated by Roger Roth. Simon & Schuster, 2001.

Yorinks, Arthur. *Mommy?* Illustrated by Maurice Sendak and Matthew Reinhart. Scholastic, 2006.

Yousafzai, Malala. *Malala's Magic Pencil.* Illustrated by Kerascoët. Little, Brown, 2017.

Zagarenski, Pamela. *The Whisper.* Houghton Mifflin, 2015.

Works Cited

Anderson, Jeff. *Mechanically Inclined: Building Grammar, Usage, and Style into Writer's Workshops.* Routledge, 2005.

Anderson, Jeff, and Deborah Dean. *Revision Decisions: Talking through Sentences and Beyond.* Routledge, 2014.

Anstey, Michèle. "It's Not All Black and White: Postmodern Picture Books and New Literacies." *Journal of Adolescent & Adult Literacy,* vol. 45, no. 6, 2002, pp. 444–57.

Arizpe, Evelyn, et al. "Picturebooks and Literacy Studies." *The Routledge Companion to Picturebooks,* edited by Bettina Kümmerling-Meibauer, Routledge, 2018, pp. 371–80.

———. "The Voices behind the Pictures: Children Responding to Postmodern Picturebooks." *Postmodern Picturebooks: Play, Parody, and Self-Referentiality,* edited by Lawrence R. Sipe and Sylvia Pantaleo, Routledge, 2008, pp. 207–22.

Atwell, Nancie. *Lessons That Change Writers.* Heinemann, 2002.

Bawarshi, Anis. *Genre and the Invention of the Writer: Reconsidering the Place of Invention in Composition.* Utah State UP, 2003.

Beckett, Sandra L. "Crossover Picturebooks." *The Routledge Companion to Picturebooks,* edited by Bettina Kümmerling-Meibauer, Routledge, 2018, pp. 209–19.

Bernabei, Gretchen S., and Dottie Hall. *The Story of My Thinking: Expository Writing Activities for 13 Thinking Situations.* Heinemann, 2012.

Bintz, William Paul, and Meghan Valerio. "Using Postmodern Picture Books to Support Middle Grades Readers Navigate Ambiguity." *Voices from the Middle*, vol. 29, no. 2, 2021, pp. 50–56.

Bishop, Wendy, editor. Introduction. *Acts of Revision: A Guide for Writers.* Heinemann, 2004, pp. v–x.

Bowden, Darsie. *The Mythology of Voice.* Boynton/Cook, 1999.

Boyne, John. *The Boy in the Striped Pajamas.* David Fickling Books, 2006.

Broach, Elise. *Questions & Answers.* https://www.elisebroach.com/q-a/. Accessed March 2024.

Cather, Willa. *My Ántonia.* Warbler Classics, 2022.

Clark, Roy Peter. *Writing Tools: 50 Essential Strategies for Every Writer.* Little, Brown, 2006.

Culham, Ruth, et al. *Using Mentor Texts to Teach Writing with the Traits: Middle School.* Scholastic, 2010.

Dean, Deborah. "Framing Texts: New Strategies for Student Writers." *Voices from the Middle*, vol. 11, no. 2, 2003, pp. 32–35.

———. *Strategic Writing: The Writing Process and beyond in the Secondary English Classroom.* 2nd ed., National Council of Teachers of English, 2017.

Devitt, Amy J. *Writing Genres.* Southern Illinois UP, 2004.

Dickens, Charles. *A Tale of Two Cities.* 1859. Union Square, 2022.

Dillard, Annie. *An American Childhood.* Perennial Library, 1988.

Dresang, Eliza T. "Radical Change Theory, Postmodernism, and Contemporary Picturebooks." *Postmodern Picturebooks: Play, Parody, and Self-Referentiality*, edited by Lawrence R. Sipe and Sylvia Pantaleo, Routledge, 2008. pp. 41–54.

Education Northwest. "Looking for 6+1 Traits?" 2024, https://educationnorthwest.org/traits.

Evans, Janet, editor. *Challenging and Controversial Picturebooks: Creative and Critical Responses to Visual Texts.* Routledge, 2015.

Farrar, Jennifer. et al. "Challenging Picturebooks and Literacy Studies." *Exploring Challenging Picturebooks in Education: International Perspectives on Language and Literature Learning*, edited by Åse Marie Ommundsen et al., Routledge, 2022, pp. 43–56.

Ferris, Dana. "'They Said I Have a Lot to Learn': How Teacher Feedback Influences Advanced University Students' Views of Writing." *Journal of Response to Writing*, vol. 4, no. 2, 2018, pp. 4–33.

Foster, Tamra C. "Using Picture Books to Enhance Content Area Reading." *UNI ScholarWorks*, Graduate thesis, University of Northern Iowa, 2007.

Frank, Anne. *Anne Frank: The Diary of a Young Girl.* Bantam Books, 1994.

Gehr, Lauren. "How to Cultivate Confident Writers through Daily Practice." *Edutopia*, 1 Feb. 2024, https://www.edutopia.org/article/daily-writing-practice-students-creates-confident-writers/#:~:text=Daily%20Writing%20Practice%20Improves%20Perspective&text=Through%20this%20activity%2C%20students%20experience,I%20going%20to%20write%20next%3F%E2%80%9D.

Gold, Judith, and Akimi Gibson. "Reading Aloud to Build Comprehension." *LD Online*, 1 May, 2001, https://www.ldonline.org/reading-aloud-build-comprehension.

Golding, Willam. *Lord of the Flies.* 1954. Penguin, 2003.

Goldstone, Bette P. "Whaz Up with Our Books? Changing Picture Books Codes and Teaching Implications." *The Reading Teacher*, vol. 55, no. 4, 2001/2002, pp. 362–70.

Gonzales, Valentina. "The Potential of Wordless Picture Books for English Learners." *Seidlitz Education*, 29 Apr. 2020, https://seidlitzblog.org/2020/04/29/the-potential-of-wordless-picture-books-for-english-learners/.

Graham, Steve. "Changing How Writing Is Taught." *American Educational Research Association*, vol. 43, no. 1, 2019, https://journals.sagepub.com/doi/10.3102/0091732X18821125.

Graham, Steve, and Dolores Perin. W*riting Next: Effective Strategies to Improve Writing of Adolescents in Middle and High Schools.* Alliance for Excellent Education, 2007.

Hadaway, Nancy L., and Terrell A. Young. "Multilingual Picturebooks." *The Routledge Companion to Picturebooks*, edited by Bettina Kümmerling-Meibauer, Routledge, 2018, pp. 260–69.

Hall, Susan. *Using Picture Storybooks to Teach Literary Devices: Recommended Books for Children and Young Adults.* Vol. 2, 2nd ed., Oryx Press, 1994.

Hayakawa, S. I., and A. R. Hayakawa. *Language in Thought and Action.* 1939. 5th rev. ed., Harcourt Brace Jovanovich, 1990.

Heard, Georgia. Heart Maps: *Helping Students Create and Craft Authentic Writing.* Heinemann, 2016.

Herrera, Luz Yadira, and Carla España. "Se hace camino al andar: Translanguaging Pedagogy for Justice." *English Journal*, vol. 111, no. 5, 2022, pp. 27–34.

Hinton, S. E. *The Outsiders.* Viking, 2006.

Hubbard, Betsy. "ICYMI: Notebooks as a Writer's Tool." *Two Writing Teachers*, 12 Nov. 2018, https://twowritingteachers.org/2018/11/12/icymi-notebooks-as-a-writers-tool/.

Hurst, James. "The Scarlet Ibis." *Tcatitans.org*, https://www.tcatitans.org/cms/lib/CO50010872/Centricity/Domain/187/Scarlet%20Ibis%20-%20Full%20Text.pdf.

Ianacone, John A. "Passion and Craft in Writing: Finding a Balance." *English Journal*, vol. 85, no. 6, 1996, pp. 17–22.

Iyer, Pico. "In Praise of the Humble Comma." *TIME*, 13 June 1988, https://time.com/archive/6712509/essay-in-praise-of-the-humble-comma/.

Kissner, Emily. *Summarizing, Paraphrasing, and Retelling: Skills for Better Reading, Writing, and Test-Taking.* Heinemann, 2006.

Kittle, Penny. *Micro Mentor Texts: Using Short Passages from Great Books to Teach Writer's Craft.* Scholastic, 2022.

Kümmerling-Meibauer, Bettina. Introduction. *The Routledge Companion to Picturebooks*, edited by Bettina Kümmerling-Meibauer, Routledge, 2018, pp. 1–8.

Lado, Ana. T*eaching Beginner ELLs Using Picture Books: Tellability.* Corwin Press, 2012.

Layne, Steven L. *In Defense of Read-Aloud: Sustaining Best Practice.* Stenhouse, 2015.

Lee, Harper. *To Kill a Mockingbird.* Heinemann, 1960.

Lewis, C. S. *The Chronicles of Narnia.* HarperCollins, 2001.

Lowry, Lois. *Number the Stars.* Clarion Books, 2011.

———. *The Giver.* Clarion Books, 1993

Macaulay, David. Caldecott Medal Acceptance Speech. *Horn Book Magazine,* vol. 67, no. 4, 1991, https://faculty.tamuc.edu/kroggenkamp/archive/MacaulayAcceptance.html. Accessed 23 May 2024.

Mackey, Margaret. "Postmodern Picturebooks and the Material Conditions of Reading." *Postmodern Picturebooks: Play, Parody, and Self Referentiality*, edited by Lawrence R. Sipe and Sylvia Pantaleo, Routledge, 2008, pp. 103–16.

Madara, Lisa Marie Ciecierski. "Using Complex Picture Books as Tools to Teach Navigating Ambiguity." *Voices from the Middle*, vol. 29, no. 2, 2021, pp. 57–61.

Marchetti, Allison, and Rebekah O'Dell. *Writing with Mentors: How to Reach Every Writer in the Room Using Current, Engaging Mentor Texts.* Heinemann, 2015.

Massey, Susan R. "The Multidimensionality of Children's Picture Books for Upper Grades." *English Journal*, vol. 104, n. 5, 2015, pp. 45–58.

McClay, Jill Kedersha. "'Wait a Second . . .': Negotiating Complex Narratives in Black and White." *Children's Literature in Education*, vol. 31, no. 2, 2000, pp. 91–106.

McEwan, Elaine K. "Teach the Seven Strategies of Highly Effective Readers." *AdLit*, 2007, https://www.adlit.org/topics/comprehension/teach-seven-strategies-highly-effective-readers#:~:text=To%20improve%20students'%20reading%20comprehension,summarizing%2C%20and%20visualizing%2Dorganizing. Accessed 17 May 2023.

McTigue, Erin, et al. "How Can We Determine Students' Motivation for Reading before Formal Instruction? Results from a Self-Beliefs and Interest Scale Validation." *Early Childhood Research Quarterly*, vol. 48, 2019, pp. 122–33.

Merga, Margaret K. "Becoming a Reader: Significant Social Influences on Avid Book Readers." *School Library Research*, vol. 20, 2017, pp. 1–21.

Moje, Elizabeth Birr, Allan Luke, et al. "Literacy and Identity: Examining the Metaphors in History and Contemporary Research." *Reading Research Quarterly*, vol. 44, no. 4, 2009, pp. 415–37.

———, Melanie Overby, et al. "The Complex World of Adolescent Literacy: Myths, Motivations, and Mysteries." *Harvard Educational Review*, vol. 78, no. 1, 2008, pp. 107–54.

Mourão, Sandie. "Interpreting and Mediating a Wordless Picturebook in Pre-primary Early English Language Learning." *Exploring Challenging Picturebooks in Education: International Perspectives on Language and Literature Learning*, edited by Åse Marie Ommundsenet et al., Routledge, 2022, pp. 59–78._

Mueller, Vicki L. "What If They Can't?" *Voices from the Middle*, vol. 12, no. 4, 2005, pp. 44–48.

Muhammad, Gholdy. *Unearthing Joy: A Guide to Culturally and Historically Responsive Teaching and Learning*. Scholastic, 2023.

Myers, Walter Dean. *Monster.* Amistad, 2001.

Newkirk, Thomas. *Literacy's Democratic Roots: A Personal Tour through Eight Big Ideas.* Heinemann, 2023.

———. "Reasoning around Picture Books." *Beyond Words: Picture Books for Older Readers and Writers*, edited by Susan Benedict and Lenore Carlisle, Heinemann, 1992, pp. 11–20.

Nikolajeva, Maria. "Emotions in Picturebooks." *The Routledge Companion to Picturebooks*, edited Bettina Kümmerling-Meibauer, Routledge, 2018, pp. 110–18.

Oczkas, Lexi D. "The Power of Reading Aloud to Your Students: Guidelines and Top 5 Read-Aloud Strategies." *Best Ever Literacy Survival Tips: 72 Lesson You Can't Teaching Without*, International Reading Association, 2012, pp. 19–28,

O'Loughlin, Judith. "Picture Books to Help ELLs Access Common Core Anchor Reading Standards." *!Colorín colorado!*, https://www.colorincolorado.org/blog/picture-books-help-ells-access-common-core-anchor-reading-standards.

Ommundsen, Åse Marie. "Cognitively Challenging Picturebooks and the Pleasures of Reading: Explorative Learning from Picturebooks in the Classroom." *Exploring Challenging Picturebooks in Education: International Perspectives on Language and Literature Learning*, edited by Åse Marie Ommundsen et al., Routledge, 2022, pp. 99–121.

Ommundsen, Åse Marie, et al. "Introduction: Exploring Challenging Picturebooks in Education." *Exploring Challenging Picturebooks in Education: International Perspectives on Language and Literature Learning*, edited by Åse Marie Ommundsen et al., Routledge, 2022, 1–20.

Osborn, Sunya. "Picture Books for Young Adult Readers." *ALAN Review*, vol. 28, no. 3, 2001, https:///doi.org/10.21061/alan.v28i3.a.5.

Österlund, Mia. "Confronting the Trauma of the Child Evacuee: Picturebooks as Entrances to Visual Literacy." *Exploring Challenging Picturebooks in Education: International Perspectives on Language and Literature Learning*, edited by Åse Marie Ommundsen et al., Routledge, 2022, pp. 268–83.

Pantaleo, Sylvia. "'Everything Comes from Seeing Things': Narrative and Illustrative Play in Black and White.'" *Children's Literature in Education*, vol. 38, no. 1, 2007, pp. 45–58.

———. "The Long, Long Way: Young Children Explore the Fabula and Syuzhet of Shortcut." *Children's Literature in Education*, vol. 35, no. 1, 2004, pp. 1–20.

———. "What Do Four Voices, a Shortcut, and Three Pigs Have in Common? Metafiction!" *Bookbird*, vol. 42, no. 1, 2004, pp. 3–12.

Pantaleo, Sylvia, and Lawrence R. Sipe. "Introduction: Postmodernism and Picturebooks." *Postmodern Picturebooks: Play, Parody, and Self Referentiality*, edited by Lawrence R. Sipe and Sylvia Pantaleo, Routledge, 2008, pp. 2–8.

Pew Research Center. "Part II: How Much, and What, Do Today's Middle and High School Students Write?" *Pew Research Center*, 16 July 2013, https://www.pewresearch.org/internet/2013/07/16/part-ii-how-much-and-what-do-todays-middle-and-high-school-students-write/#:~:text=In%20focus%20groups%2C%20many%20teachers,texting%20and%20online%20social%20networking.

Philbrick, Rodman. *Freak the Mighty.* Scholastic, 2001.

Provost, Gary. *100 Ways to Improve Your Writing: Proven Professional Techniques for Writing with Style and Power.* Berkeley, 2019.

Reese, Debbie. "Critical Indigenous Literacies: Selecting and Using Children's Books about Indigenous Peoples." *Language Arts*, vol. 95, no. 6, 2018, pp. 389–93.

Reiker, Melissa. "The Use of Picture Books in the High School Classroom: A Qualitative Case Study." Master's thesis, Rollins College, May 2011.

Roser, Nancy, et al. "The Power of Picturebooks: Resources That Support Language and Learning in Middle Grade Classrooms." *Voices from the Middle*, vol. 19, no. 1, 2011, pp. 24–31.

Schmidt, Pauline S., and Matthew J. Kruger-Ross. *Reimagining Literacies in the Digital Age: Multimodal Strategies to Teach with Technology.* National Council of Teachers of English, 2022.

Scoggin, Jennifer, and Hannah Schneewind. *Trusting Readers: Powerful Practices for Independent Reading.* Heinemann, 2021.

Silva-Díaz, Maria Cecilia. "Picturebooks and Metafiction." *The Routledge Companion to Picturebooks*, edited by Bettina Kümmerling-Meibauer, Routledge, 2018, pp. 69–80.

Sipe, Lawrence R. "How Picture Books Work: A Semiotically Framed Theory of Text-Picture Relationships." *Children's Literature in Education*, vol. 29, no. 2, 1998, pp. 97–108.

———. *Storytime: Young Children's Literary Understanding in the Classroom.* Teachers College P, 2008.

Smith, M. Cecil. "The Benefits of Writing." *Northern Illinois University Center for the Interdisciplinary Study of Language and Literacy*, https://www.niu.edu/language-literacy/_pdf/the-benefits-of-writing.pdf.

Spandel, Vicki. *Creating Writing through 6-Trait Writing Assessment and Instruction.* 4th ed., Pearson, 2005.

Stewart, Melissa, and Melanie Correia. *5 Kinds of Nonfiction: Enriching Reading and Writing Instruction with Children's Books.* Routledge, 2021.

Sundmark, Björn, and Cecilia Olsson Jers. "The Challenge of Creativity: Using Picturebook Sequencing for Creative Writing." *Exploring Challenging Picturebooks in Education: International Perspectives on Language and Literature Learning*, edited by Åse Marie Ommundsen et al., Routledge, 2022, pp. 229–45.

Tiedt, Iris McClellan. *Teaching with Picture Books in the Middle School.* International Reading Association, 2000.

Vercelletto, Christina. "Never Too Old: Embracing Picture Books to Teach Older Students." *School Library Journal*, 23 Feb. 2018, https://www.slj.com/story/never-old-embracing-picture-books-teach-older-students.

Wiesel, Elie. *Night.* 1960. Translated by Marion Wiesel. Hill & Wang, 2006.

Williams, Bronwyn T. "Action Heroes and Literate Sidekicks: Literacy and Identity in Popular Culture." *Journal of Adolescent & Adult Literacy*, vol. 50, no. 8, 2007, pp. 680–85.

Williamson, Thea. "Authoring Selves in School: Adolescent Writing Identity." *Literacy Research: Theory, Method, and Practice*, vol. 68, no. 1, 2019, pp. 250–70.

Wolfe, Tom. *The Right Stuff.* Farrar, Straus and Giroux, 1983.

Womack, Mark. "Essay 3: Informative Essay." *Dr. Mark Womack*, English 1301 Composition course, https://drmarkwomack.com/engl-1301/assignments/major-essays/essay-3-informative-essay/.

Zusak, Markus. *The Book Thief.* Knopf, 2007.

Index

Note: A page number followed by "b" denotes a text box.

Author

Deborah Dean has taught junior high, high school, and university students. The author of many books and articles, she loves thinking about how to help students of all ages develop as writers and readers. She has used picturebooks in her teaching for most of her career and can't resist a display of picturebooks if she is close to one (it takes strong arms to pull her away!). In her spare time, she likes to read (all kinds of books, including picturebooks), travel with her husband, and make cookies with her grandchildren.

This book was typeset in Adobe Garamond Pro, Adobe Clean UX, and Monarcha by Cynthia Gomez.

The typefaces used on the cover include Bodoni 72 Oldstyle and Cera Pro.

The book was printed on 70 lb., white offset paper.